Race to the Bottom

Chicago Studies in American Politics

A series edited by Susan Herbst, Lawrence R. Jacobs, Adam J. Berinsky, and Frances Lee; Benjamin I. Page, editor emeritus

ALSO IN THE SERIES:

Race to the Bottom

*How Racial Appeals Work
in American Politics*

LAFLEUR STEPHENS-DOUGAN

THE UNIVERSITY OF CHICAGO PRESS   CHICAGO AND LONDON

The University of Chicago Press, Chicago 60637
The University of Chicago Press, Ltd., London
© 2020 by The University of Chicago
Published 2020

29 28 27 26 25 24 23 22 21 20   1 2 3 4 5

ISBN-13: 978-0-226-69884-7 (cloth)
ISBN-13: 978-0-226-69898-4 (paper)
ISBN-13: 978-0-226-69903-5 (e-book)
DOI: https://doi.org/10.7208/chicago/9780226699035.001.0001

Library of Congress Cataloging-in-Publication Data

Names: Stephens-Dougan, LaFleur, author.
Title: Race to the bottom : how racial appeals work in American politics /
    LaFleur Stephens-Dougan.
Other titles: Chicago studies in American politics.
Description: Chicago : University of Chicago Press, 2020. | Series: Chicago studies
    in American politics | Includes bibliographical references and index.
Identifiers: LCCN 2019044986 | ISBN 9780226698847 (cloth) | ISBN 9780226698984
    (paperback) | ISBN 9780226699035 (ebook)
Subjects: LCSH: Stereotypes (Social psychology)—United States. |
    Race discrimination—United States. | African Americans—Race identity.
Classification: LCC HM1096 .S738 2020 | DDC 305.800973—dc23
LC record available at https://lccn.loc.gov/2019044986

Contents

Tables and Figures

Tables

Figures

CHAPTER ONE

Introduction

On April 27, 2015, West Baltimore, Maryland, erupted in unrest. The uprisings were in response to the death of Freddie Gray, an African American civilian who died while in police custody under suspicious circumstances. It was not the first time that the nation would be forced to confront the crisis of policing in black and brown communities, and it likely would not be the last. Once again, a familiar scene unfolded on television screens across the nation—black youth clashing with police amidst billowing smoke and flames, placing a national spotlight on race, justice, police brutality, and the distrust between African American communities and their local governments. As was typical of the fallout around other tense racial incidents, the nation was looking to the first black president to address the racial tension. How would he respond?

When racial fissures were previously exposed during his tenure, Obama made an effort to appear tempered and even-handed. On the one hand, he would acknowledge and appear sympathetic to African American grievance, largely through symbolic gestures, such as famously saying, "You know, if I had a son, he'd look like Trayvon,"[1] or by sending Attorney General Eric Holder to Ferguson, Missouri, to address racial unrest in the aftermath of the police shooting of Michael Brown. On the other hand, Obama would also acknowledge that "the police have a difficult job," while simultaneously criticizing any behavior that could be characterized as violent or destructive.[2] The resulting fallout was usually that Obama was criticized in conservative circles for being anti-police, while he faced criticism in liberal circles for being far too silent on an issue that disproportionately affected African Americans.

The day after the unrest began in Baltimore, Obama initially avoided commenting on what was happening only forty miles away from the

White House. Eventually, he made a fourteen-minute prepared statement during a press conference with Prime Minister Shinzo Abe of Japan. Similar to his response in previous incidents, President Obama reminded the public that the police have "a tough job." Obama, however, also condemned the "criminals and *thugs* who tore up the place."[3] It was not the first time that the president expressed that he had "no sympathy at all for destroying your own communities,"[4] but this time the president's language was different. His language was more forceful and more racially charged, given his use of "thug"—a word that carries a racial connotation.[5]

Obama, however, was not alone in his use of racially charged language. Obama's word choice was similar to that of his fellow Democrat Stephanie Rawlings-Blake, the African American mayor of Baltimore, who said, "Too many people have spent generations building up this city for it to be destroyed by *thugs*, who in a very senseless way, are trying to tear down what so many have fought for."[6] Perhaps, more surprisingly, Obama's response was also similar to that of the white Republican governor of Maryland, Larry Hogan, who referred to the protestors as "gangs of *thugs* whose only intent was to bring violence and destruction to the city."[7] All three politicians were united in their use of racially inflammatory language, referring to the protestors as "thugs" in separate statements—this, despite the diversity of their racial and political backgrounds, and political constituencies.

The word choice drew criticism and scrutiny from some black lawmakers, including Baltimore city councilman Carl Stokes, who suggested that "thug" was racially charged—a euphemism for the "N-word."[8] Linguist and conservative critic John McWhorter, while not critical of the word choice, also suggested that the word "thug" carried a racial connotation, saying in an interview with National Public Radio, "Thug is a nominally polite way of using the N-word."[9] In the face of the criticism over the use of the word, Mayor Rawlings-Blake walked back her use of the term, saying, "There are no thugs in Baltimore. Sometimes, my own little anger translator gets the best of me."[10] President Obama, however doubled down on his use of the term, communicating through White House spokesman Josh Earnest that he did not regret using the term (Earnest 2015). Obama, however, was responsible to a national electorate that was predominantly white (Krogstad 2016). Rawlings-Blake had an urban electorate that was overwhelmingly African American (Yeip

2015), which might explain why Rawlings-Blake chose to back down from her statement, while Obama doubled down on the use of the term.

Using the word had political utility, communicating to Americans that these elected officials were taking a "no-nonsense" approach to crime that was being perpetrated by mostly black youth. Hogan was reinforcing his party's reputation for being tough on crime, while Obama and Rawlings-Blake were distancing themselves from their party's reputation for being soft on crime. Obama and Rawlings-Blake were also eschewing any presumed racial allegiance with the protestors, who were overwhelmingly African American. This is just one of many examples of how politicians across the racial and political spectrum engage in a political strategy that I refer to as "racial distancing," often in surprisingly similar ways.

"Racial distancing" is the phenomenon whereby politicians convey to racially moderate and racially conservative whites that they will not disrupt the racial status quo. By "racial status quo" I am referring to the existing state of affairs that is characterized by racial inequality, with whites at the top of the hierarchy, including white dominance in political, social, and economic institutions. Racial distancing helps black politicians and white Democratic politicians disrupt the stereotype of being beholden to racial and ethnic minorities, while for white Republican politicians, racial distancing helps them reinforce their reputation for keeping intact the existing racial hierarchy.

Politicians can engage in racial distancing rhetorically, visually, and substantively. Rhetoric that invokes negative stereotypes, as in the opening example of this chapter, is one way in which politicians engage in racial distancing. In addition, language that emphasizes hard work and individualism can also be a rhetorical form of racial distancing, depending on the racial context. Because of the way in which stereotypes regarding race and hard work are intertwined in the American context, even if African Americans are not explicitly mentioned, they are often implicated in discussions of "handouts" and dependence on the welfare state. Thus, critiques of work ethic and welfare dependency can be used to create distance from racial and ethnic minorities. Racial distancing can also be visual, such as the absence of people of color in campaign advertisements and photo opportunities with politicians. Finally, racial distancing can be substantive, such as platforms or agendas in which a discussion of race is absent. Liberal or progressive candidates can engage in a form of racial distancing when they opt to focus on universal issues (Sniderman and Carmines 1997; Wilson 1987), rather than promoting policies or initiatives that directly challenge the racial hierarchy and the racial disparities that the hierarchy produces.

Scholarly and popular attention tends to focus on white Republican politicians making appeals to prejudice while ignoring the incentives that also exist for white Democratic candidates, and black candidates from either major party, to appeal to negative racial attitudes about blacks for political gain. We tend to focus on the Republican Party's exploitation of racial division because even in the post–civil rights era, the party has fielded white supremacist candidates, blatantly courted white supremacist voters, and trafficked in white nationalist rhetoric (Ehrenfreund 2015). As a result, voters' association of white Republican politicians with racism is only further solidified, while attention is detracted from how the Democratic Party, as well as black candidates of either major party, navigate some white Americans' racial animus, and how in some cases, they even exploit voters' negative racial attitudes about blacks for political gain. The focus on white Republican politicians is too narrow. That is, not only are there incentives—in my view, often overlooked—for a much broader range of politicians to appeal to racial prejudice, but the array of appeals that activate negative racial attitudes is also much larger than previously considered.

Appealing to White Americans' Racial Animus— What We Know So Far

A large body of research examines the role of negative racial appeals and race in campaigns, but none of this research considers the possibility that candidates of color might also make appeals to voters' racial animus toward racial and ethnic minorities. Studies that examine the impact of negative racial appeals in campaigns focus on how *white*, typically Republican, candidates might be advantaged when racial issues become salient in the campaign (Mendelberg 2001; Valentino, Hutchings, and White 2002; for an exception, see White 2007 and McIlwain and Caliendo 2011). In the rare instances where studies devote attention to the use of racial appeals by politicians other than white candidates (White 2007; McIlwain and Caliendo 2011), scholars still ignore the possibility that candidates of color also appeal to *negative* racial attitudes about racial and ethnic minorities to court the electoral support of whites.[11] Other research has devoted attention to the electoral prospects of black candidates in majority-white jurisdictions, such as statewide or national races (Jeffries 1999; Orey and Ricks 2007), but inevitably the focus is on how black candidates attempt to neutralize the negative racial attitudes of some whites through a strategy of deracialization or avoiding racial issues altogether. Left unexamined is whether black candidates and candidates of color more broadly, as well as white Democratic candidates, can actually *benefit* by making race salient in a campaign, by also invoking negative stereotypes about people of color, often African Americans.[12]

Obama's decision to use the word "thug," for example, was not the first time that he would use racially charged language when discussing black people. While campaigning in 2008, and well into both of his terms as president, Obama repeatedly made calls for "Cousin Pookie,"[13] "Ray Ray," "Uncle Jethro," and other fictitious black men to "get up off the couch," "pull up their pants," and take personal responsibility for their own lives, rather than making excuses or blaming racism for their circumstances.[14] The former president's messages to and about black audiences often emphasized personal responsibility, especially among black men, as the remedy for all that ails the black community, including the purported tendency of blacks to blame racism as an excuse for racial disparities. During numerous Father's Day addresses, Obama suggested that black men are particularly irresponsible, failing to understand that "responsibility does not end at conception."[15] He has also criticized African American parents for feeding their children Popeyes chicken for breakfast,[16] told the Congressional Black Caucus Foundation to "quit complaining,"[17] and admonished black parents to "put away the Xbox."[18]

Obama's practice of chastising blacks was so common that at one point he was branded "the scold of black America" (Coates 2013). He routinely espoused negative stereotypes about African Americans— namely, poor African Americans, who are doubly marginalized (Cohen 1999), given their status as both poor and black. "No excuses" was a frequent refrain in his addresses to black audiences.[19] The "no excuses" rhetoric, which he directed almost exclusively at black audiences, suggested that African Americans were especially prone to making excuses for their own individual failings and shortcomings, rather than taking personal responsibility for their behavior.

Ironically, the first black president, whose election was viewed in some circles as ushering in a "post-racial" era, was elected in part on a campaign strategy that perpetuated negative stereotypes about African Americans—thus, raising some troubling normative implications. If the nation's first black president felt compelled, or at the very least was incentivized, to espouse some of the worst stereotypes about black people to get elected, then it is indicative of the constraints that black candidates face when discussing race. This also speaks to the utility of this strategy for Obama and other politicians seeking the electoral support of racially moderate to racially conservative whites.

Much of this rhetoric is not very different from that of, say, President Ronald Reagan, who invoked stereotypes of "young bucks" relying on food stamps to buy T-bone steaks.[20] However, these types of messages from black politicians have been met with arguably less scrutiny and skepticism. Appeals that invoke negative stereotypes about people of color, delivered by people of color, are less likely to be scrutinized because they appear to be innocuous or simply "tough love" messages. Negative messages delivered by people of color also generate electoral support from a wider swath of white voters, because in some instances, racial liberals are more supportive of this rhetoric when it is delivered by a black politician rather than a white politician. Many white Americans feel that African Americans are especially in need of personal responsibility messages (Salter, Hirsch, and Schlegel 2016). At the same time, racially resentful whites are already inclined to be sympathetic to this type of rhetoric. Ironically, African American politicians, who are presumed to be the most ardent guardians of black interests, further perpetuate negative stereotypes of African Americans when they espouse negative rhetoric about the black community, thus posing a threat to the advancement of the interests of African Americans. I demonstrate later in the book that appeals that disparage African Americans delivered by African American politicians depress support for efforts to reduce racial disparities between blacks and whites.

Instances of black politicians invoking negative, often racially inflammatory stereotypes of other African Americans have been discussed or alluded to in previous scholarly works (Glaude 2016; Price 2016; Carter and Dowe 2015; Harris 2012; Gillespie 2010). However, the impact of these types of messages on white voter behavior has not been empirically tested, despite the fact that these messages are likely to reach white voters, in addition to the politicians' proximate audience of African Americans. When black politicians make critiques of the black community, often invoking inflammatory rhetoric or negative stereotypes about African Americans, these critiques are perceived as especially unusual because black politicians are stereotyped as looking out for the interests of black voters, to the point that many white voters perceive black politicians' purported racial favoritism as a political liability. Thus, a critique of black people by a black politician is likely to receive a great deal of media attention. News outlets, for example, have reported on Obama's speeches to predominantly black audiences with headlines such as "Obama to New Grads: 'No Time for Excuses," "Obama Tells Black Fathers to Step Up,"[21] and "Obama Sharply Assails Black Fathers."[22] These public critiques of black audiences help disrupt the stereotype of black politicians, especially black Democratic politicians, as being beholden to black voters, because the message gets disseminated well beyond the proximate audience of African Americans. Language that invokes stereotypes of African Americans as entitled people who complain too much and blame racism for their lack of success rather than taking personal responsibility resonates with many white Americans, many of whom believe that African Americans use racism as a crutch or an excuse (Pew Research Center 2016).

The Theory of Racial Distancing

Some readers might find it surprising that black politicians, or even white Democratic politicians for that matter, would risk alienating African American voters by engaging in racial distancing, by appealing to some white Americans' racial animus. African Americans are, after all, the Democratic Party's most loyal constituents. The vast majority of black elected officials are Democrats, and these officials also routinely rely on overwhelming support from African Americans (Tyson 2018; Dawson 1994). Why would African American Democratic politicians inject racially inflammatory symbols or rhetoric into their campaigns? Why would any candidate, black or white, Democratic or Republican, risk being perceived as racist by injecting race into their respective campaigns, often through messages that play to the worst stereotypes of black people?

Simply put, candidates across the racial and political spectrum use negative racial appeals about racial and ethnic minorities—often African Americans, but increasingly other marginalized groups such as Latinos, immigrants, and Muslims—because these appeals are an effective way of communicating to racially moderate to racially conservative whites (the overwhelming majority of whites) that they will not disrupt the racial status quo. The central theme of *Race to the Bottom* is that Republican *and* Democratic candidates, candidates of color and whites alike, implicitly and explicitly appeal to negative racial attitudes to attract the electoral support of racially moderate to racially conservative whites. However, the electoral incentives, constraints, and considerations that candidates face when appealing to negative racial attitudes are largely influenced by the candidates' race, and to a lesser degree, their partisanship. White Republican candidates are incentivized to remind white Americans that they are associated with the party that has the reputational advantage for maintaining the racial hierarchy or the racial status quo. On the other hand, candidates of color, and to a lesser extent, white Democratic candidates, are incentivized to make appeals to racial prejudice to "play against type," or upend the notion that they will disrupt the racial status quo.

The theory of racial distancing predicts that racially conservative whites and racially moderate whites will prefer candidates who signal that they will not disrupt the racial status quo, or that they will not favor their racial and ethnic minority constituents.[23] These racial signals exist on a continuum, ranging from appeals that are implicit or ostensibly not about race, such as coded references to the "inner city" or strategically placed imagery of certain demographic groups, to appeals that are explicit in nature, openly referencing racial and ethnic groups, such as "blacks," "Mexicans," or "hardworking white Americans." When it comes to distancing themselves racially, however, politicians face a balancing act—on the one hand, they must indicate to a large fraction of white voters that they will maintain the racial status quo, but they must also not appear to be blatantly racist or racially insensitive. Most white Americans, even if they are racially conservative, do not want to be seen as racist, nor do they want to be associated with a candidate who is perceived as racist. Since some racial and partisan groups are more likely to be thought of as beholden to certain demographic groups than others, the extent to which a candidate can credibly signal that she carries no special obligation to racial and ethnic minority voters without being perceived as racist is influenced foremost by the candidate's race and then her partisanship.

The racial distancing model predicts that black politicians are more likely to be perceived as looking out for the interests of blacks and thus face less scrutiny than their white counterparts when they engage in racial distancing. According to the racial distancing model, black politicians may be incentivized to use stronger signals, such as the public upbraiding of African Americans, to forcefully disrupt the stereotype of their being beholden to their black constituents. That is, in the case of black candidates of either party, a subtle signal or a "dog whistle" is less likely to be picked up by racially resentful voters than the very same signal from a white candidate. On the other hand, white candidates can racially distance with more credibility, because even when they subtly engage in racial distancing, they are presumed as less likely to disrupt the racial status quo, relative to their black counterparts. Racially inflammatory comments made about black people by white politicians are more likely to be scrutinized because whites are not a member of the group that they are disparaging.

Ignoring the ways in which politicians other than white candidates inject inflammatory racial symbols into their campaigns causes us to underestimate the prevalence of racialized communication in American politics. Departing from previous research, I provide empirical evidence of the incentives that exist for *black* candidates to inject negative stereotypes about other blacks into their campaigns when pursuing white electoral support. I focus on black candidates because the black/white divide is still the most salient racial divide in American politics. It is also routinely the greatest divide in American politics (Kinder and Sanders 1996; Sears and Savalei 2006)—what Kinder and Sanders (1996, 31) refer to as "a divide without peer."

The Electoral Environment for Black Candidates in Majority-White Jurisdictions

Despite the election of the nation's first black president in 2008, African Americans have historically been underrepresented among elected officials in the United States. At virtually all levels of government, the proportion of black elected officials has yet to reach parity with the proportion of blacks in the general population (Williams 2017). Black candidates have also had difficulty winning elections in majority-white jurisdictions. Currently, only three U.S. senators out of 100 are black.[24] There are no black governors,[25] and the majority of black members of the House of Representatives represent majority-minority districts (Lublin

2018). In fact, the overwhelming number of black elected officials represent jurisdictions where the black population is sizable, if not the majority (Swarns 2008). One reason for the low number of African Americans holding office in majority-white jurisdictions is the racial resentments of some white Americans.[26] Black politicians may thus come to see racial distancing as a strategy that helps them overcome the racial resentment of some white Americans.

The fact that most black elected officials are already concentrated in majority-minority jurisdictions also means that for black representation to increase, it will likely come from black politicians running for office in jurisdictions that are majority-white, such as in statewide races or districts that are non-majority-minority. As more candidates of color run for office in majority-white jurisdictions, they may be increasingly incentivized to tailor their messages to appeal to racially moderate and racially conservative whites. Racially liberal whites are a decided minority in the United States.[27] For example, in 2016 only about 21 percent of white Americans supported "government aid to blacks," including a minority of white Democrats.[28] Racially liberal policies such as affirmative action in the workplace and in colleges and universities were also unpopular, garnering the support of 14 percent and 13 percent of white Americans, respectively.[29]

Candidates and party leaders who are interested in winning elections in majority-white jurisdictions are often careful to not engage in behavior that they believe will alienate racially moderate to racially conservative whites. They may even go a step further by appealing to base prejudice. Past racial trends also suggest that when white social status is threatened by gains made by people of color, members of the white community tend to react by mobilizing to reverse those gains (Abrajano and Hajnal 2015; Craig and Richeson 2014; Olzak 1990). Facing these circumstances, candidates, especially black candidates who are more likely to be perceived as closely aligned with minority interests, are incentivized to demonstrate that they are not beholden to their constituents of color. In eras of clear racial polarization, candidates who are seen as closely aligned with minority interests are unlikely to garner the electoral support of many white Americans.

Previous research indicates that whites are motivated to protect America's racial hierarchy and their hegemonic position within it (Sidanius, Devereux, and Pratto 1992). One potential threat to the racial hierarchy is the growing diversification of the U.S. population. The U.S.

Census Bureau projects that, for the first time in the nation's history, native-born non-Hispanic whites will become a minority by the year 2044 (Colby and Ortman 2015). Since demographic changes are associated with heightened white anxiety and concerns about loss of status (Craig and Richeson 2014; Enos 2014), some politicians pursuing white electoral support may feel pressured to demonstrate their racially conservative bona fides. And they may do this by engaging in a strategy of racial distancing—distancing themselves rhetorically, visually, and even substantively from racial and ethnic minorities.

Of course, racial distancing is not the only strategy politicians can pursue. The increasing diversity of the nation, which is also reflected in the demographic makeup of the Democratic Party, may incentivize Democratic candidates, especially black Democratic candidates, to focus on increasing turnout among people of color, rather than pursuing support from white racial moderates and conservatives. Harold Washington, the first black mayor of Chicago, for example, focused on increasing turnout among blacks to secure electoral victory (Malcolm 1983). More recent examples of this strategy include Stacey Abrams,[30] the 2018 Democratic nominee for the governor of Georgia, and of course, President Barack Obama (Roberts 2009). In addition, Democratic candidates may focus on shoring up black support during a primary election but rely more frequently on a racial distancing approach during a general election, where the electorate is more racially conservative. A critical element of my argument, however, is that black politicians have more latitude to pursue *both* strategies simultaneously because their appeals to prejudice are less likely to be scrutinized, and less likely to be punished.

The electoral environment that black politicians encounter is also one in which many white Americans, Republicans and Democrats alike, take as a given that African Americans are less hardworking than whites, and prone to using racism as an excuse for their individual failings. Since the very founding of the nation, biological racism—the belief that blacks are inherently lazy, immoral, violent, and sexually deviant—was used to justify the institution of slavery (Knoles 2006). Thus, racialized politics was endemic to the nation from the very beginning. Although biological racism eventually fell out of fashion, it was replaced by symbolic racism, or the idea that blacks are unwilling to adhere to the American values of hard work and individualism (Sears and Henry 2003). These stereotypes about black Americans' commitment to hard work and individualism are so dominant that we continue to see them reflected in contemporary political appeals that prime negative racial predispositions. When a politician invokes race negatively, it is not uncommon for her to rely on a stereotype about African Americans' work ethic or supposed lack thereof.

Stereotypes about the purported pathology of blacks are so deeply engrained in American society that according to the 2016 General Social Survey, 42 percent of white Republicans and 28 percent of white Democrats rated African Americans as "less hardworking than whites."[31] Also, according to the 2016 American National Election Study, approximately 32 percent of white Democrats rated blacks as more violent than whites. On the other hand, 57 percent of white Republicans and 67 percent of white Trump voters rated blacks as more violent than whites.[32] Thus, depending upon the stereotype in question, a majority of white Republican voters and a nontrivial fraction of white Democratic voters endorse negative stereotypes about blacks. Furthermore, this pattern in white public opinion is unlikely to change because of generational replacement. Over three in ten white millennials, or those whites born after 1980, believe African Americans to be less hardworking than whites. Roughly 25 percent of white millennials also believe African Americans to be less intelligent than whites.[33] Negative stereotypes about blacks are so popular among both white Republican and Democratic voters, young and old, that strategic politicians, even African American politicians, are encouraged to use these stereotypes as a political tool to appeal to white voters across the political spectrum.

If blacks are perceived by many of their fellow white Americans as "takers"[34] who are unwilling to work for their fair share, then Republican politicians can easily use negative appeals about blacks to mobilize the electoral support of racially conservative whites. The prevalence of these stereotypes also encourages white Democratic candidates and candidates of color to invoke these stereotypes to neutralize the negative racial attitudes of many white Americans. Politicians and parties interested in attracting the electoral support of whites, many of whom are racially conservative, may perceive it as politically expedient to distance themselves and even denigrate African Americans, especially if the politicians themselves are also African American. Since black politicians are the most likely to be stereotyped as being preoccupied with minority interests (Hajnal 2007), they are the ones often highly motivated to signal that they are not beholden to African American voters when trying to attract white electoral support. In addition, since black politicians are perceived as overly concerned with minority interests, the racial distancing model predicts that black politicians have the latitude to deni-grate the group with less scrutiny than their white counterparts. Accordingly, both major parties face incentives to recruit candidates of color specifically to deliver racially inflammatory messages, with less fear of generating a backlash. Racially inflammatory messages from politicians of color can be used to justify the expression of prejudice by some white voters, while still allowing voters to maintain that they are not prejudiced. As a result, the Republican Party may field candidates of color with racially inflammatory messages as a means of insulating the party from the charge of racism. Political figures such as 2012 GOP presidential candidate Herman Cain and 2016 GOP presidential candidate and Secretary of HUD Ben Carson are examples of black Republican politicians who have been touted as examples that the party is not racist. In a similar vein, the Democratic leadership may also insulate their party from charges of racism by fielding candidates of color, who may have more latitude to racially distance.

Take, for example, discussions around the Democratic Party's strategy to defeat President Trump in 2020. At the time of this writing, not a single Democratic primary has been held, but the party is already wrestling with questions of how to court the electoral support of white racial moderates and conservatives, while maintaining an electoral coalition that is largely dependent on the votes of racial and ethnic minorities. One candidate, Senator Kamala Harris (D-CA), is already being touted as an example of a politician who might be able to balance this tension, by piecing together the multiracial Obama coalitions of 2008 and 2012 that eluded the Democratic Party in 2016. Harris is a woman of color, born to an Indian mother and a black Jamaican father, whose multiracial background may hold symbolic value for some voters (Silver 2019). Other symbolic trappings include the fact that she launched her presidential campaign on Martin Luther King Day, with a campaign logo that invoked Shirley Chisholm, the first African American woman to run for president (Viser and Janes 2019). Harris also graduated from Howard University, a historically black college, where she pledged the nation's oldest African American sorority (Reston 2019).

On the other hand, Harris's experience as a former prosecutor and former attorney general of California may mean that she has an established track record of not being "too liberal" on criminal justice, an issue that is highly racialized (Valentino 1999; Peffley and Hurwitz 2010). Harris's law enforcement credentials are likely appealing to some voters, who might worry about a black Democrat being beholden to her minority constituency. In fact, Harris routinely refers to herself as "smart on crime,"[35] which distinguishes her from other Democrats, who may be susceptible to the charge of being "soft on crime." Nevertheless, as a woman of color, Harris is also distinct from "tough on crime" Republicans, whose efforts to address crime are often perceived as racially motivated. The point here is that the early "buzz" that Harris's campaign has generated illustrates the incentives that political parties have to create winning electoral coalitions by fielding racial and ethnic minority candidates, who have more leeway to engage in racial distancing than their white counterparts, simultaneously mobilizing racial and ethnic minorities and not alienating whites. On the other hand, white Democratic presidential candidates will likely face the challenge of having to demonstrate their racially liberal bona fides to people of color in the Democratic primary electorate, while simultaneously trying to win back white Americans who defected to the Republican Party in 2016, many of whom have racially conservative views (Sides, Tesler, and Vavreck 2018). While black candidates, such as Senator Harris and Senator Cory Booker (D-NJ), may actually be no more liberal on race than many of their white counterparts, similar to Obama, they can distance on race while simultaneously being the physical and symbolic embodiment of opposition to Trump's race-baiting.

Candidates of color are more likely to be perceived as liberal on racial matters. Research has shown that race affects perceptions of candidates' ideologies, with black candidates being viewed as more liberal than white candidates, even when the information provided about those candidates is identical (Lerman and Sadin 2014; Sigelman 1995; Williams 1990). Therefore, black politicians who engage in racial distancing, either implicitly or explicitly indicating that they will not disrupt the racial status quo, are able to portray themselves as more conservative, and less likely to favor blacks over whites. Since the comments of those who are thought to speak against their apparent self- (or group-) interest are seen as especially credible (Kelley 1973), black politicians who speak openly and negatively about other black people are likely to be perceived as acceptable, with respect to their group loyalties, relative to black politicians who do not engage in racial distancing. Furthermore, research on persuasion indicates that speakers who are seen as credible wield greater influence (Nelson, Sanbonmatsu, and McClerking 2007; Oskamp and Schultz 2005). Therefore, a negative message about black people by a black elite seems likely to be perceived as a more influential source than the equivalent message from a white politician. Black politicians who make appeals to prejudice distinguish themselves from the "old guard" of black politicians (Gillespie 2012), such as Jesse Jackson Jr. and Al Sharpton—politicians whom many whites perceive as obsessed with racial grievance. Finally, black politicians are also likely to either defensively or preemptively mitigate the negative racial attacks against them that would likely spring from their opponents during an election campaign. One way that they might attempt to mitigate racial attacks is by engaging in racial distancing or demonstrating that they are not too closely aligned with black interests.

What about Black Voters?

To the casual observer, it might seem implausible that black politicians would inject negative stereotypes about other African Americans into their campaigns. A strategy in which black politicians espouse some of the worst stereotypes about black people seems tantamount to political suicide. Yet a strategy of racial distancing—in particular, the use of negative racial messages—is popular with black audiences for a variety of reasons. For one, this strategy speaks to the electoral environment that many African Americans have begrudgingly embraced. In other words, the sentiment among many African Americans is that black politicians are forced to distance themselves from African Americans to appeal to white voters, even if that means endorsing and reifying negative stereotypes that are associated with African Americans. As Harris (2012) indicates, many black voters were willing to engage in a "wink-and-nod agreement," or a tacit bargain with Obama, for example, whereby Obama could publicly distance himself from African Americans as a tactic to gain white electoral support. The fact that many black Americans understood Obama's use of racial distancing as key to gaining the electoral support of white Americans speaks to the precarious position of black Americans in the American political system.

Second, the use of negative racial messages by black politicians is well received by many black Americans because there is a long history within the black community of black elites chastising and policing the behavior of other African Americans, usually those African Americans who have a lower-class status within the black community. This discourse has its roots in "the politics of respectability," which was first promoted by African American elites in the late nineteenth and early twentieth century. The "politics of respectability" was a term coined by Evelyn Brooks Higginbotham (1993) in her history of the Woman's Convention (W.C.) of the National Baptist Convention. According to Higginbotham, the W.C. emphasized the reform of individual behavior and attitudes both as a goal in itself and as a strategy for reform of the entire structural system of American race relations. Messages of "racial uplift" were designed to help improve the behavior of the black masses, many of whom black elites perceived as needing guidance and correction. Middle- and upper-class black women at this time sought to inculcate in poor black migrants from the South, "temperance, industriousness, thrift, refined manners, and Victorian sexual morals" (Higginbotham 1993, 14–15). The politics of respectability also served the purpose of proving to whites that blacks were worthy of full inclusion in American society. According to Higginbotham (1993, 196), "The Baptist women spoke as if ever cognizant of the gaze of white America." In other words, well aware of the "gaze of white America," the black middle class and black elites policed the behavior of lower-class blacks as a strategy to gain acceptance from white Americans. A similar parallel exists in contemporary American politics, such that black politicians who are seeking white electoral or coalitional support may opt to police the behavior of other blacks as a way of demonstrating that they are not partial to other African Americans—thus gaining access to donors, favorable media coverage, and of course, votes.

The politics of respectability also has a history of being embraced by some of the foremost black politicians and thinkers (Gaines 1996). As Harris (2012, 102) reminds us, prominent black leaders such as W. E. B. DuBois and Booker T. Washington "were united in their view that the habits of ordinary black folk needed self-correction and supervision in order for the race to progress," although they differed on the means of achieving black progress. It is also well documented that the politics of respectability featured prominently in the civil rights movement, including ideas about which people were deemed as reputable spokespersons for the movement, as well as what constituted appropriate dress for sit-in participants (jackets for men and dresses for ladies) (Schmidt 2018). Strains of respectability politics are also evident in contemporary conversations in black barbershops, churches, and backyard barbecues, where there is a unique brand of conservatism that stresses the importance of personal responsibility and black respectability

(Harris-Lacewell 2004; Philpot 2017). Thus, these messages are familiar to African American audiences, and are not necessarily different from what many African Americans might hear from the pulpit on a Sunday morning or in an informal conversation at a family barbecue or at the beauty salon.

What distinguishes the current era of black politics from previous eras in which black elites endorsed negative stereotypes about black people is that Americans outside the black community are increasingly privy to what used to be an in-group conversation. Racially segregated patterns of life have made it such that most white Americans were previously unaware of this strand of black conservatism. As Dawson (2001, 27) reminds us, "The black counterpublic sphere is the product of both the historically imposed separation of blacks from whites throughout most of American history and the embracing of the concept of black autonomy as both an institutional principle and an ideological orientation." Ironically, it is this very segregation that in part helped foster African Americans' commitment to autonomy and personal responsibility. These ideological orientations are still quite prominent in discussions in black spaces today.

Of course, segregation still remains a key feature of American life. More African Americans, however, are running for office outside of majority-black jurisdictions (Lublin 2018). As more black politicians run for office in these spaces, the mainstream media has unprecedented access to conversations that have routinely occurred within the confines of black churches, barbershops, and beauty salons (Harris-Lacewell 2004). Furthermore, as black politicians run for office outside of majority-black jurisdictions, often for more prominent offices, such as mayor of a major city, governor, U.S. senator, or even president, they also have a larger bully pulpit or microphone to transmit these messages well beyond their proximate audience of black people. The prominence of the offices also means that they are attracting more attention from the mainstream media.

Finally, for many white Americans, the idea that a black politician would speak out seemingly against the group's interests seems counterintuitive and thus garners more attention. As Muhammad (2010, 10) notes in his book-length treatment of the social construction of black criminality, "Conservative black opinion makers and race reformers who dwelt on the self-destructive behavior of poor blacks were more likely than antiracist activists to be heralded as clear-eyed and unbiased

by their influential white peers." Similarly, modern-day personal responsibility messages help insulate black politicians from accusations of favoring blacks over whites. Personal responsibility messages, while aimed
at the proximate audience of African Americans, are also well received
by the mainstream, both liberals and conservatives.

Black politicians who engage in negative racial messaging may receive support from black audiences because the targets of these messages are often the "doubly marginalized" (Cohen 1999) members of the
community, such as absentee fathers and "Cousin Pookie." Among African Americans there is a "qualified linked fate politics," whereby not
every black person is an equally representative proxy of one's individual
interests, and thus as equally worthy of political support by other African Americans (White 2007; Cohen 1999). Many of the cheering African Americans in Obama's audiences, for example, may have thought
that Obama was not chastising them, but rather the more marginalized
members of the community, whom more affluent African Americans
may have thought were in need of "tough love."[36] Obama's position as a
member of the in-group enabled him to invoke these stereotypes or engage in what Price (2016) refers to as "black blame" with little to no scrutiny. Future black politicians seeking the electoral support of whites may
likely take a page from Obama's playbook.

One caveat, however, is that a black politician's ability to espouse
negative racial messages about blacks with little backlash from African
Americans is likely conditioned on the black candidate's partisanship.
Obama received overwhelming support from African Americans despite
endorsing negative stereotypes about African Americans, whereas black
Republicans, such as Herman Cain and Ben Carson, espoused similar
messages, but were tremendously unpopular among African Americans
(Martin 2015). The partisan label of Republican likely made many African Americans skeptical of Cain's and Carson's "tough-love messages."
Many African Americans are skeptical of black Republican politicians,
who have chosen to affiliate with a party that has a reputation for enforcing the racial status quo. African American Republican politicians
may be perceived as privileging their ideology and perhaps their self-
interest above the shared racial group interests of African Americans
(Wright Rigueur 2014; Fields 2016). For black Republican politicians,
however, it might be worth it to engender black hostility, since black Republican politicians are typically courting majority-white or near exclusively white constituencies.

Relevance of Key Findings

My theory of racial distancing makes a theoretical contribution to the race and politics literature by making a novel allowance for both Democrats and Republicans as well as politicians of color and white politicians to "distance" themselves from racial and ethnic minorities. While the theory of racial priming has never explicitly stated that only white politicians attempt to prime racial attitudes, the literature that has developed has done this to the exclusion of other groups. Previous research has relied almost exclusively on white source cues in studies of negative racial appeals. Even when the racial appeals literature has accounted for black messengers, the assumption was that black politicians either could not or would not invoke negative stereotypes about blacks for political gain. Thus, my theory of racial distancing addresses an important oversight in the literature by accounting for the racial and partisan characteristics of the messenger delivering the racial appeal, which surprisingly many of the studies of racial appeals fail to do. Research, however, has demonstrated that the messenger can be just as, if not more, important than the message itself (Kuklinski and Hurley 1994). Accounting for how the effect of a racial appeal may be conditioned by the racial characteristics of the messenger is thus important.

The failure to account for black candidates and white Democratic candidates also engaging in appeals to prejudice may have contributed to a more sanguine view of racial politics than is warranted. Although the conventional wisdom is that explicit negative racial appeals inevitably lead to a loss in electoral support, this conclusion may have been reached erroneously, thanks to an almost exclusive reliance on white, largely Republican source cues in studies of racial priming. The Republican Party has a reputation for being racially conservative, and, some might even argue, racially insensitive. Therefore, white Republican politicians are unable to build a broad electoral coalition when they make negative racial appeals about blacks. When white Republican politicians "play the race card," they boost support among racially resentful whites, but they prompt an even stronger backlash effect from racial liberals (Tesler 2016). On the other hand, when black politicians or even white Democrats engage in negative racial distancing, they are able to build a broader electoral coalition than their white Republican counterparts. Black politicians in particular are able to pick off the votes of some racially resentful whites while experiencing little to no backlash from racial liberals.

Previous research has also likely underestimated the utility of explicit negative racial appeals because the utility of these appeals has largely been tested in the context of the candidates who are more likely to be scrutinized when making negative racial appeals—white politicians. Consequently, previous scholarship has also overlooked the ways in which appeals to racial prejudice are still an integral part of campaign strategy in American politics, even among black politicians who are presumed to be looking out for the interests of black Americans. Racialized communication—specifically negative appeals about blacks—is an enduring feature of American political campaigns.

The electoral landscape of American politics has also changed since many of the seminal studies of racial appeals were conducted (Mendelberg 2001; Valentino, Hutchings, and White 2002). We elected our first African American president, the United States has experienced rapid demographic change, and some of the norms around racist speech appear to be rapidly eroding. While the universality of these norms is questionable, it is becoming increasingly evident that significant segments of the population are more comfortable with racist rhetoric than previously thought (Hutchings, Walton, and Benjamin 2010; Valentino, Neuner, and Vandenbroek 2018). We must reexamine the landscape of negative racial appeals using more geographically and demographically diverse samples, across a wider range of candidates, accounting for both the partisan and the racial characteristics of the candidates. In short, the story of negative racial appeals is incomplete and needs updating.

Race to the Bottom considers a wider range of racial appeals and a broader range of candidates than have many of the previous studies of racial appeals. Thus, my theory offers a more comprehensive account of appeals to negative racial attitudes in American politics. When we fail to think broadly about the ways in which race is injected into political campaigns, we underestimate the ways in which racial prejudice continues to pose a threat to the marginalized members of society in the political arena. That appeals that play to negative and pejorative stereotypes about African Americans continue to be such an integral part of American campaigns has damning implications for American democracy—namely, that the presumed rejection of racist rhetoric in the United States has been overstated, and thus the degree to which racial progress in the political arena has been made has also been overstated. Therefore, a comprehensive and broader theoretical framework is needed to deepen our understanding of the use of racial appeals in American politics. Racial distancing theory fills this void by making distinct predictions compared to other contemporary theories of race in electoral politics, and so contributes to our understanding of how and why candidates, including but not exclusively white Republicans, mobilize racial appeals, and the variety of possible racial attitudes that might be activated by them. I offer a more holistic yet sobering view of contemporary race relations.

I rely on a mixed-methods approach to systematically test my theory of racial distancing. I draw on examples of candidates who have engaged in racial distancing, as well as survey experiments of nationally representative and nationally diverse samples of white Americans, and the analysis of campaign ads, to offer a broader theoretical account for the subtle and not so subtle ways in which racial prejudice is strategically appealed to in American politics.

Plan of the Book

In chapter 2, I draw on the literature on racial priming, deracialization, and issue ownership to expound on the theory of racial distancing. I develop the theoretical support for the central claim of this book: that both major parties, candidates of color and whites alike, use negative racial appeals about racial and ethnic minorities strategically for their political advantage, and that these appeals work. I conclude the chapter with a discussion of my theoretical predictions for the racial distancing model, in which I forecast that the racial and partisan characteristics of politicians will influence their perceived credibility to maintain the racial status quo, as well as the latitude with which they can comfortably racially distance.

Chapter 3 is a case study of the most prominent African American politician to engage in racial distancing, President Barack Obama. I rely on newspaper accounts and a content analysis of television advertisements to establish support for the claim that the Obama campaign engaged in racial distancing, drawing comparisons between the 2008 Obama campaign and other campaigns where appropriate. I also analyze speeches to black audiences by Obama during the 2008 campaign and his two terms as president. I compare the rhetoric in his speeches to predominantly black and Latino audiences relative to whites, to support the claim that negative racial messaging was systematically deployed by Obama when speaking to people of color.

Chapter 4 begins with a discussion of several prominent black candidates, Democrats and Republicans alike, who engaged in racial distancing. I rely on journalistic sources, as well as campaign materials, to reconstruct the events surrounding some of their candidacies. The candidates include Herman Cain, Ben Carson, Artur Davis, Harold Ford Jr., Mia Love, Michael Nutter, and Allen West. In the latter part of the chapter, I test the efficacy of a racial distancing strategy, relative to deracialization, using a survey experiment conducted on a nationally representative sample of white Americans. The results of the experiment demonstrate that a deracialized message that emphasized commonality across racial lines actually resulted in *less* electoral support than messages that either implicitly or explicitly disparaged blacks, suggesting that when attracting the electoral support of white Americans, racial distancing is a more effective strategy than deracialization.

In the latter chapters of the book, I rely largely on survey experiments to test the racial distancing model relative to the racial priming hypothesis. Chapter 5 tests the negative racial messaging element of the racial distancing model across a wider range of candidates than the candidates depicted in the experiment in chapter 4. I discuss the results of two experiments that demonstrate that a candidate's race and partisanship influence the degree to which he can invoke negative racial stereotypes without losing electoral support. I find that because of partisan and racial stereotypes, white Republican candidates are perceived as the most credible when they indicate that they will not disrupt the racial status quo, but they also have the least latitude to engage in more explicit forms of distancing. On the other hand, black Democratic candidates are perceived as the least credible when they indicate that they will not disrupt the racial status quo, but they can also engage in more extreme forms of distancing with virtual impunity from whites. Since previous studies of negative racial appeals have relied almost exclusively on white Republican source cues, we have ignored the ways in which the public's response to negative racial appeals may be influenced by the racial and partisan characteristics of the politician making the appeal.

Chapter 6 examines whether an association with black images is more detrimental for some candidates than others, depending on the candidate's race and party. Specifically, I test whether a candidate's race and partisan characteristics can facilitate or hinder subtle efforts to engage in racial distancing. In other words, can an association with white imagery in a campaign mailer help politicians signal that they will not disrupt the racial status quo? I found that more implicit signals conveyed through racial imagery are not an effective tool for black candidates who want to disrupt the perception that they will be beholden to black interests. Although images in campaign advertisements can be an effective way for candidates to signal their legislative preferences and priorities to voters, African American candidates regardless of party were mostly unable to overcome the perception that they would favor blacks over whites, even when they associated themselves with counter-stereotypical images of African Americans or predominantly white images. Thus, black candidates may be incentivized to engage in more explicit forms of racial distancing to attract the electoral support of white Americans. On the other hand, white Democratic candidates were penalized by white Americans when their campaign advertisements included African Americans, but received more electoral support when their advertisements included exclusively white imagery.

Chapter 7 sums up the findings of the book and discusses racial distancing theory for dynamics that are not black-white. For example, racial distancing theory may lend itself to other racial or ethnic group divides. I also discuss the implications of racial distancing for black politics and for democratic politics more broadly.

CHAPTER TWO

The Theory of Racial Distancing

You know, I tried to talk about good roads and good schools and all these things that have been part of my career, and nobody listened. And then I began talking about niggers, and they stomped the floor. —George Wallace

After losing his first campaign for governor of Alabama in 1958, Democrat George Wallace reportedly told a friend, "I was out-niggered and I will never be out-niggered again."[1] In other words, Wallace believed that he had lost the race because he was too moderate on racial issues compared to his opponent, John Patterson. Wallace is mostly remembered in history as a staunch segregationist, but earlier in his career he was known as a moderate on race. Long before he famously declared, "Segregation now, segregation tomorrow, segregation forever," Wallace refused to make race an issue during his initial run for governor of Alabama in 1958.[2] He declined the endorsement of the Ku Klux Klan, which won him the support of the NAACP. Conversely, Wallace's opponent, Patterson, embraced Klan support and trounced Wallace in the election.

As indicated by the epigraph, by the time Wallace ran for governor again in 1962 he had realized the power of race as a political tool. This time he ran as a proponent of segregation, and he won by a land-slide. According to Wallace, when he initially ran for governor in 1958, he tried to run a campaign about "good schools" and "good roads," but his loss in that election taught him that many white voters were more receptive to a message of racial division.[3] Wallace's loss in 1958 also taught him that being "too closely" associated with African Americans, with an endorsement from the NAACP, for example, can diminish support among some white Americans. In short, George Wallace learned that capitalizing on negative racial attitudes is an effective strategy for gaining the electoral support of many white Americans. This lesson has been adopted by politicians across the racial and political spectrum today.

Simply put, parties and politicians know that candidates who inject inflammatory racial symbols into their campaigns often fare better than candidates who do not try to appeal to voters' negative attitudes about racial and ethnic minorities. However, research has not kept pace with this political reality, instead focusing on a narrow swath of the universe of negative racial appeals. Numerous studies, for example, have documented the political advantage that white Republican politicians have gained from making race salient in their campaigns, but we still have very little systematic knowledge about this practice outside of white Republican politicians, thus limiting our ability to make more generalizable conclusions about the impact of negative racial appeals in American politics.

In this chapter, I begin by explaining the theory of racial distancing. I subsequently provide empirical evidence of "racialized partisan stereotypes," or the idea that a candidate's race either enhances or tempers the stereotypes associated with her party. I argue that these racialized partisan stereotypes either enhance or limit a politician's ability to use negative racial appeals without backlash. I subsequently discuss racial priming and deracialization—the two literatures that to date have dominated our thinking about negative racial appeals. I also discuss issue ownership theory and its relevance to candidate behavior in a racialized political system. Issue ownership is not typically considered a foundational literature in the study of race and politics. However, given the distinct reputational advantages that the two major parties have with respect to matters of race, issue ownership theory offers insight into how candidates might try to emphasize or deemphasize their reputations on racial matters. I conclude the chapter by expounding on the theory of racial distancing, offering distinct predictions of candidate behavior based on the race and partisanship of the politicians. I predict that white Republican politicians are most likely to face backlash for making negative racial appeals, whereas the very same racial appeals from other types of politicians face far less scrutiny, especially when the politician is a black Democrat.

Defining Racial Distancing

As noted in chapter 1, "racial distancing" is the process whereby politicians, both black and white, and Democrat or Republican, either implicitly or explicitly indicate to racially moderate to racially conservative white voters that they will not disrupt the racial status quo. "Racial status quo" refers to the existing state of affairs that is characterized by racial inequality, with whites at the top of the hierarchy, including white dominance in political, social, and economic institutions. When it comes to distancing themselves racially, however, politicians face a balancing act—on the one hand, they must indicate to a large fraction of white voters that they will maintain the racial status quo, but they must also not appear to be blatantly racist or racially insensitive. The distancing behavior that candidates use to indicate that they will not threaten the racial status quo runs the gamut, from racially explicit rhetoric that derogates entire groups, such as President Trump referring to some Mexican immigrants as rapists, to more implicit or subtle signals, such as strategically placed demographic groups in campaign advertisements. Although candidates can racially distance in many different ways, for the purposes of this book, I focus on two elements of racial distancing—politicians' rhetorical strategy and politicians' imagery strategy.

"Imagery strategy" refers to when candidates avoid appearances at public events or advertisements with racial and ethnic minorities, while placing an emphasis on their white supporters and constituents. An imagery strategy is closer to the implicit end of the racial distancing continuum, because while there are no verbal references to race, those whom a candidate chooses to be associated with visually sends a strong message. An imagery strategy is based on the premise that there are negative political consequences to being visually or publicly associated with African Americans or other racial and ethnic minorities, depending on the racial and partisan characteristics of the politician.

By limiting or avoiding public appearances with African Americans, the candidate sends a signal about the groups to which he will be responsive. As noted by Frymer (1999, 12; emphasis added), "Many Democratic Party leaders believe their victory is threatened by their association with large numbers of African American voters. This leads them to minimize the *public appearance* of their candidates with these voters. If Democratic Party leaders believe wide segments of the public are ambivalent about black interests, they will disassociate themselves from black voters." Previous research, for example, indicates that voters are more likely to believe that candidates support African American constituents when African Americans are pictured in their campaign ads (Swigger 2012; Stephens-Dougan 2016). Thus, the inclusion or exclusion of certain demographic groups can potentially send a message about which constituents the candidate will support.

Another way in which candidates can disassociate themselves from racial and ethnic minority voters is through a rhetorical strategy. Broadly speaking, "rhetorical strategy" refers to verbal cues that distance politicians from racial and ethnic minorities. These verbal cues may include messaging that invokes negative stereotypes about racial and ethnic minorities. These messages can be either implicit or explicit in nature. As originally envisioned in the literature, an explicit verbal cue entails the use of racial nouns, such as "African American" or "Mexican" (Mendelberg 2001). Conversely, an implicit verbal cue may use coded language, such as "inner city, "tough on crime," or "sanctuary cities." Instead of employing direct references to racial minorities, some political elites use coded language and highlight issues that are ostensibly not about race but that have become associated with African Americans, such as crime or welfare (Gilens 1999; Gilliam and Iyengar 2000; Mendelberg 2001, 2008).

In a similar vein, implicit verbal cues may also include language that references the purported lack of personal responsibility, work ethic, self-reliance, and individualism among racial and ethnic minorities, most often African Americans. In the post–civil rights era, whites' prejudice toward blacks is often expressed as "a moral feeling that blacks violate such traditional American values as individualism and self-reliance" (Kinder and Sears 1981, 416). Therefore, verbal cues that invoke negative stereotypes with respect to the work ethic of African Americans are likely to be popular among whites who have negative racial attitudes toward blacks, and can be used by politicians across the racial and political spectrum, to varying degrees. At the same time however, when it comes to black politicians, verbal cues may also include efforts to present *themselves* counter-stereotypically, by emphasizing their own work ethic, as well as their commitment to American values of hard work and self-reliance. In other words, strategic black politicians may reference their own work ethic and self-reliance as a means of distancing themselves from the stereotype of their group, as unwilling to adhere to traditional American values of hard work and self-reliance. Previous research, for example, indicates that upper- and middle-class blacks often employ destigmatization strategies that emphasize individual agency as a means of indicating competence to whites (Lamont and Fleming 2005).

However, if black candidates take counter-stereotypical positions with regard to matters of race by making racially conservative appeals, will citizens recognize this and adjust their evaluations accordingly? And, just how far can these candidates go? Is it enough that they espouse racially conservative positions, or can they also directly criticize the black community? In other words, if black candidates take counter-stereotypical positions by making explicit racial appeals rather than implicit appeals, which subtly suggest criticisms of the African American community, will they succeed in generating greater support among whites?

Racial distancing theory posits that when trying to win elections in majority-white jurisdictions, candidates who signal that they will maintain the racial status quo will fare better than candidates who make no such indication. Since politics is largely about which politician can deliver resources to a voter's group, even candidates of color can gain electoral support from white Americans who have animus toward racial and ethnic minorities, as long as they signal that they will maintain the racial status quo. Racial distancing theory also posits that voters' assumptions about which candidates are more or less likely to maintain the racial status quo are informed by the stereotypes voters associate with the racial and partisan characteristics of the candidate. Candidates whose racial or partisan characteristics are associated with looking out for the interests of people of color, such as black Democratic politicians, are therefore incentivized to "signal" that they will not be beholden to racial and ethnic minorities. They may even require more explicit or extreme measures to convince white voters that they are not beholden to people of color. On the other hand, white Republican politicians, whose racial and partisan characteristics are more closely associated with racial conservativism, are still incentivized to "distance," but their motivation is different, such that they are reminding racially moderate and racially conservative white voters about their reputational advantage for maintaining the racial hierarchy and the racial status quo.

Evidence of Racialized Partisan Stereotypes

I conducted a survey experiment on a national diverse sample of 653 white Americans from the 2017 Cooperative Congressional Election Study (CCES). The aim of this study was to provide empirical evidence of racialized partisan stereotypes, or the idea that a candidate's race either enhances or tempers the stereotypes associated with her party.[4] An assumption of the racial distancing model is that voters have distinct perceptions of different politicians that are based on both the partisan and the racial characteristics of a politician. Yet the literature on partisan stereotypes and reputations has developed separately from the literature that explores racial stereotypes. One body of research has explored how racial stereotypes affect candidates', most often black politicians', electoral prospects (Sigelman et al. 1995; McDermott 1998; Piston 2010). The other line of research has examined how stereotypes about the Republican versus the Democratic Party affect voters' evaluations of candidates, as well as candidates' abilities to overcome those stereotypes (Rahn 1993; Arceneaux 2008; Nicholson 2012). We still know very little about how those partisan and racial stereotypes interact and the degree to which those racialized partisan stereotypes can hinder or facilitate politicians' use of various types of racial signals.

I hypothesize that the public has perceptions of what it means for a politician to be a "white Democrat" versus a "black Democrat," or a "black Republican" versus a "white Republican." The public also has perceptions about the propensity of these different types of politicians to maintain or enforce the racial status quo. A politician who is an African American Democrat is more likely to be perceived as favoring blacks over whites than his white Democratic counterpart, whereas being an African American Republican tempers the stereotype of a Republican politician as looking out for the interests of whites.

I hypothesize that black Democratic politicians and white Republican politicians are at extreme ends of the spectrum, with black Democratic politicians the most likely to be perceived as favoring blacks over whites, and white Republicans the least likely to be perceived as favoring blacks over whites. Black Democratic politicians should be the most likely to be perceived as favoring blacks over whites because the stereotypes associated with both their racial and partisan characteristics point in the direction of racial liberalism. In contrast, for white Republican politicians, the stereotypes associated with both their racial and partisan characteristics point toward racial conservatism. Finally, given the conflicting nature of the racial and partisan stereotypes associated with white Democratic politicians and black Republican politicians, white Democratic politicians should be less likely than black Democratic politicians to be perceived as favoring blacks over whites, while black Republican politicians should be perceived as more likely to favor blacks over whites, relative to white Republican politicians.

Respondents were randomly assigned to rate either "White Republican politicians," "Black Republican politicians," "White Democratic politicians," or "Black Democratic politicians," on whether they "Favor Whites Over Blacks," "Blacks Over Whites," or "Treat Both Groups the Same." The scale was rescaled such that a rating of "zero" indicates favoritism toward African Americans, a rating of "one" indicates favoritism toward whites, and a rating at the midpoint of the scale indicates equal treatment of both groups. Figure 2.1 presents the average rating of the politicians for the 653 white Americans in the sample.

As hypothesized, black Democratic politicians were the least likely to be perceived as looking out for the interests of whites, with an average rating of 0.31. White Democratic politicians, however, were more likely

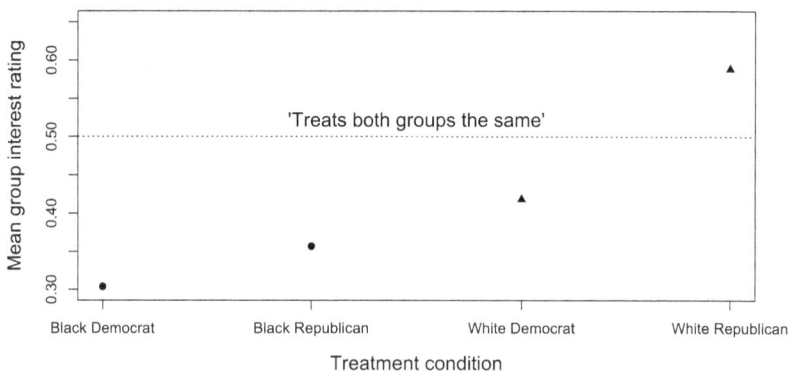

FIGURE 2.1. Respondents' Average Rating of Candidate Treatment of Blacks and Whites
Source: 2017 Cooperative Congressional Election Study
Note: The points represent the predicted rating of the candidate's treatment of blacks or whites. Respondents were randomly assigned to rate one of the following types of politicians on a seven-point scale: "Black Democratic politicians," "White Democratic politicians," "White Republican politicians," or "Black Republican politicians." "0" indicates that on average that type of politician "looks out for the interests of blacks," "1" indicates that on average that type of politician "looks out for the interests of whites," and "0.50" indicates that on average that type of politician "treats both groups the same."

than black Democratic politicians to be perceived as looking out for the interests of whites, with a mean rating of 0.43 ($p < .01$). Although the Democratic Party has a reputation of being beholden to their racial and ethnic minority constituents, it appears that the perception of this varies according to the race of the Democratic politician. It is likely that the racial cue of "white" helps undercut the perception of looking out for the interests of blacks, relative to the black Democratic politician.

Black Republican politicians were also more likely to be perceived as looking out for the interests of whites, relative to their black Democratic counterparts, with a mean rating of 0.36. Also of note is that even with the partisan cue of "Republican" black Republican politicians were more likely than their white Democratic counterparts to be perceived as looking out for the interests of blacks. This suggests that the racial cue of "black" overwhelmed the partisan cue of "Republican," such that a Republican's "racial loyalties" were presumed to be more aligned with African Americans than a Democratic politician's, when the Republican was black and the Democrat was white. White Republican politicians, on the other hand, were the least likely to be perceived as looking out for the interests of blacks. The average rating for white Republican politicians was 0.60, which is not only above the midpoint of the scale, but also separates them from black Democratic politicians by approximately one-third of the scale. A rating above the midpoint of the scale suggests that white Republican politicians are more likely than not to be perceived as looking out for the interests of whites. Conversely, black Democratic politicians are perceived as most likely to be looking out for the interests of blacks. In short, white Republican politicians and black Democratic politicians flank opposite ends of the perceived racial favoritism spectrum.

White Americans have distinct perceptions of what it means for a politician to be a "white Republican" versus a "black Republican," or a "black Democrat" as opposed to a "white Democrat." Although the Democratic Party is generally thought of as "the party of civil rights," the racial cue of "white" helped attenuate the perception that a white Democrat would look out for the interests of blacks. Similarly, the racial cue of "black" attenuated the perception that a black Republican would look out for the interests of whites. The racial distancing model is based in part on the premise that this perception of racial group favoritism, or lack thereof, then facilitates or hinders the ease with which different types of politicians use various types of appeals. In the next section, I discuss competing theories of candidate behavior as a means of situating the theory of racial distancing within the existing literature.

Competing Theories of Candidate Behavior

My discussion of competing theories of candidate behavior draws primarily on three literatures—racial priming, deracialization, and issue ownership. Each of these theories generates interesting, yet often disparate predictions about candidate behavior in a racialized two-party system. I discuss each of them in turn.

Racial Priming

Much of what we know about negative racial appeals and campaigns comes from studies that test the racial priming hypothesis (Mendelberg 2001; Valentino, Hutchings, and White 2002; Hurwitz and Peffley 2005). The racial priming hypothesis predicts that cues in the information environment, such as stereotypical imagery or racially coded language, activate or deactivate voters' negative racial attitudes, often about blacks, with consequences for voters' preferences about policy and vote choice. Examples of these cues in the information environment include negative stereotypical imagery depicting racial and ethnic minorities as criminals, and racially coded language, such as "law and order," "tough on crime," or "inner city." These stereotypical images and examples of racially coded language are connected to a bundle of associations about race, called "racial schemas." In the American context, racial schemas typically include racial stereotypes, beliefs about fairness and personal responsibility, and a sense of zero-sum group competition (Winter 2008). According to the theory of racial priming, racial schemas become relevant to public opinion when they are activated by racially coded language or negative racial imagery.

Although previous research has focused on the impact of negative or stereotypical imagery of African Americans, I argue that this approach is too narrow. Even an association with positive or counter-stereotypical portrayals of blacks can influence voters' perceptions of politicians. The reputations of the two major parties on race are so established that voters draw a different meaning from a white Democratic candidate associated with counter-stereotypical images of blacks, for example, as opposed to a white Republican candidate associated with the very same images.

Previous research (Stephens-Dougan 2016) finds that the mere presence of images of African Americans in a campaign mailer is associated with the perception that a white Democratic candidate will favor blacks over whites. Thus, even innocuous racial imagery can foster perceptions of zero-sum competition. These results also suggest that white Democratic candidates may be incentivized to engage in public distancing or minimizing their appearances with African American supporters and constituents when trying to gain white electoral support. My theory of racial distancing accounts for positive imagery because I argue that whites' negative racial attitudes about blacks are more pervasive than previously thought and are largely driven by perceptions of group competition or fears of racial group favoritism rather than simply irrational racial animus. Therefore, images of African Americans do not have to be negative to influence voters' perceptions and choices at the ballot box.

Another key element of the theory of racial priming is the notion that racial appeals are effective only when they are implicit or are ostensibly not about race. According to the theory, if the racial appeal is explicit in nature, voters will become aware of the racial content and reject the appeal. This is because an explicit appeal is perceived as violating "the norm of equality," or the prohibition against racist speech.[5] However, the racial priming hypothesis has largely been tested in the context of white candidates, which implies that only white politicians are likely to benefit from the activation of negative attitudes about blacks.

White politicians, however, face markedly different electoral considerations than black politicians. As a result of voters' perceptions of black versus white candidates, voters do not presume that white candidates will be indebted to black voters. Black candidates, especially black Democrats, are often perceived as being too attentive to racial issues, and thus may need to overcome the perception that they will be beholden to their black constituents. Furthermore, even when black candidates make negative appeals about other African Americans, they may still have a hard time convincing some white voters that they will not favor black constituents. Alternatively, white candidates may face more scrutiny when they make negative appeals about blacks that are more explicit in nature. Black people who make negative appeals about other blacks are presumed to still be looking out for the interests of black people or delivering a dose of "tough love," whereas the motives of a white politician with the identical message are more likely to be met with skepticism.

Since much of what we know about negative racial appeals has been tested in the context of white candidates, it is quite possible that we have overstated the ineffectiveness of explicit racial appeals. By focusing on the group most likely to be punished for using explicit racial appeals, we have overlooked the instances in which black candidates can reap political advantages by making explicit appeals about other African Americans. If explicit appeals are more effective than previous research has shown, we have also overstated the degree to which racist speech is socially prohibited in the post–civil rights era. In fact, work by Hutchings, Walton, and Benjamin (2010) and Valentino, Neuner, and Vandenbroek (2018) suggests that some of the norms around racist speech may have changed, such that racist speech is more accepted than previously thought. Racial distancing theory differs from this work, however, in that the focus is not whether these norms are more strongly enforced in certain parts of the country or whether these norms have devolved over time. Instead, the theory of racial distancing focuses on whether the norm against racist speech is more strongly adhered to when the message is delivered by a white politician versus a black politician, who is presumed to be more likely to be looking out for the interests of blacks. As this book demonstrates, not only are many white voters more receptive to explicit racial appeals from black politicians than from white politicians, but those whites with the most negative attitudes toward blacks are generally unperturbed by such appeals, regardless of the race of the person making the appeal.

Scholars have also explicitly stated that only Republican, presumably white, politicians are likely to benefit from a strategy of racial priming. Conversely, Democrats are assumed to not benefit from invoking negative stereotypes about blacks, since the Democratic Party is heavily reliant on the black vote. For example, according to Kinder and Sanders (1996, 10),

> The strategic problem for Democratic candidates is to maintain the loyalty and enthusiasm of black voters without alienating conservative whites: for Democratic presidential campaigns, the temptation on matters of race is silence and evasion. The strategic problem of Republican candidates is to draw the support of white conservatives without appearing to make racist appeals: the Republican temptation is racial codewords.

Kinder and Sanders neglect the possibility that black candidates, the overwhelming majority of whom are Democrats, as well as white Democratic candidates, might also succumb to the "Republican" temptation of racial codewords. *Race to the Bottom* argues that in addition to resorting to "silence and evasion," Democratic candidates, including African Americans, also make appeals to racial prejudice, in an effort to neutralize the impact of those attitudes on citizens' votes. Surprisingly, the literature on racial priming is relatively silent about how Democratic candidates should respond when their Republican opponents try to make race salient in a campaign. Clearly, the expectation is that Republicans will try to invoke race. But with the exception of Mendelberg (2001), scholars have articulated very few predictions about how Democratic (black) candidates should respond when their Republican opponents invoke race.

Mendelberg (2001) initially suggested that the successful strategy of Democratic candidates should be to rebut Republicans' negative racial appeals by calling attention to the racial nature of the appeals, but this prediction was not explicitly tested. In more recent work, however, Mendelberg (2009) describes several additional strategies candidates use when they are targeted by an implicit racial appeal, including one she refers to as "mimic." "Mimic," which is very similar to racial distancing, is when the party of the racial left (Democrats) "mimics the other party's communication, to show that despite its own relative leftward inclination on matters of race, it is no less sympathetic to white citizens' views than is its rival party" (Mendelberg 2009, 166). Tokeshi and Mendelberg (2015) cite Bill Clinton's condemnation of the rapper Sister Souljah during his 1992 campaign as an example of the mimic strategy, but again, the efficacy of the strategy was never explicitly tested.[6]

Additionally, very little has been said about how black candidates, regardless of party, might also respond to racial attacks from their white opponents. Recent research by Tokeshi and Mendelberg (2015), however, indicates that a rebuttal strategy is not equally effective across different types of candidates. They find that a rebuttal strategy is far more effective for white candidates than for their black counterparts, which underscores the importance of accounting for the racial characteristics of the messenger delivering the appeal. Also, given the expectation that Republican candidates will try to inject race into their campaigns for their political advantage, very little has been said about whether Democratic candidates, or black candidates from either major party, may adopt a preemptive strategy to combat the perception that they are beholden to their black constituents.

My theory of racial distancing revisits and extends the theory of racial priming by making a novel allowance for the racial and partisan characteristics of the messenger. In accordance with the literature on racial priming, I argue that white Republican candidates are incentivized to use racial signals to highlight their Democratic opponents' affiliation with a party that has a reputation for being beholden to racial and ethnic minorities, most notably blacks. When a Republican candidate discusses the issue of crime, for example, it likely activates both stereotypes about black criminality and the Democratic opponent's association with a national party that is perceived as "soft on crime," and accordingly not looking out for the interests of whites. Therefore, in keeping with previous racial priming research, I accept the premise that white Republican candidates benefit from making racial issues salient.

However, contrary to previous racial priming research, I offer more explicit expectations about the behavior of politicians other than white candidates. For example, I predict that white Republican politicians are uniquely able to benefit from more implicit forms of racial distancing because of the racial and partisan stereotypes associated with their group. Building on previous research that indicates that black politicians are perceived by white voters as less credible than white politicians when they claim an incident is racist (Tokeshi and Mendelberg 2015; Nelson, Sanbonmatsu, and McClerking 2007), I also predict that African American candidates of either major party are incentivized to use racial signals to powerfully and clearly send the message that they are neither overly concerned with black interests nor preoccupied with matters of race. For example, when a black candidate criticizes black people for their purported pathology, it may disrupt the existing racial schema that stereotypes a black candidate as beholden to African American constituents. My expectations about the use of negative racial appeals by Democrats also contradict previous racial priming research, which suggests that Democrats have an incentive to avoid negative racial appeals for fear of alienating their base (Kinder and Sanders 1996; Mendelberg 2001).[7]

My theory of racial distancing suggests a preemptive rather than reactive role for black candidates on racial matters. In other words, since race is the proverbial "elephant in the room," black candidates and white Democratic candidates are sometimes incentivized to preemptively send the message that they are not beholden to blacks. Candidates are most likely to use this strategy in majority-white jurisdictions in general elections. Black candidates assume that their white opponents are likely to inject race into the campaign in these areas for their own political advantage. Thus, black politicians, especially black Democrats running in majority-white jurisdictions, where white racial resentment is likely to be high, attempt to disrupt the stereotype that they are beholden to blacks. White Democrats may also engage in this preemptive strategy in general elections in majority-white jurisdictions that have, on average, moderate to high levels of racial resentment. White Republicans, on the other hand, are incentivized to remind racially resentful voters of their reputation for maintaining the racial status quo. Finally, black Republicans are similarly incentivized as their white Republican counterparts, but the fact that they are African American gives them more cover from charges of racism.

Deracialization

Another theory that offers insight into campaign strategy around race is the theory of deracialization. Since Democratic candidates are often stereotyped as being too beholden to black interests (Carmines and Stimson 1989; Frymer 1999), Democratic candidates seeking office in majority-white jurisdictions have been advised to use a "deracialization strategy." The originator of the term "deracialization," political scientist Charles Hamilton (1977), initially intended the concept as a strategy by which the Democrats could regain some of the ground they had lost to the Republicans during the 1972 presidential election. The concept was first introduced in 1973 by Hamilton at a National Urban League meeting. The meeting was designed to discuss strategies for African Americans organizing after the civil rights movement. By then, the Republican Party had successfully rolled out its infamous Southern strategy, in which Republican candidates, led by Richard Nixon, adopted coded language such as "anti-busing," and "pro–law and order." This language was intended to appeal to whites, particularly Southerners, who were uncomfortable with the pace of integration in the aftermath of the civil rights movement.

Hamilton subsequently expounded on the concept of deracialization in a 1977 position paper commissioned by the Democratic Party, in which he advised the Democrats to pursue a deracialized electoral strategy, thereby denying their Republican opponents the opportunity of using race as a "polarizing issue." Hamilton also encouraged the Democratic Party to work for "deracialized solutions" such as national health insurance and an income maintenance program. Essentially, Hamilton was encouraging the Democratic Party to emphasize those issues that had broad appeal to the electorate across racial lines. Practically speaking, much of the research on the deracialization strategy focuses on black candidates, although deracialization was originally intended as a strategy for Democrats more broadly.

Building upon the work of Hamilton (1977), McCormick and Jones (1993, 76) define deracialiazation as "conducting a campaign in a stylistic fashion that defuses the polarizing effect of race by avoiding explicit reference to race-specific issues, while at the same time emphasizing those issues that are perceived as racially transcendent, thus mobilizing a broad segment of the electorate for purposes of capturing or maintaining public office." They also suggest that deracialization entails black candidates presenting an image that is "reassuring to the white electorate" (76). Racial distancing is distinct from this definition of deracialization because the emphasis is on avoiding race, rather than engaging race in a manner that positions the candidate away from racial and ethnic minorities, which is what my racial distancing theory suggests. Furthermore, it is unclear what McCormick and Jones mean when they mention presenting an image that is "reassuring to the white electorate." They reference behavior such as avoiding the discussion of "welfare and set-asides," but they do not entertain the possibility that black politicians might also pathologize racial and ethnic minorities, which is distinct to racial distancing theory. Furthermore, their definition of racial distancing is limited to black candidates, whereas racial distancing encompasses a wider range of politicians across the racial and political spectrum.

More recent work on deracialization also suggests that black candidates would not use negative racial appeals. McIlwain and Caliendo (2011, 17), for example, say, "Put simply, we see very little evidence to suggest that minority candidates have any interest in appealing to negative stereotypes, resentments, and prejudices associated with the racial group to which they belong." Stout (2015) has a similar conclusion, arguing that voters respond positively to positive framings of race. Stout's classification of racial appeals is based on a content analysis of over 2,000 articles, which is a formidable task. However, the coding of the newspaper articles is not a direct test of the effect of a specific racial appeal on voters' evaluation of a candidate. My experiments enable me to manipulate and directly test the effect of negative racial appeals on vote choice.

Race to the Bottom builds on the theory of deracialization, arguing that deracialization, while useful, is too static to account for the contemporary manifestations of the behavior of Democratic and Republican candidates pursuing white electoral support. Previous research still has not accounted for the phenomenon whereby Republicans *and* Democrats—blacks and whites alike—invoke race but do so in a manner that indicates that they will not advance racial and ethnic minorities at the expense of whites. Racial distancing, unlike deracialization, is not simply the absence of a discussion of race. Rather, it often entails the invocation of race in a manner that signals that the politician will not disrupt the racial status quo. Racial distancing is an effort to distance the politician from racial and ethnic minorities, rhetorically, visually, or substantively. Racial distancing, unlike deracialization, is not simply about an emphasis on nonracial policy issues, but often, although not exclusively, involves a distinct *pathologizing* of racial and ethnic minorities.

Although black candidates have been advised to adopt a deracialized approach, it still remains unclear whether deracialized appeals are sufficient. Black candidates' efforts to deracialize their campaigns are often overcome by their white opponents, who attempt to garner white support by playing on white fears. Therefore, racial distancing theory posits that black candidates may have an incentive to run campaigns that are more than deracialized—rather than avoid the topic of race, they talk about race in a manner that signals that they will not be beholden to black voters. As Carter and Dowe (2015, 109) note, "If what the literature suggests about whites' racial judgments of black candidates holds, it seems highly unlikely that deracialization does the work these candidates expect." Some black candidates may therefore be incentivized to go above and beyond a strategy of deracialization, by engaging in racial distancing. My theory of racial distancing suggests that explicit racial appeals can be as effective, and in some cases more effective, for black politicians than deracialized appeals. Racial distancing suggests that black candidates do not have to avoid the issue of race altogether to be successful among white voters. Contrary to deracialization theory, black politicians can talk openly about race and racial issues. Talking about race in and of itself is not problematic—talking about race in a manner associated with racial liberalism is what is problematic when trying to gain widespread electoral support from white Americans.

The two strategies are not mutually exclusive. Many candidates primarily rely on a deracialization strategy, avoiding the discussion of racialized issues such as welfare and affirmative action or emphasizing issues that have broad appeal, such as health care or the economy. However, candidates may also use racial distancing as a complement to their dominant strategy of deracialization. In other words, some candidates may avoid race for the most part, but at crucial junctures use racial signals to indicate that they will not be indebted to racial and ethnic minorities. Harris (2012), for example, argues that Obama strategically engaged in the policing of black behavior in his campaign speeches, *after* he shored up black support, which gave his campaign confidence that he had virtually unwavering support from African Americans.

When candidates make racial appeals that invoke negative stereotypes about racial and ethnic minorities—an element of racial distancing strategy— rather than simply avoiding race, they are engaging race in a manner that is counter-stereotypical for black politicians and, to a lesser degree, white Democratic politicians, yet stereotype-consistent for white Republican politicians.[8] This means that white Republican candidates are reinforcing their reputation for maintaining and enforcing the racial status quo, while black politicians and white Democratic politicians are disrupting the stereotype of being beholden to racial and ethnic minorities. Therefore, unlike deracialization, racial distancing is not exclusively available to Democratic candidates. Both Democratic and Republican candidates, blacks and whites alike, are incentivized to demonstrate to racially moderate to racially conservative whites that they are not beholden to black voters. Like deracialization, racial distancing is a method for candidates to "enhance effectively the likelihood of white electoral support" (McCormick and Jones 1993, 76).

While deracialization and racial distancing are both approaches by which candidates can "enhance effectively the likelihood of white electoral support," black candidates in particular might prefer to engage in racial distancing above and beyond a strategy of deracialization. Black candidates may need a "stronger signal" than white candidates to disrupt the perception that they will be beholden to racial and ethnic minorities. White voters often perceive black candidates less favorably than their white counterparts (Parker, Sawyer, and Towler 2009; Sigelman et al. 1995; Williams 1990), and black candidates are also more likely to be perceived as liberal and preoccupied with minority rights (Jones 2014; McDermott 1998). Therefore, racial distancing may be more effective in helping dispel some of the negative stereotypes that are associated with black candidates, relative to a strategy of deracialization, which simply avoids the topic of race altogether.

Racial distancing may also be a preferred strategy relative to deracialization because racial distancing, particularly the use of racial messages that invoke negative stereotypes about racial and ethnic minorities, provides more information to voters about a candidate's position on racial policies. By following a deracialization strategy and avoiding racial matters, candidates are in effect providing voters with little to no information about their stance on racial matters. Research indicates that when voters lack information, they are more likely to rely on their partisan and racial stereotypes of the candidate (McDermott 1998). Since Democratic candidates and candidates of color are stereotyped as racially liberal, a deracialized strategy, which provides little to no information about a candidate's stance on racialized policies, would likely work to the detriment of candidates of color. On the other hand, when white Democratic candidates and candidates of color discuss racial matters through a strategy of racial distancing, they are providing information that helps disrupt the stereotype of the candidate as racially liberal. Counter-stereotypical behavior that provides individuating information inhibits reliance on negative stereotypes (Hurwitz and Peffley 1998; Bobo and Kluegel 1993). In short, black candidates may be especially motivated to use racial distancing in addition to, or instead of, deracialization. A racial distancing strategy provides white voters with more information, relative to deracialization, and consequently helps disrupt the stereotype of black candidates as liberal on racial matters and preoccupied with matters of race.

Issue Ownership

Petrocik's (1996) theory of issue ownership offers another approach to understanding campaign strategy. Issue ownership is the idea that the Democratic and Republican parties have developed a reputation for having strengths on different political issues. This reputational advantage is the result of each party's tendency to promote the same issues repeatedly on behalf of the groups with which they are aligned. According to the theory of issue ownership, candidates benefit from emphasizing those issues that their affiliated party "owns" through a strategy of agenda-setting (Petrocik 1996). In other words, candidates will discuss the issues on which they have a reputational advantage in an effort to encourage voters to make their decision on those grounds.

Since as early as the New Deal, and especially after the civil rights movement of the 1960s, the Democratic Party has become increasingly associated with racial and ethnic minorities, while the Republican Party has become more associated with white Americans. The two parties have also developed distinct reputations or perceived expertise on different policy issues, including race (Philpot 2004). Republicans are perceived as traditionally owning issues such as crime, law enforcement, and national security, while the conventional wisdom is that the Democratic Party owns social issues, including the issue of race (Petrocik 1996). For example, when asked in surveys, white voters consistently perceive the Democratic Party as more "pro-black" than the Republican Party. Since 1972, the American National Election Study has asked respondents to place the Democratic Party, the Republican Party, the Democratic presidential nominee, and the Republican presidential nominee, as well as themselves on a seven-point scale that ranges from "Blacks Should Help Themselves" to "Government Should Help Blacks." As indicated in figure 2.2, the majority of white Americans have consistently rated the Democratic Party and the Democratic presidential nominee in any given year as more likely to favor "aid to blacks" than the Republican Party or the Republican presidential nominee, respectively.[9] Thus, the Democratic Party "owns" the issue of government aid to blacks.

Figure 2.2 also shows that using the same scale, the majority of white Americans oppose government aid to blacks, which indicates that support for government aid to African Americans is a consistently unpopular position among white Americans. Thus, not only do the two major parties have distinct reputations with respect to this issue, but, at least among whites, the Republican Party also enjoys a reputational advantage on this matter. Although we typically think of the Democratic Party "owning" the issue of race, this Democratic reputational "advantage" on race is actually a reputational *disadvantage* among the majority of white Americans. The perceived position of the Democratic Party on "government aid to blacks," as well as the party's position on many other racial issues, is at odds with most white Americans' position on this issue. Conversely, the perceived position of the Republican Party on "government aid to blacks," as well as a host of other racial issues, aligns with the position of most white Americans. The majority of white Americans,

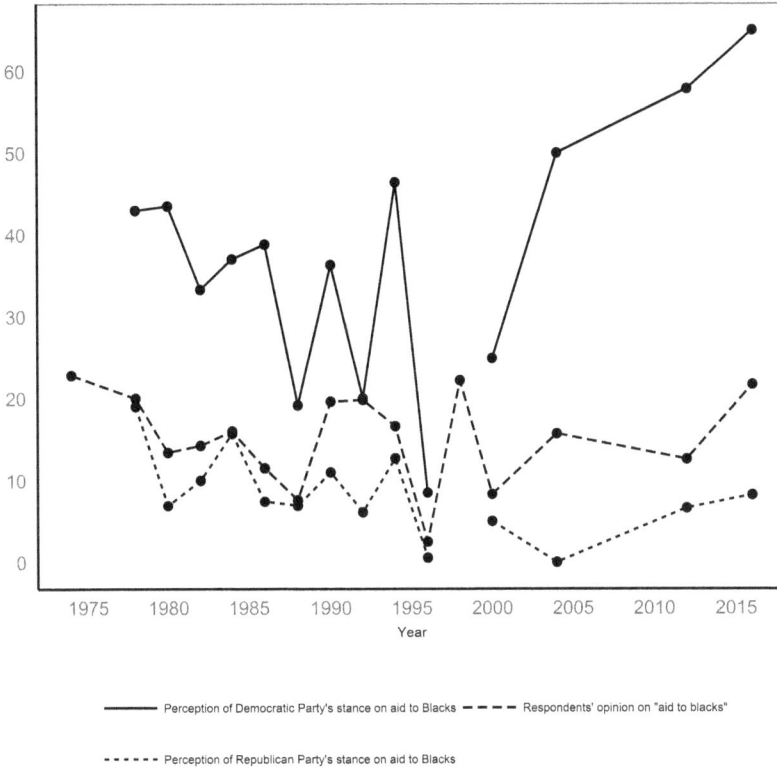

FIGURE 2.2. Respondents' Perceptions of Issue Ownership of "Aid to Blacks"
Source: American National Election Studies 1972–2016
Note: Author's calculations from the American National Election Study. Question was not asked in 1992 and 1996.

including the majority of white Democrats, for example, have also historically supported the Republican Party's opposition to affirmative action (Hillygus and Shields 2008). Yet the theory of issue ownership suggests that the Democratic Party and Democratic politicians should campaign on their racial liberalism because they "own" the issue of race.

What happens when a party "owns an issue" that is unpopular? In the case of Democrats, because of the unpopularity of racial liberalism among many white voters, Democrats running for office in majority-white jurisdictions may actually prefer to not own the issue of "aid to blacks." Conversely, the Republican Party in effect "owns the issue" or the position of racial conservatism, which works to their advantage when appealing to white voters, since many white voters are also moderate to conservative on racial issues. A major limitation of the theory of issue ownership, therefore, is that it does not account for context. Owning certain issues might be popular in some places or among some groups, while owning those very same issues might be unpopular in other places and among some other groups. The Democratic Party's reputation for a relatively progressive racial agenda is not universally popular. While racial liberalism might play well in majority-minority jurisdictions because voters of color are more likely to be racially liberal (Hutchings 2009; Kinder and Winter 2001; Kinder and Sanders 1996), a reputation for racial liberalism is likely not an advantage in many majority-white jurisdictions.

The theory of issue ownership is relatively silent about what a candidate should do when their affiliated party is at a reputational *disadvantage*. We have seen evidence of candidates trying to take the lead on issues that arguably their party does not own, such as 1988 Democratic presidential nominee Michael Dukakis campaigning with a tank to trespass on the Republican-owned issue of national security or Bill Clinton campaigning to "end welfare as we know it." However, to my knowledge, we have yet to systematically study how Democratic candidates, blacks and whites, encroach on the Republican Party's racial conservatism or reputational strength for looking out for the interests of whites.

A tension exists between the expectations derived from the theory of issue ownership and the nature of a two-party system that encourages parties to appeal to the hypothetical median voter who is most often white, and racially moderate to racially conservative. On the one hand, the theory of issue ownership suggests that Democratic politicians should focus on a progressive racial agenda, because of the party's reputational "advantage" on racial matters. On the other hand, a progressive racial agenda is at odds with the preferences of the average white voter. This is especially true in a political context in which intergroup competition is central to politics.

One way to test whether the theoretical expectations of issue ownership hold in the context of race and politics is to examine the issues on which candidates air campaign ads. If Democrats are highlighting their reputational "advantage" for racial liberalism, then we should expect to see Democrats airing more ads focused on civil rights and highlighting the Democratic Party's reputation for racial liberalism. However, if Democrats are unlikely to air ads about their reputational advantage on civil rights, then perhaps the predictions of issue ownership theory do not hold in this context. In accordance with issue ownership theory, we should expect Republicans to air more ads that highlight their reputational advantage for maintaining and enforcing the racial status quo. Although it was not developed with the race and politics literature in mind, issue ownership theory is still useful for developing theoretical predictions about what parties and candidates will choose to emphasize in their campaigns when it comes to matters of race.

My theory of racial distancing predicts that both Democratic and Republican candidates will use negative signals about blacks and other racial and ethnic minorities to appeal to racially moderate to racially conservative voters. Rather than embrace the perception that they are racially progressive, Democrats instead shy away from their reputation of racial liberalism by distancing themselves from blacks—at least when it is strategically advantageous—which is an idea that has been articulated by Frymer (1999). However, to my knowledge, this book marks the first empirical test of this strategy, while also accounting for a wide range of racial and partisan characteristics of the politicians using the strategy.

In sum, the theories of racial priming, deracialization, and issue ownership are useful because they generate clear, albeit conflicting, predictions about which of the two parties we can expect to use negative racial appeals about blacks for their political advantage. The racial priming literature suggests that Republicans will inject race into campaigns by positioning themselves against issues associated with blacks. The intent behind this strategy would be to prime racial prejudice as a consideration that would negatively affect evaluations of Democratic candidates. Implicit in the theory is the notion that black candidates would also not inject race into their campaigns by positioning themselves against issues associated with blacks. The theory of issue ownership, on the other hand, would suggest that Democrats would talk about racialized issues positively to highlight their strength on civil rights. Their goal would be to make those issues more important as evaluation criteria in the minds of sympathetic voters. Conversely, Republicans would avoid talking about these issues, because they are not a traditional area of strength for them. Meanwhile, the deracialization literature suggests that Democrats, especially black Democrats, would avoid talking about racial issues altogether, to prevent Republicans from exploiting these issues to their political advantage.

The Theoretical Expectations of the Racial Distancing Model

My theory of racial distancing is based on three core tenets. First, candidates running for office in majority-white jurisdictions have an incentive to "signal" that they are not beholden to the interests of racial and ethnic minorities. In other words, they must indicate that they will not disrupt the racial status quo or challenge the racial hierarchy in a way that benefits racial and ethnic minorities at the perceived expense of whites. Second, however, candidates must also indicate that they are not racially insensitive, or at the very least they must have some measure of plausible deniability of being racist (toward blacks).[10] Third, a candidate's race and partisanship close or open different options for racial distancing.

The first tenet is based on two premises: (1) race—specifically, black-white relations—has long been at the center of American politics (Hutchings and Valentino 2004; Carmines and Stimson 1989), and intergroup competition is endemic to the American political system; (2) most white Americans, who constitute the majority of the electorate, are moderate to conservative on racial issues. Thus, party leaders frame their messages to appeal to these racially conservative voters. Candidates who have been perceived as too liberal on racial issues or too concerned with racial equity have historically not fared well in national and statewide elections (e.g., Walter Mondale, Michael Dukakis, Bill Bradley). Democratic Party leaders are further incentivized to racially distance because they perceive racial distancing as a strategy that is less risky than trying to appeal to their African American base. Although there may be concerns that racial distancing could alienate the Democratic Party's base of African Americans, I argue that because African Americans are a captured minority (Frymer 1999), the Democratic Party's strategy is likely perceived as "less risky" than appeals associated with racial liberalism. This risk aversion is especially palpable after high-profile losses, such as the 1984, 1988, and even 2016 presidential elections. As Frymer (1999, 41) has articulated, "Party leaders shy away from more volatile and less certain appeals to black voters in favor of appeals to a hypothetical median white voter." I contend that a prevalent way to appeal to this median white voter is to employ the strategy of racial distancing.

The second tenet of the theory of racial distancing suggests that candidates must show that they are not racially insensitive toward African Americans in particular.[11] Whites are known to impression-manage their responses to racial matters, because of concerns about appearing racist (Kuklinski, Cobb, and Gilens 1997; Mendelberg 2001; Jost, Banaji, and Nosek 2004). Most white voters do not want to be thought of as racist (Berinsky 2002), nor do they wish to be associated with a candidate who is perceived as racist. In turn, candidates often demonstrate that they are not racist by making symbolic gestures toward racial and ethnic minorities (Philpot 2007). They also rely on implicit or racially coded messages that have a measure of plausible deniability of being racist. According to Mendelberg (2001), in the post–civil rights era a norm of racial equality has developed, making publicly racist statements unacceptable. Mendelberg defines the norm of racial equality as "the prohibition against making racist statements in public" (2001, 17), personal repudiation of "the sentiments that have come to be most closely associated with the ideology of white supremacy—the immutable inferiority of blacks, the desirability of segregation, and the just nature of segregation in favor of whites" (19), and commitment to "basic racial equality [and] in particular to equal opportunity" (18). In other words, a social prohibition exists against espousing ideas that may indicate a belief in the biological or inherent inferiority of blacks, which means that in the post–civil rights era, candidates are incentivized to at least appear as if they have embraced the norm of racial equality. This also means that in the post–civil rights era, politicians may continue to appeal to negative predispositions about African Americans, but rather than being critiqued for their "inherent inferiority," blacks are criticized for their lack of work ethic and unwillingness to adhere to American values. Short of using racial epithets, a candidate will likely have some measure of plausible deniability that his appeal or comments were not about race (Bonilla-Silva 2010). However, the race and partisanship of the candidate will influence the degree to which voters will believe the claim that the comments were not about race, as well as the degree to which the comments are perceived as egregious. As I will demonstrate later, black candidates are less likely than their white counterparts to be perceived as violating the norm of racial equality, even if their comments derogate other black people.

Therefore, the third tenet of the theory is that candidates' race and, to a lesser degree, their partisanship can open and close different options for racial distancing—specifically their *credibility* and *latitude* to engage in racial distancing. "Credibility" refers to the degree to which voters believe a candidate who signals that she will not disrupt the racial status quo. "Latitude" refers to the degree to which a candidate can engage in racial distancing without experiencing scrutiny or backlash from racially liberal whites and people of color. Depending on a candidate's race and partisanship, she may be more or less likely to be stereotyped as looking out for the interests of whites versus blacks, which then affects her credibility when she racially signals, as well as the latitude that she has to racially signal without scrutiny or backlash. That is, white Republican candidates are presumed to be committed defenders of the racial status quo. However, Democrat candidates (especially black Democrats) are presumed to champion the interests of racial minorities to the detriment of the racial status quo.

The third tenet is based on the parallel processing model of stereotypes, as well as the justification-suppression model of prejudice. A parallel processing model of stereotyping suggests that when stereotypes overlap, individuals will be more likely to recognize the connections between multiple stereotypes, and this can increase the strength of an overall stereotype (Kunda and Thagard 1996). Democrats, for example, have a reputation for being racially progressive, to the point that it is a perceived handicap for them among some white voters. Likewise, black politicians are more likely to be stereotyped as more liberal than their white counterparts (Sigelman et al. 1995; Williams 1990). According to Hajnal (2007, 3), white voters in particular "expect a black leader to redistribute income, encourage integration, and generally channel resources toward the black community." Therefore, in the case of black Democratic politicians, both the partisan and the racial stereotypes that voters apply to them point to racial liberalism. The stereotypes reinforce each other, increasing the strength of the overall stereotype of black Democratic politicians as racially liberal and preoccupied with race.

In contrast, both the partisan and the racial stereotypes that voters apply to white Republican politicians point to racial conservatism; they reinforce each other, which increases the strength of the overall stereotype of white Republican politicians as racially conservative, and perhaps even racially insensitive. Given the nature of these racial and partisan stereotypes, I expect that black Democratic politicians will have the least credibility when they signal that they will not disrupt the racial status quo, whereas white Republican politicians will have the most credibility when they engage in such distancing. I also expect that black politicians will have more latitude to engage in racial distancing, experiencing less scrutiny and backlash for this behavior from racially liberal whites and people of color than their white counterparts. Since black politicians are more likely than white politicians to be perceived as looking out for the interests of blacks versus whites, even when black politicians disparage blacks, they are able to do so without much scrutiny or backlash from voters. In the case of black Republicans and white Democrats, I expect that the stereotypes associated with their racial group will supersede their partisan stereotype, such that black Republicans will be perceived as more likely to favor blacks over whites, relative to their white Republican counterparts. Similarly, white Democrats will be less likely to be perceived as favoring blacks over whites, relative to their black Democratic counterparts.

My expectations about the latitude with which politicians can engage in racial distancing are also informed by the justification-suppression model of prejudice (Crandall and Eshleman 2003). According to the justification-suppression model, people are often highly motivated to seek out justifications that allow the unsanctioned expression of their prejudices. A justification is a "psychological or social process that can serve as an opportunity to express genuine prejudice without suffering external or internal sanction" (Crandall and Eshleman 2003, 425). A black politician who invokes negative stereotypes about racial and ethnic minorities helps justify the expression of those stereotypes by white voters.

In short, black Democratic politicians are most likely to be perceived as looking out for the interests of blacks, relative to other types of candidates, because both their partisan and their racial stereotypes are associated with racial liberalism. As a result, they are the least trusted to maintain and enforce the racial status quo. However, they also have the most latitude to engage in racial distancing without scrutiny or backlash from racially liberal whites and people of color. On the other hand, both the partisan and the racial stereotypes for white Republicans are associated with racial conservatism. This means that voters are more likely to believe white Republican politicians when they signal that they will not disrupt the racial status quo, relative to other politicians. However, white Republican politicians are also more likely to be scrutinized for using racial signals, relative to other types of candidates, because of stereotypes of them as not only racially conservative, but also racially insensitive. Finally, for black Republican politicians and white Democratic politicians, the stereotypes associated with their respective racial and partisan groups conflict, such that black Republicans will be perceived as more racially liberal than their white co-partisans, while white Democrats will be perceived as more racially conservative than their black co-partisans. In short, given the reputations of the two major parties on race, as well as stereotypes of black versus white candidates, candidates' ability to use different appeals is contingent on largely their race, and to a lesser degree, their partisanship.

I test my theory mostly through a series of survey experiments. I manipulate the type of appeal, the race of the candidate, and sometimes the candidate's partisanship to examine voter-level reactions to different distancing strategies. I find that racially moderate and racially conservative whites are more receptive to candidates who direct personal responsibility messages specifically to African Americans. Many white voters are more likely to support a candidate who is willing to "put African Americans in their place," and this is especially true when the candidate is black. I also provide evidence of politicians engaging in racial distancing outside of the survey experiment setting, as a means of providing not only external validity but also richness and context.

Measuring Negative Racial Attitudes toward African Americans

Throughout the book I talk at length about the incentives for politicians to appeal to racially moderate and racially conservative whites. By "racially moderate and racially conservative whites," I am referring to white Americans who answer in the affirmative to survey items designed to capture negative racial attitudes toward African Americans. I rely primarily on two metrics, the racial resentment scale and a question that measures the endorsement of the negative stereotype of African Americans as lazy.

The racial resentment scale is a Likert scale that was developed by Kinder and Sanders (1996) to distinguish between white Americans who harbor resentment or hostility toward African Americans—white racial moderates and conservatives—and white Americans who are racially sympathetic—white racial liberals. The scale is constructed on the basis of the following four statements:

"Irish, Italian, Jewish, and many other minorities overcame prejudice and worked their way up. Blacks should do the same without any special favors."

"Generations of slavery and discrimination have created conditions that make it difficult for blacks to work their way out of the lower class."

"Over the past few years, blacks have gotten less than they deserve."

"It's really a matter of some people not trying hard enough; if blacks would only try harder, they could be just as well off as whites."

The scale is coded from 0 to 1, such that those individuals who score at or around the midpoint of 0.50 are classified as "racial moderates." People who score above the midpoint are classified as "racial conservatives," whereas people who score below the midpoint are classified as "racial liberals." The average racial resentment score for white Americans is consistently around 0.65, and the median is consistently around 0.62.[12] If we rely on the standard of the racial resentment scale, most white Americans are racially moderate to racially conservative.

Critics of the racial resentment scale argue that it is actually capturing "principled conservatism" (Sniderman and Carmines 1997; Sniderman and Piazza 1993), while others argue that the scale means different things for liberals and conservatives (Feldman and Huddy 2005; Huddy and Feldman 2009). But the scale still does a remarkably good job of distinguishing between white Americans who express hostility toward blacks and those who do not express hostility toward African Americans (Kinder and Sanders 1996; Tesler and Sears 2010). Furthermore, even if one does not believe that the racial resentment scale is capturing what it claims to capture, most white Americans would still be classified as racially moderate to racially conservative, given that most white Americans oppose most governmental efforts to reduce racial inequality.[13]

Aside from the racial resentment scale, I also rely on a metric that measures the degree to which respondents adhere to negative stereotypes about African Americans. This metric is commonly used on nationally representative surveys, such as the American National Election Study and the General Social Survey. Respondents are asked to rate how hardworking blacks and whites are on seven-point scales, ranging from 1 (lazy) to 7 (hardworking).[14] A difference score is subsequently constructed by subtracting the score respondents gave blacks from the score they gave whites. The difference score enables researchers to examine how a respondent views blacks relative to whites. If respondents rate their own group as more hardworking than African Americans, then the rating is indicative of prejudice toward African Americans, whereas if the scores are equal, then it suggests that respondents are not exhibiting prejudice toward African Americans. One virtue of using this measure of prejudice is that unlike the racial resentment scale, it cannot be confounded with conservative ideology. A potential limitation of this measure, however, is that social desirability pressures may limit self-reporting. Thus, this measure is likely underestimating the number of white Americans who are prejudiced toward African Americans. Nevertheless, in 2016, approximately 42 percent of white respondents in the American National Election Study rated African Americans as lazier than whites.

In short, the takeaway here is that regardless of whether we are relying on the racial resentment scale or the anti-black stereotype measure, a nontrivial sum of white Americans consistently express racial attitudes indicative of unfavorable views toward African Americans. Drawing on Blumer's (1958) group position model, I assume that many white Americans who express animus toward African Americans do so not merely out of irrational prejudice, but also out of a commitment to maintaining the racial hierarchy, or their "group position" vis-à-vis African Americans and other minorities. In contemporary American politics, however, racial animus is expressed primarily in the language of individualism—not group position. As noted by Kinder and Mendelberg (2000, 60), "Prejudice's public expression and private language are preoccupied with black Americans' specifically individualistic shortcomings: that blacks fail to display the virtues of hard work and self-sacrifice that white Americans claim as central to their own lives and to their society." Many white Americans who are hostile toward racial and ethnic minorities may couch that hostility in language about minorities' purported lack of hard work and self-reliance, even if they are primarily concerned about competition over resources and status. Furthermore, as noted by Bobo and Tuan (2006), many Americans conflate perceived group competition with the belief that racial and ethnic minorities do not adhere to rugged individualism and hard work.

Concluding Remarks

The main takeaway here is that racial distancing theory predicts voters' reactions to negative racial appeals, conditioned on the racial and, to a lesser degree, the partisan characteristics of the candidate making the appeal. Specifically, racial distancing theory predicts that when white candidates engage in racial distancing, they are more likely to be believed that they will enforce and maintain the racial status quo, relative to their black counterparts. However, they are also more likely to be scrutinized or receive backlash from racially liberal whites and people of color, relative to their black counterparts. But despite my expectations about the role of the race of candidates in racialized communication, surprisingly, much of the relevant literature does not account for the racial and partisan characteristics of the messenger. The failure to consider the incentives for a wider range of candidates to invoke race negatively for political gain likely means that we have made erroneous conclusions about the efficacy of explicit racial appeals—namely, we may have been too quick to conclude that explicit racial appeals are universally rejected. Since the racial priming hypothesis has been largely tested in the context of white politicians, we may have overstated the inefficacy of explicit racial appeals, because white politicians are more likely than black politicians to be punished for the use of explicit appeals.

Contrary to previous theories of candidate behavior, specifically racial priming, deracialization, and issue ownership, the theory of racial distancing predicts that Democrats and Republicans, blacks and whites, will all make appeals to racial prejudice. White Republicans will make these appeals to keep race salient in the minds of voters. Black politicians, and, to a lesser degree, white Democratic politicians, will use these negative appeals to disrupt the stereotype that they are overly concerned with racial issues. Candidates are most likely to use racial distancing in majority-white jurisdictions, where racial resentment is higher than in more racially diverse areas. White Republican candidates want to remind white voters that their Democratic opponents are too "liberal" on matters of race, while Democratic candidates and black candidates want to distance themselves from the stereotype of Democrats and blacks as beholden to black voters.

When previous studies have examined the impact of negative racial appeals in campaigns, the emphasis is invariably on how Republican candidates might be advantaged when racial issues are made salient in the campaign (Mendelberg 2001; Valentino, Hutchings, and White 2002; for an exception, see White 2007). Left unexamined is whether Democratic candidates and black candidates more broadly can actually benefit by making race salient in a campaign, by doing so in a manner that signals that they are not beholden to African Americans. It is well documented that candidates who are perceived as liberal on matters of race have found it difficult to win elections in majority-white jurisdictions. But less attention has been devoted to whether their perceived liberalism gives them more latitude to use negative racial messages to their political advantage. I expect candidates who make negative racial appeals about blacks to be more "electable" than those who do not make those types of appeals. In fact, although it is commonly believed that racially resentful whites will not support black candidates, electoral support for blacks is actually more nuanced—black candidates and candidates of color more broadly can and do gain acceptance from racially resentful whites, as long as they are perceived as not threatening the racial status quo.

I address these expectations over the course of the book by developing and systematically testing my theory of racial distancing, which is based on three core tenets. First, candidates running for office in majority-white jurisdictions have an incentive to "signal" that they are not beholden to the interests of racial and ethnic minorities. In other words, they must indicate that they will not disrupt the racial status quo or challenge the racial hierarchy in a way that benefits racial and ethnic minorities at the perceived expense of whites. Second, candidates face a balancing act in which they must signal that they will not disrupt the racial status quo while also indicating that they are not racist. Third, a candidate's ability to use negative racial appeals is either facilitated or thwarted by her race and partisanship.

In chapter 3, I examine the case of the most prominent politician to engage in racial distancing, President Barack Obama. Obama's election was supposed to usher in a post-racial era, but by routinely engaging in racial distancing, he reinforced the stereotype that African Americans are more in need of personal responsibility than any other group of Americans. As I demonstrate in the next chapter, Obama was more likely to invoke the rhetoric of personal responsibility when talking with predominantly black audiences than when he was talking with majority-white audiences.

CHAPTER THREE

Obama as Racial Distancer

I was trying to think about who he was tonight. It's interesting: he is post-racial, by all appearances. I forgot he was black tonight for an hour. . . . I think it was the scope of his discussion. It was so broad-ranging, so in tune with so many problems, of aspects, and aspects of American life that you don't think in terms of the old tribalism, the old ethnicity.
— Chris Matthews

After President Obama's first State of the Union address, host of the MSNBC television show *Hardball*, Chris Matthews, said that he "forgot that the president was black." The liberal host also went on to say, "It's [Obama's race] something we don't even think about."[1] Matthews's comments were intended as praise but were naive at best, suggesting that blackness is a handicap that needs to be overcome. Matthews's comments also suggest that Obama did such a good job of deracializing his campaign, or avoiding any discussion of racial matters, that some people "forgot" he was black. Although the express purpose of a deracialization strategy is not to make voters forget that a candidate is black, deracialization is a campaign strategy whereby candidates deemphasize racial issues, choosing instead to focus on issues that have broad appeal. According to Matthews, President Obama's first State of the Union address was "so broad-ranging, so in tune with so many problems, of aspects, and aspects of American life that you don't think in terms of the old tribalism, the old ethnicity," which is indicative of a deracialized strategy as outlined by scholars (Hamilton 1977; McCormick and Jones 1993). For example, McCormick and Jones (1993, 76) suggest that when using a deracialized strategy, candidates should avoid explicit references to issues that have become racialized, such as welfare and affirmative action, thus presenting an image that is "reassuring to the white electorate."

Although deracialization was originally intended as a strategy for Democratic candidates in general, practically speaking, scholarly and popular interest has tended to focus on the deracialization strategies of black Democratic politicians, rather than Democrats more broadly. Much of this interest in deracialization was sparked by black Democratic candidates who were elected to office in majority-white jurisdictions as "historic firsts" on "Black Tuesday," Election Day, November 1989. These included L. Douglas Wilder as governor of Virginia, the nation's first black governor since Reconstruction; David Dinkins as mayor of New York; and Norman Rice as mayor of Seattle. More recently, however, the focus has shifted to a new cohort of black candidates who came of age in the post–civil rights era and who have pursued office in majority-white jurisdictions (Gillespie 2010).[2] These candidates include Harold Ford Jr., who lost a close election in 2006 for one of Tennessee's U.S. Senate seats; former governor of Massachusetts Deval Patrick; and of course, President Barack Obama. However, just because these black Democratic candidates received significant support from white voters, does it mean that they ran exclusively deracialized campaigns?

Previous research suggests that many of the black politicians who were presumed to be examples of deracialized politicians were in fact not deracialized. Summers and Klinkner (1996), for example, cited numerous examples of racially targeted campaigning and issue development to argue that John Daniels, the first black mayor of New Haven, Connecticut, was not a deracialized politician. Henderson (1996) contended that the first African American mayor of Baltimore, Kurt Schmoke, transcended race, but was not deracialized. More recently, Franklin (2010) argued that Harold Ford Jr., in his 2006 run for the U.S. Senate, adopted fiscally conservative policies when campaigning in predominantly white areas, but he also used race-conscious appeals that were attractive to liberal and progressive African Americans when those messages were *contained* in African-American jurisdictions, a phenomenon Franklin refers to as "situational deracialization."

In a similar vein, I argue that President Obama did not run a purely deracialized presidential campaign in 2008. Instead, Obama, like many "deracialized politicians," often went far and above deracialization, by rhetorically, visually, and substantively disassociating himself from other African Americans through a strategy of racial distancing. By "racial distancing" I am referring to the process by which candidates indicate either implicitly or explicitly that they will not disrupt the racial hierarchy, often through appeals that deride racial and ethnic minorities. Racial distancing and deracialization are not mutually exclusive, because racial distancing is a strategy that can be engaged in as a complement to a strategy of deracialization. The statements politicians make on the stump, what their campaign ads claim and what they charge of their opponents, whom they choose to speak to and whom they avoid, are all avenues through which candidates racially distance.

In this chapter, I use the Obama's 2008 presidential campaign, as well as his tenure as president, as an illustrative case of a black politician who engaged in racial distancing. Previous research has generally focused on Obama's avoidance of race, or on his engagement with race around themes of unity and universalism. Far less attention has been devoted to ways in which Obama invoked race, often through negative stereotypes about the African American community (for an exception, see Harris 2012 and Price 2016). Obama won the votes of many white Americans, along with overwhelming support from racial and ethnic minorities—especially African Americans, even though he distanced himself from them. In some instances, he perpetuated negative stereotypes about blacks. Although no one campaign strategy can be entirely responsible for a candidate's victory, and no one theory can completely explain a phenomenon, it is important to examine how the understudied phenomenon of racial distancing also may have contributed to Obama's victory. Without examining the ways in which Obama, the nation's first African American president, engaged race in a manner that appealed to some voters' negative racial predispositions about blacks, we ignore the ways in which his campaign strategy may have been detrimental to African Americans and the advancement of their interests.

President Obama is also a useful lens through which we can learn about how black candidates successfully appeal to the animus of some white Americans because Obama's success likely presages the rise of more black candidacies in heterogeneous electorates. Thus, as more African Americans pursue office in areas where whites constitute the majority, it is important to examine which types of appeals from black candidates resonate with white voters. The empirical evidence indicates that appeals from black politicians that openly criticize black people appear to resonate with many racially resentful whites as much, if not more than, appeals that only implicate blacks. Appeals that either implicitly or explicitly criticize black people are successful because many white Americans take as a given that black Americans are less hardworking and more prone to criminality and sexual promiscuity than their white counterparts.

Although Obama's 2008 presidential campaign was not exclusively deracialized, for a variety of reasons it is frequently cited as an example of a perfectly executed deracialized campaign. After all, the Obama campaign's chief strategist, David Axelrod, had already developed a reputation for running deracialized campaigns by "packaging black candidates for white voters," including Deval Patrick, former governor of Massachusetts (*The Economist* 2008). Also, after Obama's surprising victory in 2008 in the predominantly white Iowa caucuses, there were declarations that Obama "transcended race." Historian and social critic Manning Marable (2009) wrote of Obama's campaign, "Obama minimized the issue of race, presenting a race-neutral politics that reached out to White Republicans and independents." It is also widely accepted that Obama explicitly discussed race only when he was forced to—most notably in his "A More Perfect Union" speech, which was a response to the release of tapes in which Obama's former pastor, Reverend Jeremiah Wright, made controversial comments about the United States. In short, the prevailing notion is that it was the deracialized nature of his campaign that enabled Obama to construct a winning coalition of whites and people of color.

Yet, despite the perception that Obama "transcended race," less than one month before the 2008 presidential election, a poll conducted by CBS/New York Times found that 20 percent of whites thought that if Obama were elected, his administration's policies would favor African Americans and other minorities, which was even higher than the percentage of Americans at the time who erroneously believed Obama was a Muslim (Pew Research Center 2010).[3] Only 12 percent of Americans surveyed in October 2008 thought that Obama was a Muslim. The fact that one month before the election 20 percent of white Americans thought that Obama's policies would favor blacks over whites helps explain why some black Democratic candidates choose to engage in racial distancing.[4] Obama was also subjected to other racialized stereotypes that may have motivated him to racially distance. Parker, Sawyer, and Towler (2009), for example, note how the language of deservingness of the presidency and discussions of Obama's purported lack of patriotism were thinly veiled allusions to Obama's race that were used to diminish Obama's support among white voters. Previous research also indicates that Obama's very presence made race "chronically accessible," such that voters' racial predispositions were almost inevitably activated as a result of Obama's very presence on the ballot, and by the historic nature of his potential election (Tesler and Sears 2010). Thus, some voters could not divorce their racial attitudes from their assessments of Obama, despite his campaign's efforts to neutralize negative racial predispositions and mobilize positive racial predispositions.

The Obama campaign, well aware of the ways in which Obama's race could work to his disadvantage, was incentivized to go above and beyond a strategy of deracialization, to more forcefully combat the stereotype of him as a black Democrat preoccupied with black interests. President Obama engaged in two elements of racial distancing that are the focus of this book—a "rhetorical strategy" and an "imagery strategy"—in some cases, deriding other African Americans. A rhetorical strategy entails racial messaging that invokes negative stereotypes about African Americans, often using language of personal responsibility and work ethic. It can also entail allusions to the politician's own commitment to hard work and individualism, as a means of distancing herself from the stereotype of blacks "not playing by the rules." An imagery strategy is the avoidance of appearances at public events with African Americans or events where the interests of African Americans were the focus, instead placing an emphasis on white supporters. An imagery strategy may also entail minimizing the appearance of African Americans in campaign materials and advertisements.

Obama's Imagery Strategy

One way in which campaigns convey racial signals is through the people whom they choose to address or whom they choose to avoid. Therefore, it is useful to examine the places where Obama gave speeches, as well as the invitations he declined. It is also helpful to compare some of the speaking engagements that Obama declined to the speeches that the other contender for the Democratic nomination, Hillary Clinton, chose to accept. Given that the 2008 Democratic presidential nomination was highly contested, with both campaigns vying for the support of heavily African American Democratic electorates in some of the early primaries, such as South Carolina, examining which invitations Obama accepted as well as those he declined is especially illuminating. Although this metric is by no means a definitive indication of a racial distancing strategy, it does offer some insight into how the candidates prioritized their time. Whom candidates choose to speak to and whom they avoid indicates which voters politicians deem worthy of persuading, which voters they have already persuaded, and which voters they have written off.

It is interesting to note, for example, that during the primary season two of the high-profile African American affinity events Clinton spoke at, Obama declined to attend. These events were the commemoration of the fortieth anniversary of the passing of Dr. Martin Luther King Jr. in Memphis, and the State of the Black Union Forum in New Orleans. Perhaps Clinton may have felt more pressure to shore up black support than Obama because she is not African American. Clinton may also have had more latitude as a white politician to reach out to black voters, without alienating racially resentful white voters. Research indicates white leaders may speak publicly about race to build electoral support across racial lines (Judd and Swanstrom 1994; Hutchings et al. 2004).[5] As an African American Democrat, Obama may have been more vulnerable to the criticism of being overly concerned with minority interests, and thus declined to attend some events that were African American–focused, particularly the State of the Black Union Forum.

Obama's decision to not attend the State of the Black Union Forum is illuminating, not only because it is suggestive of a strategy of racial distancing, but also because of the fallout that took place around his decision. In an open letter that appeared in the *Chicago Sun-Times*, Obama cited his need to focus on his presidential run ahead of the March 4, "Super Tuesday," primaries as his reason for not attending the February 2008 State of the Black Union Forum. Modeled on the 1972 National Black Political Convention and broadcast on C-SPAN, the State of the Black Union Forum was hosted annually for a decade by African American political pundit Tavis Smiley. Past participants have included Al Sharpton, Jesse Jackson Jr., and Congressman John Conyers, all of whom fit the mold of the "old guard" of black politicians.

Obama offered to send his wife, Michelle Obama, in his stead, but this offer was reportedly declined by Smiley. Obama stated in the letter, "The exchange of ideas raised at this annual symposium are invaluable as our nation strives to address the critical issues facing not just African Americans, but Americans of *every race*, background and political party." He went on to say, "I am committed to touching *every voter* and earning their vote."[6] Obama's letter and his decision to not attend the forum implicitly "signaled" that he was not beholden to African Americans. Attendance at such a high-profile "black event" was likely to have confirmed the stereotype of a black candidate primarily concerned with black interests.[7] Obama's decision to decline Smiley's invitation in an open letter also meant that many people were exposed to Obama's rationale for not attending the forum, going far beyond Smiley, and even the African American community at large. The open letter was also likely to reach white Americans, who would learn that Obama was not beholden to African Americans.

The events that unfolded after Obama declined to attend the forum are also telling because they suggest that blacks who might have been critical of Obama's racial distancing might have opted to not critique it for fear of intense backlash from other African Americans. Prior to his public critiques of Obama during the 2008 campaign, Smiley was a very popular figure in the African American community. He had served as an aide to the first black mayor of Los Angeles, Tom Bradley, and hosted popular programs on Black Entertainment Television and National Public Radio. During the 2008 presidential campaign, Smiley was also a featured commentator on the Tom Joyner Morning Show (TJMS), a nationally syndicated radio show that reached a predominantly African American audience of over 10 million listeners weekly via more than 100 radio stations. Smiley used his platform on the TJMS to encourage African Americans to hold Obama accountable, for example, saying after Obama's victory in the Iowa caucus, "Don't fall so madly in love [with Obama] that you surrender your power to hold people accountable. I'm not saying overlook Senator Obama, but you better be ready to look him over."[8] On the TJMS, Smiley was also critical of Obama's decision to not attend the State of the Black Union Forum, and to not travel to Memphis for the ceremonies marking the fortieth anniversary of the assassination of Martin Luther King Jr. However, Smiley was essentially shunned by many African Americans— reportedly even receiving death threats— after expressing skepticism about Obama and criticizing Obama's decision to not attend the forum and other black-centered events. Smiley eventually resigned from the TJMS, citing fatigue, but according to Joyner, Smiley "couldn't take the heat" or the intense criticism from fellow African Americans for not offering unwavering support to Obama.[9]

The reported backlash that Smiley experienced for his public critiques of Obama may have taught the Obama campaign that Obama could racially distance with virtual impunity from the African American community. In fact, in an interview with *The Atlantic*, Obama campaign adviser Anita Dunn said, "Tavis Smiley had become the object lesson for everyone." In other words, African Americans defecting from the group paid social costs (White, Laird, and Allen 2014). According to Harris (2012), black voters had struck a tacit bargain with Obama whereby he could publicly distance himself from African Americans as a tactic to gain white electoral support.

Comments in *The Atlantic* from an unnamed Obama campaign adviser also suggest that the campaign had indeed made efforts to distance the candidate from blacks in order to make Obama more palatable to white voters. The unnamed adviser reportedly said, "You could get intensity in the African American community by giving them a candidate they could see as being able to win. You didn't have to speak to them in a way that would make white people nervous."[10] The campaign may have been concerned about making "white people nervous," and thus may have even taken steps to not only avoid racial issues, as suggested by a deracialization strategy, but to also signal both implicitly and explicitly that they would not be beholden to black voters.

Television Advertisements as Imagery Strategy in the 2008 Obama Presidential Campaign

Another way to assess Obama's use of a strategy of racial distancing is by systematically assessing his television advertisements. I conducted a content analysis of television advertisements from 2008 that were sponsored by the Obama campaign, while also making comparisons to the advertisements aired by the McCain and Clinton campaigns. Storyboards of television advertisements with transcribed text of the verbal message were collected by the Wisconsin Advertising Project (WAP). WAP also coded the ads to determine which issues were mentioned, as well as the frequency with which each ad was aired in the various media markets, and the estimated costs for airing the ads.

The content analysis was designed to assess the percentage of Obama's 2008 television advertisements that mentioned implicitly racialized policies such as welfare, capital punishment, crime, and drugs, as well as explicitly racial policies, such as affirmative action and civil rights.[11] According to deracialization theory, candidates who are executing a deracialized strategy should avoid racialized issues that have become linked to African Americans. If Obama executed a purely deracialized campaign, then we should see evidence that he avoided racialized issues in his television advertisements even when compared to other Democratic candidates or to his Republican opponent, John McCain.

The 2008 Obama campaign created approximately 200 unique ads. These ads aired multiple times across multiple media markets. Of the approximately 582,000 television advertisements aired by the Obama campaign, less than 1 percent mentioned the terms "race" or "civil rights." This finding is in line with previous research that finds that Obama spoke about race less in his first two years as president than any other president since John F. Kennedy (Gillion 2015). None of Obama's advertisements mentioned affirmative action, which may simply be an indication that affirmative action is not as politically salient as it was in earlier decades, such as when then the infamous "Hands" ad was aired.[12] In fact, none of the ads ever mentioned "race," racial disparities, or "African Americans" explicitly. The few advertisements that did include the term "civil rights" used the term to reference Obama's previous work as a "civil rights lawyer" or as a lawyer "defending civil rights." Contrary to what might be predicted by issue ownership theory, Obama did not spend much time highlighting his party's reputation for owning the issue of civil rights.

The Obama campaign, however, was not unique in the lack of attention devoted to race or civil rights issues. The Clinton and McCain campaigns did not air *any* ads that mentioned the terms "race," "civil rights," "affirmative action," and "African Americans." Race and civil rights have historically not been very high on the political agenda, so it is not surprising that these issues did not have a very prominent role in any of the presidential campaigns. Nevertheless, examining the attention candidates devoted to these explicitly racial topics helps us determine whether candidates avoided racialized issues altogether, or just those racial issues that are associated with a liberal racial agenda.

Despite the relatively little attention that was devoted to explicitly racial themes, the results indicate that the Obama campaign did not avoid all racial issues. Television advertisements sponsored by the Obama campaign that mentioned implicitly racial themes, such as welfare, crime, capital punishment, and drugs, were more common than advertisements about the explicit racial themes of race and civil rights. Seven percent of the advertisements aired by the Obama campaign mentioned the implicitly racial topic of welfare. Less than 1 percent of the advertisements mentioned crime, and none of the advertisements mentioned capital punishment or drugs. The two major ads that the Obama campaign aired about crime, "Absolute Lie" and "What I Believe," were both rebuttal ads, as their titles suggest. These rebuttals ads were aired in response to charges from the McCain campaign that Obama was soft on crime.[13] The Republican Party has traditionally owned the crime issue, and Democrats have been vulnerable on it, so it is not surprising that the McCain campaign would take steps to portray Obama as soft on crime. Obama's rebuttal advertisement, "Absolute Lie," mentioned that Obama was endorsed by the National Association of Police Organizations and included language about Obama passing "laws to toughen sentences." The other rebuttal advertisement, "What I Believe," included language that said, "I believe people who break the law should be punished." Neither ad included negative stereotypical imagery. Obama, however, was taking a counter-stereotypical stance for a Democrat, by touting his "tough on crime" credentials.

Obama's advertisements about welfare appear to be more preemptive than his ads about crime, because unlike Obama's crime ads, the two ads that discuss welfare, "Dignity" and "Country I Love," are not rebuttal ads. The proactive nature of the welfare ads might be indicative of an awareness from the campaign that Obama as a black Democratic politician was vulnerable on the issue of welfare. Accordingly, Obama's advertisements on welfare had a negative valence. In other words, these were ads indicating opposition to welfare or cutting the welfare rolls, not ads in support of the welfare state. Obama's advertisement "Dignity," for example, is typical of how welfare was discussed in Obama's television advertisements.[14] The ad begins with an announcer stating, "He [Obama] passed a law to move people from welfare to work. He slashed the rolls by eighty percent." The ad also goes on to mention that as president, Obama "will never forget the dignity that comes from work." Thus, Obama's message around welfare and work runs contrary to the negative stereotype of African Americans as unwilling to work and failing to adhere to American values. The advertisement also stands in sharp contrast to the stereotype of African American Democratic politicians as preoccupied with their racial and ethnic minority constituents, since none are pictured. "Dignity" was one of most frequently aired ads of the 2008 Obama campaign, second only to an ad about health care, the campaign's signature issue.

Another ad that typifies how Obama discussed welfare in television advertisements is "Country I Love." "Country I Love" was Obama's first television ad of the 2008 general election, and it ran in several key

battleground states, including Florida, Ohio, Pennsylvania, and Michigan. The ad references implicitly racial themes, such as "cutting taxes for
working families."[15] The viewer is also informed that Obama was raised
with "values straight from the Kansas heartland," including "working
hard without making excuses," which runs counter to the stereotype of
African Americans as making excuses and not supporting the American
value of hard work. Obama also reminds the viewer that he "passed laws
moving people from welfare to work." The reference to "moving people
from welfare to work" emphasizes Obama's counter-stereotypical position on the racialized policy of welfare (Gilens 1999). "Country I Love"
also signaled that Obama would not be beholden to African Americans,
because the sixty-second advertisement does not include any discernible
African American faces, or any other people of color, save for the candidate himself.[16]

Of course, as noted earlier, the majority of advertisements that the
2008 Obama campaign aired were not about the implicitly racialized
topics of welfare or crime. The majority of the ads aired on those topics
during the 2008 election season, however, were sponsored by the Obama
campaign. The Obama campaign sponsored 93 percent of the ads that
aired on those implicitly racial topics. Rather than avoid altogether the
issues of welfare and crime, as suggested by the theories of racial priming, deracialization, and issue ownership, the *Democratic* Obama campaign ran advertisements about welfare and crime more frequently than
his Republican opponent. Although airing an ad about an implicitly racial topic does not necessarily mean that a candidate is engaging in racial distancing, the ads that the Obama campaign aired about welfare
and crime visually, substantively, and rhetorically distanced the candidate from African Americans, which is indicative of a racial distancing
strategy. Racial distancing theory predicts that Democratic candidates,
especially black Democratic candidates, take steps that are sometimes
preemptive, such as airing ads about their counter-stereotypical positions on issues such as welfare and crime, to disrupt the notion that they
will be beholden to their racial and ethnic minority constituents.[17]

In contrast, less than 1 percent of the advertisements sponsored by
the McCain campaign were about any of these implicitly racial topics,
while the Clinton campaign did not air any television advertisements
that mentioned the implicitly racial themes of welfare, crime, drugs,
and capital punishment. While implicitly racial themes such as welfare,
crime, and drugs were included in only a small fraction of his advertise-

ments (7 percent), not only did Obama air more advertisements about welfare, crime, and drugs than John McCain and Hillary Clinton, but he also aired more ads about those implicitly racial topics than the two previous Democratic nominees combined.[18] Again, these results are contradictory to the predicted expectations of the theory of racial priming and issue ownership. According to the theory of racial priming, a Democratic candidate would either be silent or avoid racialized issues such as welfare or crime, while the theory of issue ownership suggests that a candidate would not run ads on issues for which their party did not have a reputational advantage.

Obama's Rhetorical Strategy

Previous research (Harris 2012) indicates that after Obama secured black support and had received significant buy-in from the black community, his speeches to African Americans adopted a more scolding tone, which likely reflects a change in his standing within the African American community. When Obama's presidential campaign began, he was a virtual political unknown to most African Americans. Furthermore, many black political elites had already pledged their support to the Clinton campaign or were undecided. Obama spent time building political capital with the African American political establishment, which is reflected in his early speeches to African American audiences. According to Harris (2012), after Obama established his authenticity within the African American community, as well as his political viability, his speeches to African American audiences increasingly adopted a tone of chastisement.

The first documented speech that Obama gave as a presidential candidate to a majority African American audience or at an African American affinity event was at the commemoration of Bloody Sunday in Selma, Alabama, in March 2007. In this speech, Obama discussed the obligations of what he referred to as the "Joshua generation," or the post–civil rights generation of African Americans. He bolstered his connection to older generations of black leaders by attributing his success, and that of others like him, to the sacrifices made by older African Americans, such as Congressman John Lewis. "I'm here because somebody marched," he said. "I'm here because you all sacrificed for me. I stand on the shoulders of giants."

Obama also described the work that lay ahead for the Joshua generation, implicitly positioning himself as its standard-bearer, a metaphorical Joshua, who would lead African Americans into the promised land. He openly highlighted racial disparities in health care and education, noting, "Blacks are less likely in their schools to have adequate funding. We have less-qualified teachers in those schools. We have fewer textbooks in those schools." Yet, despite the attention to racial disparities in the speech, the omnipresent "Cousin Pookie" also made an appearance: "I also know that, if Cousin Pookie would vote, get off the couch and register some folks and go to the polls, we might have a different kind of politics."[19]

As in many of his speeches to predominantly black audiences, Obama acknowledged racial disparities while simultaneously scolding African Americans for being irresponsible. Absentee fatherhood, another common theme in Obama's speeches to black audiences, was also mentioned in the speech. Personal responsibility and "black blame" (Price 2016) are not central to the speech, however, as they were in later speeches. Obama spent the bulk of the speech paying homage to the civil rights generation of black politicians. Overall, the speech focused on establishing his credentials in the black community, as well as establishing his role as a black politician, whose biracial ancestry would help him build a multiracial coalition that would address racial disparities in the United States.

In his other early addresses to majority-black audiences, including an address to the National Conference of Black Mayors, a speech at the historically black Hampton University, and a speech entitled "Changing the Odds for Urban America," Obama continued to invoke the theme of the Joshua generation. He spoke openly about racial disparities, and offered structural solutions, such as "investing in minority-owned businesses" and funding prisoner recidivism programs. However, Obama would also invoke negative stereotypes about African Americans, making references to Cousin Pookie and the like. According to Harris (2012), Obama was more likely to deploy personal responsibility messages after he had shored up black support, which came after his victory in the South Carolina primary in January 2008. Obama beat Clinton by more than 30 points because of overwhelming support from black South Carolinians, and shortly thereafter, African American congressman and civil rights hero John Lewis changed his endorsement from Clinton to Obama.

One day after receiving the endorsement from Congressman John Lewis, during a stump speech in Beaumont, Texas, Obama chastised a predominantly black audience for feeding their children Popeyes for breakfast:

> I know hard it is to get kids to eat properly but I also know that if folks [are] letting our children drink eight sodas a day, which some parents do, or, you know, eat a bag of potato chips for lunch or Popeyes [fried chicken] for break-fast . . . Y'all have Popeyes out in Beaumont? I know some of y'all got that cold Popeyes out for breakfast. I know. That's why y'all laughing . . . You can't do that. Children have to have proper nutrition. That affects how they study, how they learn in school.[20]

Earlier in the speech, Obama also criticized black parents for not in-stilling proper educational values in their children, saying, "It's not good enough for you to say to your child, 'Do good in school.' And then your child comes home, you've got the TV set on, you've got the radio on, you don't check their homework, there's not a book in the house, you've got the video game playing." Obama's 2008 speech in Beaumont, with its references to Popeyes, presumably fried chicken, played to negative stereotypes about African Americans. Specifically, the speech suggested that blacks are irresponsible, perhaps, even pathological, particularly when it comes to parenting. The theme of personal responsibility is also very evident in the speech, as Obama focused on the impact that paren-tal decisions about nutrition have on children's ability to study and learn in school. Absent from the discussion was any mention of structural fac-tors that also influence children's ability to study and learn, such as ac-cess to healthy, affordable food, or well-trained teachers.

Throughout the campaign, Obama continued to invoke race in his speeches to predominantly black audiences, often through negative ra-cial stereotypes. Yet, it is the conventional wisdom that Obama never discussed race on the campaign trail until March 18, 2008, when he gave what is widely thought of as his first and perhaps only "speech on race," "A More Perfect Union."[21] Obama was pressured into formally addressing the issue of race in this speech after controversial tapes of his longtime pastor, Reverend Jeremiah Wright, surfaced. Through this speech Obama aimed to dispel the notion that Wright—and, by ex-tension, he himself—was anti-white and anti-American. Obama drew on his biracial heritage, as "the son of a black man from Kenya and a

white woman from Kansas," as someone uniquely equipped to understand the racial grievances of black and white Americans alike. He condemned Wright's statements as "divisive," while at the same time arguing that he could "no more disown him [Wright] than I can disown my
white grandmother." The speech, like many of Obama's other speeches
that touched on race, acknowledged racial disparities and structural inequalities, while simultaneously urging African Americans to take personal responsibility, "For the African American community, that means
embracing the burdens of our past without becoming victims of our
past." "A More Perfect Union" confronted race more directly than any
of Obama's other speeches and included explicit racial pronouns such as
"black" and "white" a record forty-one times—more than any other re-
corded speech by Obama.[22] Thus, his speech was widely heralded as the
beginning of a "national conversation on race."

Race to the Botton argues, however, that Obama had already been
talking about race for quite some time, often using racially inflammatory language, such as in his February 2008 speech in Beaumont, Texas.
This rhetoric would continue well into his first and second terms as president. At the 2009 NAACP centennial convention, for example, he told
the predominantly black audience, "We can't tell our kids to do well in
school and then fail to support them when they get home. You can't just
contract out parenting. For our kids to excel, we have to accept our responsibility to help them learn. That means putting away the Xbox—
putting our kids to bed at a reasonable hour. It means attending those
parent-teacher conferences and reading to our children and helping
them with their homework."[23] Obama's comments once again suggested
that African Americans were not responsibly assuming their roles as
parents, instead opting to "contract out parenting." Obama's speeches to
predominantly black audiences frequently invoked the themes of absentee fathers and personal responsibility, while also relying on the racialized tropes of "Cousin Pookie," "Uncle Jethro," and "Cousin Ray Ray."

During his second term, Obama continued to deliver racially inflected personal responsibility messages, often to the members of the
black community who were seemingly the least likely to need a reminder
about the importance of personal responsibility. For example, he delivered the 2013 commencement speech at historically black, all-male
Morehouse College, where he once again emphasized the need for personal responsibility in the black community, saying, "But along with collective responsibilities, we have individual responsibilities. There are

some things, as black men, we can only do for ourselves." Later in the speech, he noted, "And I have to confess, sometimes I wrote off my own failings, as just another example of the world trying to keep a black man down. But one of the things you've learned over the last four years is that there's no longer any room for excuses."[24] His comments support the stereotype of African Americans using racism as an excuse, which is a belief endorsed by many racially moderate to racially conservative whites.

The idea that Obama was more likely to lecture or chastise black audiences than other groups has been noted by several black elites, including civil rights activist Jesse Jackson and Congresswoman Maxine Waters. Jackson, for example, was caught on tape saying that he wanted to castrate Obama for "talking down to black people."[25] Jackson apologized for his comments, but the message was clear that Jackson was critical of the way that Obama was addressing black audiences. Jackson's comments came on the heels of Obama's Father's Day speech at the Apostolic Church of God, a predominantly black church that he and his family visited a week after officially severing their ties with their former pastor, Jeremiah Wright. During the speech Obama lambasted absentee black fathers and black parents. Obama criticized black fathers, saying, "We need fathers to understand that responsibility does not end at conception." Obama was also critical of African American parenting, saying, "Don't get carried away with that eighth-grade graduation. You're supposed to graduate from eighth grade!"[26]

At first glance, it might appear problematic for a black candidate who initially had trouble gaining political support from the African American community to receive criticism from civil rights icon Jesse Jackson. However, this type of criticism from Jesse Jackson likely worked in Obama's favor among white voters, for many of whom Jesse Jackson has consistently been an unpopular figure. In effect, Jackson's comments enabled Obama to distinguish himself from the old guard of black politicians, whose focus on racial injustice and inequality is unpopular among many white Americans. According to Price (2016), "Jackson had inadvertently set Obama up for his own Sister Souljah moment."[27] Jackson's "hot mic" comment was the most reported-on campaign story of the week (Tesler 2016). Thus, many white Americans were likely exposed to Obama being critiqued by the most prominent black figure of the post–civil rights era, save for Obama himself. A poll indicates that of the respondents interviewed by the Pew Research Center between July 11 and July 14, 2008, 48 percent said that they had heard a lot about "Jesse Jackson being overheard making a crude comment about Barack Obama," while 29 percent said they heard a little about this story. Only 22 percent of respondents reported hearing nothing at all.[28] Although Jackson's comments were inadvertent, they provided an opportunity for Obama to distance himself from many Americans' notion of the stereotypical African American politician.

Obama also received similar criticism from Representative Maxine Waters, albeit in less crude language than that of Jesse Jackson. In President Obama's 2011 address to the Congressional Black Caucus Foundation, he told the predominantly black audience, "Take off your bedroom slippers, put on your marching shoes. Shake it off. Stop complaining. Stop grumbling. Stop crying."[29] Waters argued that Obama never speaks the same way publicly to other organizations representing other key voter blocs—for instance, Hispanic groups—as he does to blacks:

I'm not sure who the president was addressing. I found that language a bit curious because the president spoke to the Hispanic Caucus, and certainly they're pushing him on immigration. And despite the fact that he's appointed Sotomayor to the Supreme Court, he has an office for Excellence for Hispanic Education right in the White House. They're still pushing him. He certainly didn't tell them to stop complaining.[30]

Representative Waters's comments suggest that Obama was singling out African American audiences for chastisement and that Latinos were not receiving similar messages from the president. Waters likely compared how Obama addressed predominantly black audiences to the way he addressed predominantly Latino audiences, because both groups are marginalized, faring similarly by many socioeconomic indicators, such as poverty, high school graduation, and homeownership rates. Thus, to the extent that one perceives personal responsibility and work ethic as the solutions to these problems, then African Americans should be no more likely to be targeted with those messages than Latinos. If Obama, however, invoked themes of personal responsibility and chastised black audiences for perceived laziness and immorality more than he did for Latinos, then it suggests that he perceived African Americans as uniquely in need of messages about personal responsibility.

I analyzed all of the speeches that Obama delivered at African American affinity events, such as the NAACP annual convention, or to predominantly black audiences, including at predominantly black churches or historically black colleges and universities, in 2007–12. This time frame encompasses his first presidential campaign and his first term in office. I subsequently compared the speeches that Obama gave to predominantly black audiences to speeches he gave to Latino audiences or at Latino affinity events, such as the National Council of La Raza. Latinos are selected as a comparison group because they are also a marginalized group with similar rates of unemployment, high school graduation, and homeownership (Traub et al. 2017). Finally, I compared the African American affinity speeches to the speeches that Obama gave to "mainstream" audiences where presumably the audience was majority-white.

For each speech delivered to a majority-black or Latino audience, a white audience speech was found that closely resembled the context of its match in several different ways. Speeches were matched on subject matter (e.g., a speech to the National Hispanic Prayer Breakfast was matched to the National Prayer Breakfast). Audience size was also considered, such that a speech given at a historically black college or university was matched with a speech given at a predominantly white institution of similar size (for a similar approach, see Dupree and Fiske 2019). I also accounted for the approximate timing, where possible.[31] Another comparison group of white audience speeches was also created, whereby I took a random sample of the speeches that Obama delivered to white audiences.[32] The number of speeches delivered to majority-minority audiences was a small fraction of the total number of speeches he delivered. Thus, the sample size was determined by the number of speeches delivered to minority audiences that were available in online archives.

I relied on computerized text analysis to determine whether Obama's speeches to black audiences were more likely to include language about personal responsibility or cultural deficiency, such as "responsibility," "culture," and "fathers." The words were read in the context of the speech to avoid any false positives or type 1 errors. I, along with a research assistant, then coded the context surrounding the words to ensure that they were in fact being used in a manner that invoked personal responsibility or cultural deficiency.[33] For example, "responsibility" appeared in speeches to blacks, whites, and Latinos, but sometimes it was used to talk about government or corporate responsibility, while at other times it was used to talk about individual or personal responsibility. I am interested only in the cases where it is used to invoke individual responsibility. Examples of language that was coded as invoking personal responsibility include the following: "If we don't seize more responsibility in our own lives"; "and to realize that responsibility does not end at conception"; "a sense of personal responsibility, and self-respect, to pass."

I also examined whether inspirational and aspirational rhetoric were more prominent in Obama's speeches to predominantly white audiences. The 2008 Obama campaign slogan was, after all, "Change We Can Believe In." Obama also frequently invoked language of "hope and change" on the campaign trail. I expect that "hope" and "change" would be subject to a racialized pattern of communication because research indicates that politicians are more likely to invoke language around systemic change when speaking to white audiences than black audiences. Conversely, rhetoric to blacks is often couched in tempered expectations (Phoenix 2019). Therefore, I also used text analysis to see whether the words "hope" and "change" were used more frequently in Obama's speeches to white audiences than in his speeches to black or Latino audiences. Of course, "hope" and "change" do not capture the universe of inspirational and aspirational rhetoric, just as "culture," "responsibility," and "father" do not capture the universe of personal responsibility rhetoric. Nevertheless, any difference in the prevalence of the use of these words that coincides with the race of the audience at the very least indicates that Obama was more likely to use certain words with some audiences than he was with other types of audiences.

As indicated in table 3.1, Obama's speeches to predominantly black audiences were more likely to rely on racially inflected personal responsibility messages, while his speeches to white audiences were more likely to include inspirational or aspirational rhetoric. The vast majority of Obama's campaign speeches were delivered to majority-white audiences, which is to be expected, since the majority of the electorate is white. When Obama did address black audiences, however, his rhetoric took on a different tone than when he was addressing majority-white audiences.[34] I found that Obama used the word "responsibility" an average of 1.65 times per speech to black audiences, as compared to 1.28 times in his speeches to Latinos, and 1.17 times in his speeches to whites. The difference in both instances was statistically significant ($p < .05$).[35] Other words that suggest an invocation of personal responsibility, such as "work" and "excuses," were also used more frequently to black audiences, relative to white or Latino audiences.

TABLE 3.1 **Prevalence of Personal Responsibility Rhetoric and Aspirational Rhetoric in Obama Speeches (2007–2012)**

	Blacks vs. whites	Blacks vs. Latinos
Personal responsibility rhetoric		
Responsibility	1.65 vs. 1.17**	1.65 vs. 1.28
Work	6.56 vs. 5.37**	6.56 vs. 0.57
Culture	0.22 vs. 0.28	0.22 vs. 0.35
Father	1.37 vs. 0.37***	1.37 vs. 0.64**
Excuses	0.34 vs. 0.17	0.34 vs. 0.35
Aspirational rhetoric		
Hope	1.93 vs. 1.65	1.93 vs. 1.14*
Change	2.87 vs. 3.89	2.87 vs. 3.14

Note: Cell entries indicate the number of times a given word was used on average by type of audience. Obama delivered a total of thirty-two speeches to African American audiences during 2007–12, and fourteen speeches to Latino audiences.

* $p < .10$; ** $p < .05$; *** $p < .01$ for a z-test of proportions.

Conversely, use of the words "hope" and "change" was more mixed. The word "change" was used an average of 2.87 times in Obama's speeches to black audiences, as compared to 3.89 times in his speeches to whites, and 3.14 times in his speeches to Latino audiences ($p < .05$). That "change" was invoked less frequently in speeches to black audiences corresponds with Phoenix (2019), who argues that politicians use language that tempers expectations more frequently when talking to black audiences, as compared to white audiences. "Hope," on the other hand, was used more frequently in speeches to black audiences, at a rate of 1.93 times, as compared to 1.65 times to white audiences, and 1.14 to Latino audiences. These differences did not attain conventional levels of statistical significance.

Obama's speeches to black audiences often acknowledged racial disparities and structural barriers to racial progress, but a consistent theme in his speeches to African Americans was that they had "no excuses." Again, this is not very different from conversations that routinely take place within indigenous black spaces, such as the black church and historically black colleges and universities. What distinguishes Obama's speeches, and the rhetoric of other black politicians, is that what used to be an in-group conversation is being broadcast well beyond the proximate audience of African Americans. While it is impossible to know the intention of this rhetoric, as more black candidates pursue office outside of majority-minority jurisdictions, this rhetoric is increasingly subject to what Higginbotham (1993) refers to as "the white gaze."

As a member of the in-group, Obama may have felt more comfortable critiquing African Americans. He may have also genuinely believed that African Americans are uniquely in need of personal responsibility messages. The possibility still remains, however, that he was using these messages to strategically distance himself from black voters. While it is impossible to definitively identify the motivation behind this rhetoric, it is still important to examine the impact of this type of rhetoric on voter behavior. Therefore, several of the experiments discussed throughout the book enable us to examine the impact of personal responsibility rhetoric by a black politician on white voters' perception of the politician. Although the experiments do not directly test the impact of personal responsibility rhetoric on voters' evaluations of Obama per se, the experimental results suggest that messages that chastise purported black pathology are more popular among whites than the conventional wisdom suggests, and even more so when the messenger is African American.

Racial Signals Employed against Black Candidates

Thus far in this chapter, I have focused on the different ways in which President Obama engaged in racial distancing, often employing racially inflammatory rhetoric and symbols. Obama's racial distancing did not take place in a vacuum, however. Therefore, I would be remiss to not also acknowledge the way in which racial stereotypes were employed *against* Obama. Examining the use of racialized attacks against black politicians helps contextualize the electoral environment in which black politicians operate. This electoral environment in some cases likely encourages them to racially distance either preemptively or defensively. In this section, I use the 2008 and 2012 Obama candidacies as a lens for examining the racial signals that are often employed against black politicians by their white opponents. If the 2008 and 2012 Obama campaigns are any indication, black candidates are likely to experience attacks from their opponents in which the opponent links the black candidate to negative stereotypes around black criminality, irresponsibility, poor work ethic, or racial grievances, thus making them likely to either defensively or preemptively mitigate the negative racial attacks that are lodged against them.

One notable racialized attack against Obama occurred during Hillary Clinton's 2008 presidential bid. In an interview with *USA Today*, Hillary Clinton relied on the tired trope of lazy African Americans by contrasting her support from white Americans to Obama's lack of support from whites. Citing a poll from the Associated Press, she said, "It found how Senator Obama's support among working, hard-working Americans, white Americans, is weakening again."[36] Clinton rejected the notion that her comments were racially divisive, but arguably her comments played to the stereotype of black people being lazy by equating white Americans with hardworking Americans. Also, during the 2008 campaign, after Obama won the South Carolina primary, Bill Clinton compared Obama's victory to that of Jesse Jackson's caucus win twenty years earlier, saying, "Jesse Jackson won South Carolina in '84 and '88. Jackson ran a good campaign. And Obama ran a good campaign here."[37] Bill Clinton's comments were seen by some as an effort to stoke racial resentment, by associating Obama with the more racially liberal, and often reviled, Jackson.

Of course, Democrats are not alone in stoking resentments about blacks for political gain, because, as noted earlier, it is well documented that Republican politicians engage in these practices as well. During the 2012 presidential election former House leader and Republican presidential candidate Newt Gingrich routinely referred to President Obama as "the most successful food stamp president in American history" on the campaign trail. Gingrich also noted that if the NAACP invited him to their annual convention he would attend and "talk about why the African American community should demand paychecks and not be satisfied with food stamps."[38] Previous research demonstrates that the food stamp program has become identified as a "black" social welfare program over time, such that the mere mention of "food stamps" or "welfare" activates many white Americans' negative attitudes toward African Americans (Gilens 1999; Williams 2003; Winter 2008). By associating Obama with food stamps, Gingrich was likely making negative racial attitudes toward blacks more salient in the decision calculus of many white Republican primary voters. Gingrich, despite his use of racially inflammatory language, went on to win the South Carolina Republican primary in 2012, shortly after doubling down on his use of the term "food stamp president."[39]

Former Republican senator from Pennsylvania and presidential hopeful Rick Santorum also drew attention to negative stereotypes about African Americans during his 2012 presidential bid by associating African Americans with the old trope of laziness. During a campaign stop in Iowa, Santorum told a mostly white audience that he did not want to "make black people's lives better by giving them someone else's money; I want to give them the opportunity to go out and earn the money." Santorum later denied that his comments were about black people and claimed to have said "blah people" instead.[40] Santorum's comments did not explicitly mention Obama, but his comments could be interpreted as implying that Obama, who was president at the time, was trying to make black people's lives better by giving them someone else's (white people's) money, rather than giving them the opportunity to go out and earn money.

In a similar vein, in September 2012, Republican presidential nominee Mitt Romney told an audience of donors that "47 percent" of the country was comprised of "takers" who would inevitably vote for Obama and his entitlement society (Klein 2012; Corn 2012). Obama's supporters, Romney claimed, were people who "are dependent upon government, who believe that they are victims, who believe the government has a responsibility to care for them, who believe that they are entitled to health care, to food, to housing, to you-name-it." Again, the implication is that black people, or at the very least, Obama supporters, many of whom are people of color, want to depend on government assistance, rather than adhering to the American value of hard work.

Romney also engaged in racial distancing by airing a television advertisement, "The Right Choice," the summer before the 2012 presidential election. The ad falsely accused Obama of doing away with the work requirements that accompany welfare benefits.[41] "Under Obama's plan you wouldn't have to work, and you wouldn't have to train for a job. They just send you your welfare check." The language in the ad was juxtaposed with images of exclusively "hardworking white Americans" or, at the very least, white Americans engaged in what appeared to be blue-collar factory work, wiping away sweat from their brows. The message was clear—welfare recipients, whom many white Americans falsely perceive as predominantly black, would just receive a check in the mail, at the expense of hardworking whites.

The comments from Bill and Hillary Clinton, Newt Gingrich, Rick Santorum, and Mitt Romney are not an exhaustive list of the ways in which Obama's opponents deployed negative racial stereotypes about blacks against him. However, they do highlight that negative stereotypes about blacks were a fairly common feature of the attacks against Obama by his opponents. These racialized attacks against Obama suggest that black candidates who are running for office in majority-white jurisdictions may likely face attacks that play to negative stereotypes of African American candidates and African Americans more broadly. Black candidates are well aware of this dynamic and may make efforts to overcome these attacks, not just by avoiding racial issues, but by taking more deliberate actions to demonstrate that not only do they work hard, but they are not partial to African Americans, many of whom are perceived as not working hard and making excuses.

Concluding Remarks

This chapter drew on the 2008 and 2012 Obama campaigns as an example of a black Democratic candidate who engaged in racial distancing, above and beyond a strategy of deracialization. Rather than avoid racial issues altogether, Obama often injected race into his speeches, referencing racialized tropes, such as "Cousin Pookie" and "Popeyes chicken." I also demonstrated that Obama's speeches to black audiences were more likely to include the rhetoric of personal responsibility even when compared to his speeches to another marginalized group, Latinos. Obama's television advertisements were also more likely to include references to the racialized issues of welfare and crime than those of either McCain or Clinton, and even more than the previous two Democratic presidential nominees combined.

The electoral environment in which Obama operated, however, was also highly racialized. Obama's opponents associated him and his supporters with the racialized stereotype of poor work ethic, referencing "hardworking white Americans," referring to him as "the food stamp president," and falsely suggesting that he rolled back welfare reforms implemented under Bill Clinton. The racialized attacks that Obama experienced may have prompted him in some instances to engage in racial distancing, as a means of defending himself from racialized attacks, such as his television advertisements on the racialized issue of crime, which were rebuttals to attack ads that made the charge that Obama was soft on crime.

Other racialized behavior on the campaign trail, such as speeches that invoked negative racial stereotypes, seemed proactive, rather than reactive. Obama routinely relied on racially inflected personal responsibility messages to black audiences, but for the most part these messages were met with very little scrutiny. Without devoting attention to the ways in which blacks, even black Democratic politicians, contribute to the reification of negative stereotypes about African Americans, we underestimate the threat that racial distancing poses to the advancement of African American interests.

In chapter 4, I discuss several cases of black politicians, Democrats and Republicans alike, who have also engaged in racial distancing. These politicians have pursued offices as diverse as the president, congressman/congresswoman, and mayor. I have included a discussion of these politicians to illustrate the depth and breadth with which racial distancing occurs in American politics. In other words, President Obama was not an anomaly.

CHAPTER FOUR

Racial Distancing on the Campaign Trail and in the Lab

The previous chapter focused on the most prominent black politician in American history, President Barack Obama. In that chapter I argued that Obama engaged in racial distancing, despite the dominant characterization of him as a purely deracialized candidate. Similarly, in this chapter I draw on examples of other black politicians who also engaged in racial distancing. I focus primarily on these candidates' rhetorical strategy, in which they racially distance by either criticizing purported black pathology or by drawing attention to their own "counter-stereotypical" work ethic and competence. I discuss cases of African American politicians who have pursued offices as diverse as the presidency, Congress, and mayorship, demonstrating the breadth and scope with which racial distancing is employed by African American politicians. In short, racial distancing is not a phenomenon that is limited to the Obama presidency. These cases are by no means intended to demonstrate causality, but rather to show that the behavior portrayed in the experiments throughout the book has a grounding in real candidate behavior. I conclude by providing empirical evidence from a survey experiment that suggests the utility of a racial distancing strategy for black politicians, relative to deracialization. The results of the survey experiment indicate that a message from a black Democratic politician that implicitly or explicitly invokes negative stereotypes about African Americans can actually produce more electoral support than a deracialized message from a black Democratic politician that emphasizes universalism.[1]

Racial Distancing on the Campaign Trail

I suspect that black politicians use opportunities to prime stereotypes about blacks to show white voters that they don't mind upbraiding their co-ethnics. These appeals often invoke negative stereotypes about blacks regarding work ethic, criminality, and dependency. Black politicians also draw attention to their own work ethic and individualism, in sharp contrast to the stereotype of black politicians as incompetent. Messages that invoke individualism also stand in contrast to the stereotype of African Americans more generally as unwilling to work hard and "play by the rules."

Take, for example, the two black Republican politicians who most recently pursued the presidency, Herman Cain and Ben Carson. When Cain ran in 2012 and Carson in 2016, they each entered a crowded Republican primary field, against mostly white opponents. Cain and Carson were initial frontrunners among the Republican presidential candidates in their respective presidential runs, outpolling establishment Republicans, including Jeb Bush, Mitt Romney, and Marco Rubio. While arguing that black people focus too much on race, Cain and Carson ironically engaged race openly and fairly often. They used race-specific language and racial nouns, but in a manner that indicated that they would not disrupt the racial status quo. Throughout their respective campaigns, Cain and Carson were dismissive of explanations that attributed racial disparities between whites and blacks to discrimination or even the historical legacy of slavery.

One example of Cain invoking rather than eschewing race is when he defined himself in an interview as "an ABC"—"an American black conservative." He said, "By the way, it's OK to call me black . . . I am an American black conservative. An ABC. OK. It's OK. It's OK. I'm not hyphenated."[2] Cain was not eschewing racial nouns as a deracialization strategy would suggest. He was distancing himself from the stereotype of black politicians as obsessed with minority rights, political correctness, and the redress of racial grievances. Cain also routinely chastised African Americans for being "brainwashed" because of their overwhelming support for the Democratic Party. He contrasted the behavior of African Americans with his own behavior, describing himself as having "left the Democratic plantation."[3] His comments implied that black voters lacked political sophistication and were unable to think for themselves. This is an old trope that dates back as far as the antebellum period. African Americans were routinely described as too unintelligent to care for themselves. Instead they required the paternal care of benevolent masters. The inclusion of the word "plantation" is also an example of racially inflected language, because "plantation" draws attention to the institution of slavery and thus race. Cain was also dismissive of the existence of racism, saying in an interview, "They [African Americans] weren't held back because of racism. People sometimes hold themselves back because they want to use racism as an excuse for them not being able to achieve what they want to achieve."[4]

In another example of a black Republican candidate engaging race, Ben Carson during his 2016 presidential campaign suggested that racism was not a problem on the right. Instead he argued that racism was more of an issue on the left, saying, "It [racism] is mostly with the progressive movement who will look at someone like me, and because of the color of my pigment, they decide that there's a certain way that I'm supposed to think. And if I don't think that way, I'm an Uncle Tom and they heap all kinds of hatred on you. That, to me, is racism."[5] Ben Carson also distanced himself from Obama, arguing that "Obamacare was the worst thing to happen to the nation since slavery."[6] The choice to compare Obamacare to slavery is odd at best. It is also an example of a black candidate invoking race by mentioning slavery, rather than avoiding race. Carson also went on to rail against Obamacare and political correctness in a speech at the 2013 National Prayer Breakfast, with Obama sitting only a few feet away from the podium. The speech received over three million views on YouTube, made Carson a darling of the Tea Party movement, and prompted an editorial from the *Wall Street Journal* drafting Carson to run for president.

Media mogul Rupert Murdoch also expressed support for a Carson run for president, tweeting, "Ben and Candy Carson terrific. What about a real black president who can properly address the racial divide. And much else."[7] It is unclear what Murdoch meant by "a real black president," but a Carson run for president was likely so attractive to Tea Party members and the Republican establishment alike because as an African American Republican, Carson could espouse a racially conservative message with less fear of generating a backlash. Racially conservative messages that dismiss racism as a cause of racial disparities indicate that the candidate is not overly concerned with "black interests" and distinguish the black candidate from the "old guard" of black politicians. These types of racially conservative messages also play to the stereotype of African American dependency and unwillingness to work hard. Racially resentful whites see blacks as a group less willing to work hard to get ahead, instead using racism as an excuse to benefit from undeserved government support. When an African American politician endorses these sentiments, racially resentful whites feel more comfortable endorsing these sentiments as well.

At the congressional level, black Republicans, such as Congresswoman Mia Love and former congressman Allen West, have also engaged in racial distancing. Mia Love, the first black person to represent Utah in Congress, initially drew significant attention because of her unusual demographic profile. Not only is she a black woman Republican, but she is a member of the Church of Latter-Day Saints, a religious denomination in which African Americans account for less than 5 percent of members.[8] While campaigning in 2012, Love said that if elected, she would join the Congressional Black Caucus (CBC), and "try to take that thing apart from the inside out." She described the CBC as characterized by demagoguery, saying, "They sit there and ignite emotions and ignite racism when there isn't. They use their positions to instill fear" (Romboy 2012). Love's statements dismissed the existence of racism, while also distancing her from the "old guard" of black politicians who founded the CBC and from black voters more generally.

Love also drew on her identity as the child of Haitian immigrants to emphasize her commitment to the American values of hard work and individualism. Prominently featured on Love's website was a video of her talking about one of her father's favorite statements to her, which was also a statement that she routinely referenced on the campaign trail: "Mia, your mother and I never took a handout. You will not be a burden to society. You will give back."[9] This statement from Love's father dispelled the stereotype of an African American politician who would advocate for the expansion of the welfare state. The rhetoric also highlighted Love's personal commitment to individualism, which I argue is a form of racial distancing.

Similarly, former Republican congressman Allen West also engaged in racial distancing throughout his 2010 campaign to represent the Twenty-Second Congressional District of Florida. During an interview with conservative newspaper the *Washington Times*, he expressed his disdain for affirmative action and argued that Democrats' social welfare policies have enslaved the "mind and will" of blacks. West went on to say, "Republicans have allowed black communities to be taken over by a voice of victimization, a voice of dependency."[10] These statements would be classified as "explicit racial appeals," because they used racial nouns. They were also derogatory in nature and invoked stereotypes of African Americans as lazy and dependent on government. Through his use of rhetoric, West was able to distinguish himself from other black politicians, who are typically expected to highlight racial inequality and build support for liberal policies to address this inequality.

In a different interview, with the conservative *Weekly Standard*, West is also quoted as saying, "I hate big-tent. Í hate inclusiveness. And I hate outreach." This language runs contrary to the universal language of the classic deracialized approach. Again, West's language is counter-stereotypical, as black elites are often expected to raise the public's consciousness about racial inequality. Also, since the Democratic Party is often perceived as the party of "big-tent inclusion," West distinguished himself from most African American politicians, the overwhelming majority of whom are affiliated with the Democratic Party.[11]

West also took decidedly conservative positions on immigration, which is an issue ripe with racial implications. For example, he told a crowd of Tea Party protesters outside a day-labor center in Jupiter, Florida, "You must be well-informed and well-armed, because this government we have right now is a tyrannical government. And it starts with illegal immigration." He went on to say, "We cannot allow them [immigrants] to come here and depress our wages."[12] The racial priming hypothesis would suggest that such rhetoric could make immigration more accessible in voters' minds (Mendelberg 2001) and thus a more important part of their decision calculus. Throughout the campaign, West also depicted his opponent as being "soft on immigration" and "supporting amnesty for illegal immigrants." Although his white Democratic opponent, Ron Klein, disputed such claims, West's incendiary rhetoric helped him frame his opponent and the election.[13]

The results from the 2010 election to represent Florida's Twenty-Second Congressional District, as well as the results from the 2014 election to represent Utah's Fourth Congressional District, offer evidence that an African American candidate does not necessarily have to adopt a deracialized approach to win elections in majority-white jurisdictions. In fact, because both districts were overwhelmingly white (76 percent and 84 percent, respectively), neither West nor Love had to worry about appealing to both black and white voters. Instead they could adopt very conservative positions on racial issues, without fear of offending black voters or sparking a countermobilization effort by a significant number of African Americans. Although members of the CBC John Lewis and Alcee Hastings did campaign for West's opponent, the district's African American population was so small that they did not constitute a significant voting bloc in the district. Furthermore, a lack of support from the CBC likely only further solidified both West's and Love's antiestablishment persona, further distinguishing them from "traditional" African American politicians.

The cases of Cain, Carson, Love, and West have a few elements in common. All are African American Republicans who quickly rose to national prominence, despite making racially inflammatory statements. They were quick to disassociate themselves from the CBC and the "old guard" of black politicians, while simultaneously discussing race openly and frequently. It was not uncommon for them to make references to slavery, for example, or to talk about black people openly. Rather than eschewing race, they talked openly about it, often with a perceived expertise status, because they were black. They all ran in districts that were overwhelmingly white, or in the Republican presidential primaries, where the electorate is also overwhelmingly white. Another common thread is that all of these politicians were virtual political unknowns prior to running for office, which may have incentivized them to demonstrate that they were challengers of the racial status quo, thus helping them gain status and legitimacy within the party.

The very presence of these black Republicans on the ballot arguably made race an issue in their respective elections. As African American Republicans and Tea Party affiliates, they were uniquely positioned to garner support from the Tea Party, a movement that was frequently characterized as having racist motivations. Cain, Carson, Love, and West could all be used as an example of the inclusiveness and diversity of both the Republican Party and the Tea Party. It is plausible that both parties on the right may have been interested in highlighting their diversity, and these black Republicans may have provided an opportunity to achieve this goal.

Of course, black Democratic politicians also engage in their own form of racial distancing. The very fact that voters are more likely to associate the Democratic Party with racial liberalism incentivizes black Democrats to engage in racial distancing as well. Also, racial distancing by black Democrats seems to be met with virtual impunity by white Americans. Racial distancing for black Democrats, however, is a riskier proposition than it is for their black Republican counterparts. Black Democrats are more reliant on the support of African Americans than are black Republicans, and thus they risk depressing black turnout when they engage in racial distancing. As we will see in the cases of Michael Nutter, Harold Ford Jr., and Artur Davis, black Democrats other than President Barack Obama have engaged in their own fair share of racial distancing, but sometimes to their own detriment.

In 2007 Michael Nutter won a closely contested five-way primary for mayor, which was virtually equivalent to winning the general election in the heavily Democratic city of Philadelphia. The former councilman focused much of his campaign on Mayor John Street, even though Street was term-limited and could not run for office again. Nutter presented himself as a reformer, contrasting himself with Street, whose administration was plagued by charges of corruption. Tom Ferrick Jr., a columnist for the *Philadelphia Inquirer,* wrote of Nutter, "He is really a post-modern black candidate."[14] Street, on the other hand, was an "old guard" black politician, who once caused controversy by telling an NAACP conference, "Let me tell you: The brothers and sisters are running the city . . . Don't you let nobody fool you; we are in charge of the City of Brotherly Love."[15] Street's comments were widely interpreted as evidence of what many white voters fear under black leadership—a black takeover.

In a city where crime was the number one issue for voters, Nutter distinguished himself from the other candidates in the race, including two African Americans, by coming out heavily in favor of "stop and frisk" policing, which has been criticized as a tactic that promotes racial profiling. While the other black candidates in the Democratic primary criticized Nutter for trampling on civil liberties, and not devoting enough attention to inner-city black concerns, Nutter's standing in the polls continued to rise. Nutter appealed to blacks and whites alike, earning a plurality of both groups—37 percent of the white vote and 40 percent of the black vote—to win the primary. In fact, according to the *Philadelphia Inquirer,* Nutter won the largest percentage of white votes ever cast for an African American in a Philadelphia mayoral primary (Epstein 2013).

After his electoral victory in 2007, criticisms of Nutter for not being sufficiently concerned with African American interests continued into his time in office. The most blatant example of Nutter engaging in racial

distancing, however, was during a now infamous speech at Mount Carmel Baptist Church in Philadelphia in 2011, in which he publicly lambasted black youth and their parents. The remarks were delivered in the
aftermath of a violent flash mob involving hundreds of black youth who
destroyed property and physically assaulted bystanders. While it is well
within the purview of a mayor to speak out against criminal activity,
Nutter's comments arguably went well beyond the issue of crime, and at
times were racially inflammatory. During the speech Nutter made statements that arguably a white Republican politician, or a white Democratic politician for that matter, would have been unable to make without
being heavily scrutinized, and without being labeled as a racist: "If you
go to look for a job, don't go blame it on the white folks, or anybody else.
If you walk in somebody's office with your hair uncombed and a pick in
the back and your shoes untied and your pants half down, tattoos up and
down your arm, on your face, on your neck, and you wonder why somebody won't hire you. They don't hire you because you look like you're
crazy. That's why they're not hiring you."[16]

Nutter's comments suggest that black people blame black unemployment on "white folks" and racism rather than accepting personal responsibility. According to Nutter, if black youth would just "pull their
pants up" and avoid getting tattoos, they would find gainful employ-
ment. While Nutter's comments were met with cheers and amens by the
audience at Mt. Carmel Baptist Church, it seems unlikely that a similarly situated white politician would be able to make the same comments
without backlash. My point here, however, is not that white politicians
should be allowed to disparage black people, just like some black politicians. Instead, I am simply highlighting that black politicians' inflammatory racial comments are met with less scrutiny than those of their white
counterparts. Nutter's message not only played to stereotypes of black
people blaming unemployment on racism rather than their own appar-
ently "pathological" behavior, but his identity as an African American
offered legitimacy to negative stereotypes about blacks. Black politicians
are able to uniquely reap political gains by publicly disparaging other
black people, while similarly situated white politicians are not able to
benefit to the same degree by making similar comments.

Another striking example of racial distancing comes from another
African American Democrat, Harold Ford Jr., during his 2006 run to
represent Tennessee in the U.S. Senate. This race is probably best known
for the infamous "Call Me" ad, an attack ad aired against Ford and spon-

sored by the Republican National Committee. The ad was heavily criticized for its negative racial undertones—particularly for promoting the
stereotype of black men as sexually promiscuous predators in pursuit of
white women. The NAACP argued that the ad exploited "a powerful
innuendo that plays to pre-existing prejudices about African American
men and white women."[17] The "Call Me" ad, however, was only one of
a series of racially charged attacks aimed at Ford during his 2006 senate race. A political action committee, Tennesseans for Truth, also sponsored a radio ad that said, "[Ford's] daddy handed him his seat in Congress and his seat in the Congressional Black Caucus, an all-black group
of congressmen who represent the interest of black people above all others."[18] This radio ad in particular was an attempt to depict Ford as a politician who would look out only for the interests of African Americans,
which, as noted earlier, is a stereotype of African American politicians.
In addition, some political observers believed that a Republican Party–
sponsored circular in eastern (and largely white) Tennessee counties,
which urged residents to vote to "preserve your way of life," was also
racially coded. Other forms in which race was invoked included a radio commercial criticizing Ford with African drums beating in the background, and a campaign flyer that darkened Ford's skin color.[19]

Ford never addressed the racial undertones of any of these advertisements. Referring to Republicans, he said, "You have to ask them about
race. I don't focus on those things," which suggests that he was reluctant to engage the issue of racism, a classic deracialization tactic (Persons 2017). While Ford was reluctant to make the charge of racism, it
does not mean that he was disinterested in engaging the issue of race
in other ways. Ford made his own racial appeals that were examples of
classic racial distancing rather than mere deracialization. Long before
President Trump promised to "build that wall," Ford took a very prominent and conservative stance on immigration. He frequently referred
to having signed legislation to build a fence along the Mexican border
to keep "illegal immigrants" out. He distanced himself from African
Americans as well by not making many public appearances with them—
limiting most of his outreach to blacks through phone banking, and appeals by political surrogates, such as African American clergy and labor
activists (Franklin 2010). Ford also made an effort to highlight his purported white ancestry by asserting that his paternal grandmother was
white, which surprised many observers, including members of his own

family, who claim that she was black. Ford's revelation may have been an attempt to make him more palatable to white voters. There is some evidence that part of what makes some black candidates who are pursuing white electoral support more viable is that they can point to white ancestry, as was the case with President Obama (Ehrenstein 2007; Helman 2007).

Ford ran unopposed in the Democratic primary, which gave him the opportunity to run an early general election campaign and visit the more rural parts of the state. During one of these trips, he visited the "Lil' Rebel," a roadside bar with a large Confederate flag displayed outside. The bar is known among Tennesseans to be an outpost for Confederate sympathizers. The congressman was photographed in a camouflage hat outside of the Lil' Rebel, giving a "thumbs-up," with a Confederate flag displayed prominently in the background—a campaign stop that he reflected on fondly throughout the campaign.[20] Given the association of the Confederate flag with racial intolerance, Ford's choice to give a "thumbs-up" in front of the flag was more than a tacit endorsement of the flag—it was a racial signal that indicated that he was not beholden to African American voters. Ford distinguished himself from the "old guard" of black politicians, who were probably more likely to picket than they were to patronize such an establishment. Ford went on to lose the race by a slim margin of 50,000 votes in a contest that was infused with race. While the onslaught of racial attacks certainly did not help his cause, Ford was also unable to mobilize African American Tennesseans, despite having been a five-term congressman from a majority-black district. Previous research indicates that his racial distancing made many African Americans lukewarm toward his candidacy (Franklin 2010).

Yet another example of a black Democrat who has engaged in racial distancing is former Alabama congressman Artur Davis. Davis represented Alabama's Seventh Congressional District from 2003 through 2011. Davis originally made a name for himself by challenging black Democratic incumbent and civil rights activist Earl Hilliard in 2000 to represent the majority-black district. Despite being handily defeated in 2000, in 2002 Davis narrowly defeated Hilliard in the Democratic primary, prompting a runoff, which Davis went on to win. Davis was able to benefit from a decennial redistricting effort that introduced new voters into the district, many of whom were white, and many of whom had no political loyalties to the incumbent. Hilliard also inadvertently helped Davis build his brand as a black politician who was different from the "old guard" of black politicians by criticizing Davis for "not being black enough."

In 2012 Davis went on to run for governor of Alabama. During his gubernatorial campaign, he downplayed matters of race and emphasized his independence from Democratic Party orthodoxy. He caused controversy, including within his heavily minority congressional district, by voting against Obamacare—the only black Democrat in Congress to do so, of which Jesse Jackson said, "You can't vote against health care and call yourself a black man."[21] Davis also refused to sit for the endorsement screenings of the state's two dominant black Democratic organizations, the Alabama Democratic Conference and the Alabama New South Coalition. Davis's response drew criticism that he was snubbing African Americans in order to court white votes. Joe Reed, the Alabama Democratic chairman and an influential Alabama Democratic power broker, ended up rallying support for Davis's white primary opponent, then agriculture commissioner Ron Sparks, who won in a stunning landslide.

Davis and Ford were both black congressmen in the South who previously represented majority-minority districts prior to running for statewide office. They may have been especially motivated to show that they were not beholden to African American voters, given that their previous political experience was gained representing a majority-black district. The experiences of Davis and Ford, however, suggest that black Democrats have to be cautious about not alienating black voters with a strategy of racial distancing. If black candidates go too far with a strategy of racial distancing, they may be able to pick off some racially conservative whites, but at the expense of black turnout.

The cases of Davis, Ford, and Nutter, who were all rising stars in the Democratic Party, suggest that black Democrats who engage in racial distancing, similar to their black Republican counterparts, can also rise to national prominence. As the Democratic Party struggles with the tension around "identity politics," one way that it has opted to resolve this tension is to field candidates of color, who are also able to espouse racially conservative messages with less fear of generating a backlash than their white Democratic counterparts. White voters within the Democratic Party seem relatively unperturbed by the sometimes racially inflammatory rhetoric of black Democratic politicians. However, if these black Democrats go too far, they will isolate the very voters who make up a lot of their base—African Americans. In short, racial distancing is a strategy that is engaged by black and white politicians, Democrats and Republicans alike.

I would be remiss, however, if I did not acknowledge some cases in which black politicians pursuing office in majority-white jurisdictions did not engage in racial distancing. Currently the U.S. Senate has more black members than ever in its history—three: Cory Booker (D-NJ), Kamala Harris (D-CA), and Tim Scott (R-SC)—two of whom, at the time of this writing, are running for the 2020 Democratic presidential nomination. Arguably, none of these black politicians engaged in racial distancing as a means of entering the Senate. Considering the paucity of black politicians elected to statewide offices, at first glance, these three cases might be exactly where we would expect black politicians to have engaged in racial distancing, thus teaching us a few lessons about scope conditions of the theory of racial distancing.

The case of the lone black Republican senator currently serving in the Senate, Tim Scott, is illustrative of the confluence of contextual factors that influence racial distancing. Scott, unlike the previously mentioned black Republicans, had an established decades-long history of representing jurisdictions that were overwhelmingly white. Prior to joining the U.S. Senate, he had also established a reputation that suggested that he would not challenge the racial status quo. Scott served on the Charleston County Council for thirteen years and was even council chairman for one year prior to being elected to the U.S. House of Representatives. He served two terms in the House prior to representing South Carolina in the Senate. All of his previous political experience was representing majority-white jurisdictions.

Scott's previous political experience representing majority-white jurisdictions helped him establish his credentials as an elected official who would not show favoritism toward African Americans. Previous research indicates that positive experiences with black leadership diminish white Americans' concerns about black politicians favoring blacks over whites (Hajnal 2007). Scott also took stances on racialized issues that helped establish his credentials as a politician who would not disrupt the racial status quo. For example, in 2001, as the lone African American member of the Charleston County Council, Scott was a vocal defender of the council when the U.S. Department of Justice sued Charleston County for racial discrimination. Scott also opposed the creation of single-member districts, which was the Department of Justice's proposed means of achieving African American representation on the council.[22]

Speaking about his opposition to single-member districts, Scott said, "I don't like the idea of segregating everyone into smaller districts. Besides, the Justice Department assumes that the only way for African-Americans to have representation is to elect an African-American, and the same for whites. Obviously, my [white] constituents don't think that's true." Scott's stance on the racial discrimination suit helped establish his racially conservative bona fides, and distinguished him from the "old guard" of black politicians. By the time Scott was elected to the U.S. House of Representatives as part of the Tea Party insurgency of 2010, he declined to join the Congressional Black Caucus, only further solidifying his reputation as a defender of the racial status quo. The fact that he was affiliated with the Tea Party also helped reinforce his credentials as a defender of the racial status quo (Parker and Barreto 2013).

In 2013, Scott became the first African American since Reconstruction to represent a Southern state in the U.S. Senate, after he was appointed by Governor Nikki Haley to fill a vacancy. By this time, there was very little need to engage in a strategy of racial distancing. He was appointed to the Senate and did not have to stand for an election, thereby removing the electoral incentives to engage in racial distancing. Scott subsequently won a special election in 2014 to complete the term and was elected to a full term in 2016. Since Scott was initially appointed to his statewide office, by the time he faced his first election to the Senate, he already had the benefits of incumbency, including name recognition and an established reputation as someone who would not challenge the racial status quo. Furthermore, he was a Republican running in a very conservative state.

The other two African American senators currently serving in the Senate were also elected in contexts that might have diminished their incentives to engage in racial distancing. Like Scott, Cory Booker (D-NJ) also won a special election in 2013 to fill a vacancy. Booker subsequently won a special election in 2014 to complete the term and was elected to a full term in 2016. Booker never faced a formidable challenger and was already well known throughout New Jersey, having served two terms as the mayor of Newark, the state's largest city. Although Newark has a large black population, Booker had already branded himself as a politician who would not be beholden to his black constituents. As Gillespie (2012) illustrates, during the 2002 Newark mayoral race, Booker distinguished himself from the stereotype of a black politician preoccupied with black interests, having engaged in a contentious battle with the incumbent and old guard black politician Sharpe James. Booker was also notoriously unpopular with many of the black residents of Newark, in part because he was perceived as a carpetbagger and opportunist, supported by largely outside (white) interests. Therefore, it was well known throughout the state that Booker did not fit many voters' stereotype of a black politician, which diminished incentives for Booker to engage in racial distancing.

The other African American currently serving in the U.S. Senate is Kamala Harris (D-CA). Like Scott and Booker, Harris ran in an open-seat race to fill a vacancy after a retirement. In a crowded field of thirty-four candidates, including seven Democrats, twelve Republicans, and fifteen third-party candidates, Harris, along with Loretta Sanchez, defeated the other thirty-two candidates to advance to the general election. Not only was Harris running against another Democrat in the general election, but her opponent was also a woman of color, thus making the circumstances around the election less than typical. By the time she ran for the U.S. Senate, Harris had wide name recognition, having served as the state's attorney general for six years. Her position as the attorney general also enabled Harris to establish her "law and order" credentials, thus helping dispel concerns about partiality to racial and ethnic minority communities. Harris is also biracial, of black and Indian heritage, which might also help distinguish her from the old guard of black politicians. Finally, California is a majority-minority state, which also diminished any incentives Harris may have had to engage in racial distancing. In other words, given that white Americans are in the minority in the state, there was less of an incentive to signal racial moderation to white voters as a means of getting elected.

I argue that racial distancing seems to be as viable a strategy as de-racialization, if not more so for many black candidates, Democrats and Republicans alike, but it does not necessarily occur in all circumstances in which a black candidate is running for office in a majority-white jurisdiction. As the cases of Scott, Booker, and Harris illustrate, some black candidates can attain prominent offices without engaging in racial distancing—largely because the circumstances surrounding their election are atypical, or because they previously established their racial conservative bona fides. Nevertheless, racial distancing among black politicians is perhaps surprisingly common, and in many instances does not appear to result in detrimental consequences for black candidates who engage the strategy. Both Cain and Carson, for example, were initial frontrunners among the Republican presidential candidates. Mia Love quickly rose to national prominence, gaining a coveted speaking role at the 2012 Republican National Convention. Allen West was successfully elected to the U.S. House of Representatives in 2010, and likely would have been reelected had the demographics of his district not changed because of redistricting. Michael Nutter was elected to serve two terms as the mayor of the fifth largest city in America. And although he was unsuccessful in his bid for the U.S. Senate, Harold Ford Jr. lost by only a slim margin of 50,000 votes in a race where almost two million votes were cast. Thus, from the evidence gathered on the campaign trail, racial distancing at the very least does not appear to automatically sink black candidates' chances of pursuing electoral victory. Although racial distancing does not guarantee a black politician electoral victory, the aim here was to provide illustrative examples of black politicians using racial distancing. These examples also help to foreshadow the messages that are used in the survey experiments discussed later in the book. The focus on black candidates in this section has highlighted the most understudied aspect of the use of racial cues in American campaigns—the use of racial distancing by African American politicians, Democrats and Republicans alike. In the next section, we will see what impact these racial signals have on white voters when black Democratic politicians pursue this strategy, relative to a message of deracialization.

Comparing Deracialized, Implicit, and Explicit Campaign Statements

Proponents of deracialization and its close cousin, universalism, argue that policies that aim overtly at protecting or advancing the interests of particular racial groups are especially politically vulnerable (Wilson 1987). Therefore, proponents of universalism contend that policies should be couched in race-neutral or color-blind terms as a means of diminishing white opposition to these policies. In a similar vein, supporters of deracialization advise that Democratic candidates, especially black Democratic candidates, should avoid racialized topics, such as welfare and affirmative action, as a means of projecting a reassuring image to the white electorate. The conventional wisdom is that if black candidates talk about race, they will lose white electoral support.

Implicit in the deracialization literature is the assumption that if a black candidate discusses race, she is doing so in a manner that calls for the redress of racial grievances. Less examined is the possibility that black candidates of either major party might discuss race in a manner that appeals to some white voters' negative racial predispositions. However, from the previous section in this chapter, it is evident that it is not uncommon for some black politicians to routinely use racially inflammatory language. It is also assumed that candidates who use the language of universalism and inclusivity, as the deracialization literature suggests, fare better than candidates who invoke race, but this has not been tested empirically. Far less attention has been devoted to the impact of rhetoric that invokes negative racial stereotypes about blacks delivered by black candidates.

Contrary to the deracialization literature and the conventional wisdom on racial appeals, racial distancing theory argues that candidates, especially black candidates, are rewarded for demonstrating that they are not beholden to African Americans. Candidates signal that they are not beholden to blacks, often through messages that invoke negative stereotypes about blacks, using racially inflammatory language. Essentially, racial distancing theory makes the controversial claim that black Democrats who either implicitly or explicitly criticize other black people with personal responsibility messages and exhortations to "get off of the couch" and the like fare better than black Democrats who take a deracialized approach, using the language of universalism. This expectation is based on the premise that messages that invoke negative stereotypes about blacks have a long-standing history of political utility in American politics. When politicians invoke negative stereotypes about blacks, negative racial attitudes are often primed such that they become a more consequential factor in voters' decision calculus. Thus, there is no reason to assume that black candidates cannot also benefit from invoking these stereotypes, even more so than from an appeal to universalism.

I fielded a survey experiment of a nationally representative sample of approximately 500 whites in September 2016 to test the hypothesis that a deracialized appeal from a black Democratic candidate garners *less* electoral support from white voters than an appeal from a black Democratic candidate that derides African Americans, either implicitly or explicitly. The data were collected by GfK (Growth from Knowledge).[23] I examine white Americans' receptivity to a race-neutral message that encourages people to vote and work together, as compared to get-out-the-vote messages that either implicitly or explicitly promote stereotypes of black laziness. This is a hard test of the racial distancing theory because instead of testing implicit and explicit racial signals relative to an unrelated control message, we are comparing an implicit and explicit racial appeal relative to a message that emphasizes universalism. Given the presumed American commitment to the norm of racial equality and support for the American creed, a deracialized message that emphasizes American ideals around working together should be popular, relative to messages that emphasize negative stereotypes about African Americans. The results of the deracialization experiment discussed in this chapter, however, find the exact opposite—I find that many white Americans were *more* supportive of a black Democratic candidate who signaled either implicitly or explicitly that he was not beholden to African Americans, even relative to a universalistic message that emphasizes the common good.

The sample was evenly split between men and women. Forty-six percent of respondents identified as Democrats, while 53 percent identified as Republicans. Thirty-six percent of the sample reported having a bachelor's degree or higher, and the median income of the sample was between $75,000 and $84,999. The respondents were randomly assigned to a fictitious Internet article that depicted a fictitious black candidate for the U.S. House of Representatives. The article reports on a speech that the black Democratic candidate delivered, encouraging voters to get to the polls in support of the candidate.

There were three versions of the article—an explicit message, an implicit message, and a deracialized message. As indicated in table 4.1, the explicit version meets the standard for an explicit racial appeal, because it uses the racial noun "black" to reference black voters (Mendelberg 2001). In the explicit version of the article, the headline was "Democratic Candidate to Black Voters: 'Get to the Voting Booth.'" In the implicit version, there is no use of racial nouns, such as "black" or "African American." Instead, race is signaled implicitly through the term "inner-city," a term that previous research has demonstrated is racially coded (Hurwitz and Peffley 2005). The headline was "Democratic Candidate to Inner-City Voters: 'Quit Complaining and Get to the Voting Booth.'" Finally, the deracialized headline was "Democratic Candidate to Voters: 'Get to the Voting Booth.'" The deracialized version makes no reference to race, implicitly or explicitly.

Creating a message that was deracialized proved especially challenging because the message had to be devoid of race but still comparable to the implicit and explicit treatments. I made voter mobilization the focus of the candidate's message because it is a subject that was not racialized at the time of data collection (September 2016). Terms such as "working together" and "across the state" were included to convey universalism. Accompanying each article was a picture of a black candidate named Michael Smith, which was used to indicate the candidate's race (African American), while his partisanship (Democrat) was conveyed in the headline of the article. The implicit and explicit versions of the article are largely patterned on Obama's 2011 address to the Congressional Black Caucus Foundation, in which he told the predominantly black audience, "Take off your bedroom slippers. Put on your marching shoes," ahead of his reelection campaign.

The tone and the target of the appeal in the implicit and explicit versions, however, differ from the deracialized version. The implicit and explicit versions have a tone of castigation, relative to a more neutral tone in the deracialized version. The target of the appeal in the implicit and explicit versions is "inner-city voters" and "black voters," respectively, whereas the target in the deracialized version is simply "voters." Therefore, by simultaneously changing the tone and the target of the appeal, it is not possible to determine whether any differences between the implicit and explicit versions, relative to the deracialized version, can be attributed to the target, the tone, or both. Nevertheless, the experiment is still useful, because it demonstrates that messages that castigate a target group are more popular than a message that embraces universalism.[24] The experiment is also useful in testing the racial priming hypothesis, because we can examine differences in the response to the implicit and explicit appeals, which are consistent in terms of both tone and target. Subsequent experiments discussed in later chapters of the book, however, keep the tone and target consistent across all treatments.

Respondents answered questions about their racial predispositions in a pre-test questionnaire. Specifically, all participants answered questions from the racial resentment scale (Kinder and Sanders 1996)[25] consisting of four agree/disagree statements: "Generations of slavery and discrimination have created conditions that make it difficult for Blacks to work their way out of the lower class"; "It's really a matter of some people not trying hard enough; if blacks would only try harder they could be just as well off as whites"; "Over the past few years, Blacks have gotten less than they deserve"; and "Irish, Italian, Jewish, and many other minorities overcame prejudice and worked their way up. Blacks should do

TABLE 4.1 **Experimental Conditions in the Deracialization Experiment**

Implicit/Explicit

Headline: Democratic Candidate to Inner-City/Black Voters: "Quit Complaining and Get to the Voting Booth"

1st paragraph: Michael Smith, who is a Democrat campaigning to represent the state in the U.S. Senate, delivered a fiery speech last night. He spoke to inner-city/Black voters, urging them to "quit complaining and get to the voting booth."

2nd paragraph: Smith also outlined his vision for creating jobs in the state. "I have experience running successful businesses that moved many residents in this state from welfare to work. If elected I will continue to create jobs that offer a hand up and not a handout."

3rd paragraph: Another issue that Smith's speech touched on was education. "In order to be successful our schools need resources. But inner-city/Black kids also need to learn the value of hard work and not complaining."

4th paragraph: Smith frequently urges inner-city/Black audiences to address their problems by working on their own behavior, rather than "waiting on government solutions."

5th paragraph: In fact, Smith spoke to the audience about the need for them to "get off of the couch and get to the voting booth! If you don't vote, you can't complain." Of course, Smith is hoping that when voters do get to the voting booth, they cast a vote for him.

6th paragraph: The candidate also pressed voters to channel their frustrations by "rolling up their sleeves and getting their hands dirty." "I don't have time to feel sorry for myself and neither do you. Quit grumbling. Quit complaining. We've got work to do!"

Final paragraph: Throughout the campaign Smith has branded himself as a straight-talking politician who isn't afraid to speak his mind.

Deracialized

Headline: Democratic Candidate to Voters: "Get to the Voting Booth"

1st paragraph: Michael Smith, who is a Democrat campaigning to represent the state in the U.S. Senate, delivered a fiery speech last night. He spoke to voters, urging them to "get to the voting booth."

2nd paragraph: Smith also outlined his vision for creating jobs in the state. "I have experience running successful businesses that created jobs for everyone. If elected I will continue to create jobs that offer a hand up for everyone across the state."

3rd paragraph: Another issue that Smith's speech touched on was education. "In order to be successful our schools need resources."

4th paragraph: Smith frequently urges audiences to address their problems by exercising their right to vote and working together, rather than "waiting on government solutions."

5th paragraph: In fact, Smith spoke to the audience about the need for them to "get to the voting booth! If you don't vote, you can't make change." Of course, Smith is hoping that when voters do get to the voting booth, they cast a vote for him.

6th paragraph: The candidate also pressed voters to channel their frustrations by "rolling up their sleeves and getting their hands dirty. I don't have time for apathy and neither do you. Together we've got work to do."

Final paragraph: Throughout the campaign Smith has branded himself as a straight-talking politician who isn't afraid to speak his mind.

the same without any special favors." Aside from the racial resentment scale, I also used a battery that assesses the degree to which respondents endorse negative stereotypes about African Americans. Respondents were asked to rate blacks on a seven-point scale from "hardworking" to "lazy." They were also asked to rate whites on the same seven-point scale, as a means of determining whether they thought that blacks were, on average, lazier than whites.[26] I subsequently took the difference of the scores between blacks and whites, such that positive scores indicated that respondents thought that whites were more hardworking than blacks, whereas scores of 0 indicated that respondents perceived whites and blacks as equally hardworking or lazy. Finally, negative scores indicated that respondents thought that blacks were more hardworking than whites.

To avoid any priming effects from the pre-test questionnaire, there was a one-week lag time between the first and second waves of the study. During the second wave of the study, subjects received the experimental treatment (mock news article) and the post-treatment questionnaire. After reading the article, participants were asked how likely they were to vote for candidate Michael Smith. Finally, all subjects were thoroughly debriefed after completion of the study so that they understood the article they read was fictitious and that "Michael Smith" was not running for the U.S. House of Representatives.

Table 4.2 displays the results of two models used to estimate the relationship between exposure to the various types of messages and likely vote, as well as voters' evaluation of the speech. The first column displays the results for likely vote. On a scale of 0 to 100, respondents were asked to indicate how likely they were to vote for the candidate depicted in their respective articles, with a higher number indicating a greater willingness on the part of the respondents to vote for the candidate. The results displayed in table 4.2 indicate that support for the candidate with the deracialized message was rather lukewarm, with an average likely vote of 52. It is not surprising that electoral support for Michael Smith in the deracialized condition is unenthusiastic. After all, the candidate depicted in the experiment is fictitious, and voters received very little substantive information about the candidate and his qualifications.

However, if voters are simply nonplussed about a candidate for whom they have very little information, then we should not expect to see much, if any difference, between the racialized conditions and the deracialized condition. In fact, if any difference emerges between the deracialized and racialized conditions, we might expect that voters would react *more* negatively to the candidate depicted in the explicit condition, given the presumed American commitment to the norm of racial equality. The results displayed in table 4.2, however, do not support this expectation. Instead, we see that the candidate depicted in the explicit condition

TABLE 4.2 **Impact of Experimental Treatments on Likely Vote and Speech Rating**

	Likely vote	Speech rating
Implicit	66***	58***
	(3.15)	(2.77)
Explicit	67***	60***
	(2.98)	(2.58)
Constant	52	46
	(5.70)	(5.17)
N	515	515
R^2	0.08	0.08

Note: Standard errors are in parentheses. All models include controls for partisanship, ideology, gender, education, and region.
* $p < .10$; ** $p < .05$; *** $p < .01$ for a two-tailed test.

received the most support. The average likely vote for the black Democratic candidate with the explicit message was 67, while support for the black Democratic candidate with the implicit message was 66, as compared to 52 for the black Democratic candidate in the deracialized condition. Unlike the support for the black Democrat in the deracialized condition, support for the black Democratic candidates in the racialized conditions is well above the midpoint of 50, indicating that, on average, white Americans in the sample were more likely than not to vote for the candidates with racialized messages. Exposure to the black Democratic candidates in the racialized conditions was associated with an increase in support for the candidates of more than 10 percent of the scale, relative to the black Democratic candidate depicted in the deracialized condition. The difference between the deracialized message and either the implicit or explicit message was statistically significant ($p < .00$), while the difference between the implicit and explicit message did not attain traditional levels of statistical significance ($p < .33$). Thus, a message that implicitly or explicitly derided blacks was associated with warmer feelings toward the black Democratic candidate and an increased likelihood of supporting the candidate. Also evident is that contrary to the racial priming hypothesis, the black Democratic candidate with the explicit message did not lose support, relative to the black Democratic candidate with the implicit message.

Respondents were also asked to rate excerpts from the speech on a scale from 0 to 100, with higher numbers indicating a more favorable rating of the speech. As indicated by the second column of table 4.2, respondents were also more likely to rate the speeches that either implicitly or explicitly derided blacks higher than the deracialized message. The average rating for the speech with the deracialized message was 46, but 58 and 60 for the implicit and explicit versions, respectively ($p < .00$). As table 4.2 indicates, overall, voters responded more favorably toward the black Democratic candidate with either an explicit or an implicit message, relative to the deracialized message.

Another major hypothesis of this chapter, and the book more generally, is that racial distancing helps black Democratic candidates in particular to build a broader electoral coalition. The reasoning is that black Democratic candidates, who are generally stereotyped as being racially liberal, benefit from dispelling that stereotype for voters. White racial liberals and the Democratic coalition more broadly are less likely to punish black Democratic candidates for explicit messages, relative to other types of candidates, while at the same time, white racial conservatives from either major party are likely to be more receptive to messages that derogate African Americans. Thus, black Democratic candidates can draw electoral support from white Republican voters, who might initially be inclined to oppose a black Democratic candidate, while still generally maintaining the support of their Democratic voters. In light of these expectations, in table 4.3 I also present the results by voters' party identification.

As indicated in table 4.3, the black Democratic candidate depicted in the experiment gained support with the racialized messages among both Republican and Democratic voters, while the deracialized message was the least popular message. Voters were more likely to vote for a black Democratic candidate when his message either implicitly or explicitly signaled that he would not be beholden to African Americans, relative to the deracialized, universalistic message. Among Democratic voters, support for the black Democratic politician with the implicit message was 10 points higher than support for the black Democrat with the deracialized message ($p < .05$), while support for the black Democrat with the explicit message was somewhat less enthusiastic than support for the black Democrat with the implicit message, but still notably higher than the electoral support for the black Democrat in the deracialized condition. The average likely vote for the black Democrat with the explicit message was 55, as compared to 47 in the deracialized condition ($p < .10$).

TABLE 4.3 **Impact of Experimental Treatments on Likely Vote and Speech Rating by Partisanship**

	Likely vote		Speech rating	
	Democrats	Republicans	Democrats	Republicans
Implicit	57**	88***	55***	76***
	(4.19)	(4.35)	(4.09)	(3.44)
Explicit	55*	94***	55***	79***
	(4.23)	(4.13)	(3.85)	(3.50)
Constant	47	73	45	61
	(7.80)	(12.37)	(7.46)	(9.91)
N	243	262	243	262
R^2	0.05	0.15	0.08	0.14

Note: Standard errors are in parentheses. All models include controls for partisanship, ideology, gender, education, and region.

* $p < .10$; ** $p <. 05$; *** $p <.01$ for a two-tailed test.

Among Republican voters, support for the black Democrat with the deracialized message was notably higher than Democratic voters' support for the candidate. The average likely vote for the black Democratic candidate with the deracialized message was 73 among Republican voters, compared to 47 among Democratic voters. The fact that the deracialized, universal message from a Democratic politician received more support among Republican voters than it did among Democratic voters is surprising. It is plausible that even though the candidate was a Democrat, his rhetoric around not "waiting on government solutions" did not resonate with Democratic voters, who are more likely to support government intervention, relative to their Republican counterparts. This might help to explain why baseline support for the black Democratic candidate in the deracialized condition was higher among Republican voters than it was among Democratic voters. What is more surprising, however, is the enthusiastic support among Republican voters for the black Democrat with the explicit message, even relative to the black Democratic politician with the implicit message. Among Republican voters, average support for the black Democrat with the explicit message was 94, as compared to 88 in the implicit condition ($p < .10$) and 73 in the deracialized condition ($p < .01$). According to the racial priming hypothesis, a message that openly uses racial nouns should be less popular than an implicit message. In this case, however, Republican voters were actually more supportive of a black Democratic candidate when he used racial nouns.

Similar patterns emerge for voters' ratings of the speech. Among Democratic and Republican voters, alike, the speech of the black Democratic politician with the deracialized message received the lowest rating. The average rating for the deracialized speech was 45 among Democrats and 61 among Republicans, while the ratings for the racialized versions of the speech were noticeably higher. Democrats rated both the implicit and the explicit versions of the speech 10 points higher than the deracialized version ($p < .01$), while among the Republican voters, the ratings were even higher relative to the deracialized version. Republican voters rated the implicit version of the speech 15 points higher than the deracialized version ($p < .01$), and the explicit version even higher, at about 18 points more than the deracialized version ($p < .01$). These results once again underscore that the explicit message was especially popular among Republican voters.

How does the black Democratic candidate fare, however, when we look at the message by the respondents' level of racial resentment, rather than by the partisanship of the respondents?

I estimated a regression model where I interacted racial resentment with exposure to the different conditions in the experiment. Figure 4.1 displays the predicted probability of voting for the candidate as a function of respondents' level of racial resentment. The panel on the left displays the results for racial liberals, meaning those respondents who were below the median level of racial resentment. The center panel displays the results for the respondents who were at the median level of racial resentment, and the right panel displays the results for the respondents who were above the median level of racial resentment.[27] As indicated in figure 4.1, the racially liberal respondents in the sample were more likely to vote for the black Democratic candidate with the racialized messages, relative to the deracialized message, but this did not attain traditional levels of statistical significance.

The more racially conservative respondents in the sample, those respondents with a racial resentment score above the median, reacted more positively to the black Democratic politician with the explicit message, relative to the black Democratic politician with the deracialized message. Respondents with racial resentment scores above the median were more likely to vote for the black Democratic candidates with

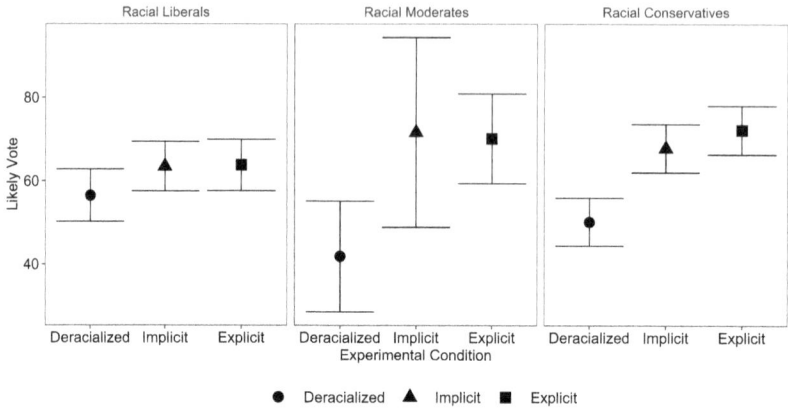

FIGURE 4.1. Predicted Probability of Voting for the Candidate as a Function of Racial Resentment
Source: 2016 GfK Deracialization Study
Note: The points represent the predicted probability of voting for the black Democratic candidate by the type of message as a function of racial resentment. 95 percent confidence intervals. Estimates from the full model appear in table A.4.1 in the appendix.

the implicit and explicit messages, relative to the deracialized, universal message ($p < .05$). If anything, according to the racial priming hypothesis, the *implicit* message should have activated racial resentment, and not the explicit message. However, as indicated by the results in figure 4.1, racially conservative respondents reacted as positively to the explicit message as they did to the implicit message ($p < .05$).

Figure 4.2 displays a similar pattern of results, but instead of examining the likelihood of voting for the candidate as a function of respondents' racial resentment, this figure displays the likelihood of voting for the candidate as a function of their endorsement of the negative stereotype of African Americans. Respondents in the left panel are those respondents who rated blacks as more hardworking than whites (pro-black), respondents in the center panel are those respondents who rated blacks as equally hardworking or lazy (neutral), and respondents in the right panel are those who rated whites as more hardworking than blacks (anti-black).[28] Again, we see that across the levels of negative attitudes about African Americans, white respondents were still more likely to prefer the racialized message, regardless of whether it was implicit or explicit, relative to a deracialized message of universalism, but this was only statistically significant for respondents who had either neutral or anti-black attitudes.

Overall, the results from this experiment suggest that a deracialized message that avoids racialized themes such as welfare does not result in automatically better outcomes for a black Democratic candidate, relative to a message that engages in racial distancing. Although the messages in which the candidate engaged in racial distancing played to negative stereotypes about African Americans, they were still more popular than a message that focused on universal benefits and working together—both among white Democratic voters and among white Republican voters. The racialized messages were also associated with higher levels of electoral support across various levels of negative attitudes about blacks. In other words, regardless of whether respondents had negative or neutral attitudes about blacks, they were still more likely to vote for a black Democratic candidate when he told black people to "get off the couch," relative to a message that emphasized "working together." Furthermore, a small minority of racial liberals did not make a distinction between the three types of messages. The conventional wisdom is that a black candidate should avoid the topic of race altogether, but the results from this experiment suggest that a black candidate can talk about race and receive support from white voters, even relative to a message of universalism.

There is reason to be cautious, however, about the interpretation of these results. As noted earlier in the chapter, the tone of the message in

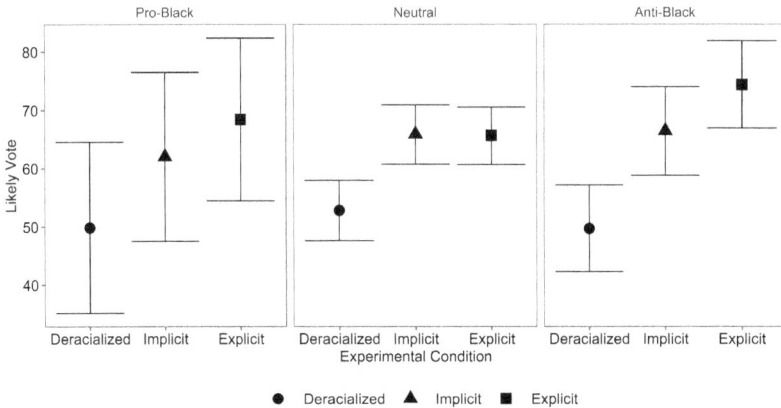

FIGURE 4.2. Predicted Probability of Voting for the Candidate as a Function of Negative Stereotype Endorsement

Source: 2016 GfK Deracialization Study

Note: The points represent the predicted probability of voting for the black Democratic candidate by the type of message as a function of negative stereotype endorsement. 95 percent confidence intervals. Estimates from the full model appear in table A.4.2 in the appendix.

the implicit and explicit versions was arguably more forceful than in the deracialized message. Therefore, it is difficult to determine whether voters were more enthusiastic about the implicit and explicit messages because of the tone of the messages or because those messages were directed specifically at African Americans. The experiment discussed in the next chapter will help us to disentangle those effects.

Concluding Remarks

In this chapter, I provided evidence of politicians engaging in behavior that is indicative of racial distancing. I discussed several black politicians, Democrats and Republicans, who campaigned for office at various levels of government. These candidates engaged in racial distancing by rhetorically, visually, and substantively distancing themselves from other African Americans. Contrary to a deracialization strategy, whereby a candidate would avoid a discussion of racial issues, these candidates engaged race by discussing racialized themes, such as racism, slavery, and immigration. In addition, rather than eschewing racial nouns, some of them routinely referenced their racial identity, drawing attention to the fact that they were black, while simultaneously distinguishing themselves from other black politicians, most notably, President Barack Obama and the Congressional Black Caucus.

Race to the Bottom argues that black candidates are incentivized to go above and beyond a strategy of deracialization by engaging in racial distancing, whereby they employ racial themes but do so in a manner that signals that they are not beholden to their racial and ethnic minority constituents, especially African Americans. The results of a survey experiment conducted on a nationally representative sample of approximately 500 white Americans indicate that the deracialized message was consistently the least popular message among white voters, relative to a message that signaled either implicitly or explicitly that the black Democratic candidate would not be beholden to African American voters. Thus, the evidence presented in this chapter indicates that deracialization may not always be the optimal strategy for black Democratic candidates who are trying to attract the electoral support of white Americans, especially white Republican voters. In short, black candidates do not necessarily have to avoid a discussion of race, as the deracialization strategy suggests. Talking about race in and of itself is not necessarily problematic for white voters because a message that openly played to negative stereotypes of African Americans from a black Democratic candidate was even more popular than a message of universalism from a similarly situated black Democratic politician. White Republican voters were actually more supportive of the black Democratic politician when he openly referred to "Black people," even relative to a message that referenced "people in the inner city." Perhaps even more surprising is that explicit and implicit racialized messages were more popular than a universal message, even when people had neutral attitudes toward blacks, and regardless of whether these attitudes were measured with the racial resentment scale or by a metric of negative stereotype endorsement. Previous research has suggested that explicit racial cues should be associated with a decline in electoral support, but previous theories have not accounted for the unique ways in which a candidate's race and partisanship can either facilitate or hinder their use of racial cues.

Since my theory of racial distancing makes a novel allowance for the racial and partisan characteristics of the messenger, it enables me to offer a broader theoretical account of racial appeals in contemporary American politics than has previously been studied. In the next chapter, I examine whether voters' reactions to more overt forms of racial distancing—namely, messages that implicitly or explicitly play to negative stereotypes about blacks—are influenced by the interaction of the race of the candidate and to a lesser degree the candidate's partisanship. One of the studies discussed in chapter 5 builds on the survey experiment discussed in this chapter. I manipulate both the race *and* partisanship of the candidates, thus allowing for a more comprehensive test of the theory of racial distancing. Furthermore, the tone and targets of the appeal are consistent across treatments, which enables us to test whether there is something politically beneficial about suggesting that *blacks in particular* are in need of personal responsibility.

CHAPTER FIVE

Race, Partisanship, and Rhetoric

We have got this tailspin of culture, in our inner cities in particular, of men not working and just generations of men not even thinking about working or learning the value and the culture of work, and so there is a real culture problem here that has to be dealt with. — Representative Paul Ryan (R-WI)

During a 2014 interview on a conservative radio show, Representative Paul Ryan (R-WI), who would become Speaker of the House in 2015, suggested that there is something about men in the inner city in particular not valuing work. According to Ryan, "there is a real culture problem" that needs to be addressed. Ryan was reflecting on a report entitled "The War on Poverty: 50 Years Later" and issued by the House Budget Committee, which Ryan chaired at the time. Ryan never mentioned race or African Americans, but his reference to the inner city was perceived by many as "dog-whistle" politics. Previous research indicates that "inner city" is a racial codeword for African Americans (Hurwitz and Peffley 2005), which is why Ryan's comments were met with backlash in liberal circles. Congresswoman Barbara Lee (D-CA) called Ryan's comments "a thinly-veiled racial attack," while then former Speaker of the House Nancy Pelosi (D-CA) said the comments were "shameful and wrong."[1]

Ryan denied that the comments had any racial undertones, saying the next day, "It never even occurred to me. This has nothing to do with race whatsoever."[2] Similar protestations typically abound after white Republican politicians have made comments that are racially inflammatory. However, what is perhaps more interesting about the controversy surrounding Ryan's comments is the observation by writer for the *The Atlantic* Ta-Nehesi Coates that Ryan's rhetoric did not sound very different from exhortations to black personal responsibility that have come from prominent African Americans. According to Coates,

> A number of liberals reacted harshly to Ryan. I'm not sure why. What Ryan said here is not very far from what Bill Cosby, Michael Nutter, Bill Clinton, and Barack Obama said before. The idea that poor people living in the inner city, and particularly black men, are "not holding up their end of the deal" as Bill Cosby put it, is not terribly original or even, these days, right-wing. From the president [Obama] on down there is an accepted belief in America—black and white—that African American people, and African American men, in particular, are lacking in the virtues of family, hard work, and citizenship.[3]

In a rejoinder to this critique, *New York* magazine writer Jonathan Chait defended Obama against Coates's criticism on the grounds that Obama had a very different perspective from Paul Ryan, who believes that liberal policies are responsible for the "cycle of poverty." By contrast, according to Chait, "Obama's habit of speaking about this issue primarily to black audiences" is Obama "seizing upon his role as the most famous and admired African American in the world to urge positive habits and behavior."[4] Indeed, Obama acknowledges that not only does he address predominantly black audiences differently than he does predominantly white audiences, but as an African American man, he views himself as being uniquely positioned to urge positive habits and behavior among African Americans:

> On this whole family-character values-structure issue. It's true that if I'm giving a commencement at Morehouse that I will have a conversation with young black men about taking responsibility as fathers that I probably will not have with the women of Barnard. And I make no apologies for that. And the reason is, is because I am a black man who grew up without a father and I know the cost that I paid for that. And I also know that I have the capacity to break that cycle, and as a consequence, I think my daughters are better off.[5]

Defenders of Obama and defenders of Ryan, although from disparate political camps, are united by the argument that such exhortations at their worst do no harm. However, the results presented in this chapter suggest that the defenders of such exhortations may be shortsighted—failing to acknowledge the harm that is done to our democratic politics when politicians find it politically expedient to chastise African Americans about personal responsibility. In some instances, such rhetoric has downstream consequences, diminishing support for public policies that might address disparities between blacks and whites. When politicians decide that not only do black people need to hear messages about "getting off the couch" more than anything else, but that black people also need to hear these messages more than any other racial or ethnic group, those politicians are contributing to a long history in which blackness is conflated with poverty and dysfunction, while whiteness is conflated with virtue and wealth.

In this chapter, I discuss the result of two survey experiments in which I explore the impact of negative racial appeals about blacks outside of the context of a white Republican messenger. In the first and most comprehensive experiment, I test the racial distancing model, which posits that a candidate's race and partisanship can open or close different options for racial distancing. I manipulate the race of the candidate (black or white), the partisanship of the candidate (Democrat or Republican), and the type of message (implicit or explicit), relative to a control condition devoid of any racial content. I demonstrate that white Republican candidates are the most likely to be penalized for explicitly invoking negative stereotypes about blacks, while a black Democrat is the most likely to be advantaged by invoking negative stereotypes about African Americans. This experiment builds on the experiment from the previous chapter in a number of ways. First, I am testing the racial distancing hypothesis across a wider range of politicians—African Americans and whites, Democrats and Republicans, instead of only black Democratic candidates. Second, the tone and targets are more consistent across the treatments in this experiment, which ensures that any differential results can be attributed to the treatment.

Contrary to the racial priming hypothesis, I also show that an explicit appeal does not automatically result in a loss of support for a politician. In fact, a message that targets African Americans as needing to work harder was associated with an increase in electoral support among a significant fraction of whites, relative to a message that said, "People need to work harder." Respondents with negative attitudes toward blacks were receptive to explicit racial appeals when the source of the message was counterintuitive (e.g., a white Democrat or an African American politician from either major party), whereas racial liberals did not punish explicit appeals when the messenger was black. Therefore, the behavior of racial liberals in the sample is actually quite similar to that of Jonathan Chait, who was quoted earlier in this chapter making a distinction between the rhetoric of President Obama and the rhetoric of Paul Ryan. In other words, racial liberals seem to be more willing to give black politicians a pass for racially inflammatory rhetoric, relative to white politicians who make very similar inflammatory statements. Since previous tests of the racial priming hypothesis have overwhelmingly tested voters' reaction to negative explicit racial appeals in the context of white, often Republican messengers, we have ignored the ways in which black politicians can also use these types of appeals to their political advantage. The second experiment is similar in that I also test the racial priming hypothesis, but with a smaller range of candidates (white Democrats and black Democrats). Again, I find that contrary to the racial priming hypothesis, an explicit racial appeal does not automatically mean a loss in electoral support.

In both studies, respondents read an Internet news article about a fictitious candidate running for office, who recently gave a speech about education. The race of the candidate was conveyed by a picture (black or white), and the partisanship of the candidate was referred to in either the headline, the body of the article, or sometimes both. Of course, the dynamic nature of campaigns cannot be fully captured within an experiment, but using this method does allow for careful control of the information that the respondents receive. The controlled environment of an experiment enabled me to provide a realistic amount of information about the candidates to respondents, while also identifying how voters perceive candidates differently on the basis of the candidates' race and partisanship. Ultimately, an experimental design is a very good option for studying how white voters react to a variety of racial appeals from white Republican, white Democratic, black Republican, and black Democratic politicians.

Voters' Reactions to Racial Appeals by Candidates across the Racial and Political Spectrum

In the first study that I will discuss, Study 1, subjects were randomly assigned to one of twelve conditions, in which I manipulated the race of the candidate (black or white), their partisanship (Republican or Democratic), and their message (devoid of racial content, implicitly racial, or explicitly racial). The conditions are outlined in table 5.1. The aim here is test whether candidates who are invariably assumed to be penalized by negative racial attitudes are able to neutralize, or even use to their advantage, those very same negative racial attitudes.

The experiment was fielded on a nationally diverse sample of approximately 1,800 adult white Americans in February 2018. The sample was reflective of the general population of adult whites in the United States, with 42 percent identifying as Republicans, 40 percent as Democrats, and 19 percent as Independents. The sample was 52 percent female, and 31 percent of the respondents resided in the South. Educational attainment for the sample was similar to that of white Americans nationally, with 34 percent of respondents holding a bachelor's degree or higher. The median income was $60,000–$69,999. The survey firm YouGov fielded the study.[6]

Respondents were randomly assigned a fictitious Internet news article that reported on a candidate who was running for governor and had recently made a speech about education. The candidate was depicted as one of four types of politicians: a black Democrat, a black Republican, a white Democrat, or a white Republican. For each of the four types of politicians, the politician was described as delivering a race-neutral control message, an implicit message, or an explicit message, making for a total of twelve conditions—four control messages, four implicit messages, and four explicit messages. Regardless of which condition respondents were assigned, the candidate was identified as Michael Harris. The name Michael Harris was chosen because, according to data from the Social Security Administration, both the first name Michael and the surname Harris are popular among both black and white Americans, thus contributing to the plausibility of there being a black Republican, white Republican, white Democratic, or black Democratic politician with that name.

The headline in the race-neutral control condition read, "Democratic/Republican Candidate Speaks at Education Forum, Urging People to 'Work Harder!'" while the headline in the implicitly racial condition read, "Democratic/Republican Candidate Speaks at Education Forum, Urging People in the Inner-City to 'Work Harder!'" The inclusion of the term "inner city" signals "black" without actually using racial nouns such as "black" or "African American," thereby meeting the definition of an implicit appeal (Mendelberg 2001; Hurwitz and Peffley 2005). The headline in the explicitly racial version was the same as the implicit version, except instead of referencing "people in the inner-city," it referred to "black people" openly. The aim here was to keep the language as consistent as possible across all conditions, such that any difference in effects could be attributed to the treatment. I was especially interested in testing whether a message that referenced the need for black people to work harder, either implicitly or explicitly, would garner more support than a message that did not allude to African Americans. In other words, is it politically advantageous for politicians to focus on the perceived lack of work ethic among African Americans, rather than simply espousing support for the American value of hard work more generally?

Ideally, I would have liked to test voters' reaction to a message encouraging black people to take personal responsibility, relative to a message encouraging *white people* to do the same. A message that openly refers to white people needing to take personal responsibility, however, seems far-fetched at best and would have diminished the external validity of the study.[7] A message of "Work harder" also has somewhat of a conservative bent, to which Republican voters might respond more favorably. In an effort to keep the articles as similar as possible across the conditions, I opted to include the message of "Work harder" in all the conditions. The articles in the respective control conditions also needed to be crafted in such a way that the answers of respondents in the control versions could be compared to the answers of the respondents in the implicit and explicit conditions. Therefore, similar to the implicit and explicit versions of the article, the control version of the article was about the fictitious politician Michael Harris.

Across the conditions, three of the four paragraphs were identical, save for whether the article referred to the politician as a Democrat or as a Republican. Aside from the headline, the manipulation of language came in the third paragraph, where race was invoked implicitly or explicitly, or not at all (control condition). For example, in the implicitly racial condition, Michael Harris said, "I'm tired of people in the inner-city blaming the government for problems that they created. People in the inner-city need to learn the value of hard work. Work harder!" whereas in the explicit version, Harris is quoted as saying, "I'm tired of Black people blaming the government for problems that they created. Black people need to learn the value of hard work. Work harder!"

The control condition was similar to the implicit and explicit conditions, except it did not include any racial modifiers. The fictitious politician was reported as saying, "I'm tired of people blaming the government for problems that they created. People need to learn the value of hard work. Work harder!" Given the way in which hard work is conflated with whiteness in the American context, however, some respondents may have perceived the language in the control conditions as racialized. Therefore, I tested the premise that respondents may have perceived the language in the control conditions as racialized by regressing the various treatments on respondents' perception that the candidate "tried to appeal to racial feelings." If respondents perceived the language in the control condition as racialized, we would expect to see a statistically significant relationship between exposure to any of the four control conditions and the perception that "the candidate tried to appeal to racial feelings." None of the control conditions, however, had a significant relationship with this variable, which indicates that the language in the control conditions was not perceived as racialized. There was, however, a statistically significant relationship between the perception that the candidate was "trying to appeal to racial feelings" and exposure to the treatments in which the candidate was depicted as using either an implicit or an explicit message, regardless of whether the candidate was depicted as black or white. In other words, people in the study perceived language about "people in the inner-city" and "black people" needing to work harder as racialized but did not perceive language that simply referred to "people" as needing to work harder as racialized.

After reading the articles, the respondents answered a series of questions, including regarding their likelihood of voting for the candidate and whether they thought that the candidate would look out for the interests of blacks versus whites if he was elected to office. Respondents were also asked some standard racial attitudes questions, including how hardworking or lazy they thought blacks were on average, relative to their white counterparts, as well as the standard racial resentment battery.[8] Finally, respondents were invited to answer open-ended questions about what they liked or disliked about the candidate.

The first test of this chapter's main hypothesis is that white Americans will be more likely to vote for a black candidate who invokes personal responsibility rhetoric toward African Americans, relative to a black candidate who invokes personal responsibility rhetoric not directed specifically at African Americans. African American politicians are stereotyped as being beholden to their African American constituents, while African Americans more broadly are stereotyped as unwilling to adhere to the American values of hard work and individualism.

TABLE 5.1 **Experimental Manipulations in Study 1**

Control

    Headline: Democratic/Republican Candidate Speaks at Education Forum, Urging People to "Work Harder!"

    1st paragraph: Democratic/Republican candidate Michael Harris announced last week that he will be running for governor. Harris is running to replace the current governor, whose governorship will end because of term limits.

    2nd paragraph: Harris has already started campaigning. Last night he made a stop at an education forum, where he gave a speech outlining his plan for the state's education policy. The initiative is called Vision 2025. Recent polls suggest education will be one of the most important issues for voters in the state.

    3rd paragraph [manipulation]: Harris' speech focused largely on the role of parenting on improving educational outcomes. The Democrat/Republican told the audience, "Parents are responsible for their children failing to achieve in school. If parents would work harder, communities would be more successful! I'm tired of people blaming the government for problems that they created. People need to learn the value of hard work. Work harder!"

    Final paragraph: The Democratic/Republican candidate is expected to be a major contender in the race. Harris is a Yale-educated lawyer who has been active on a variety of issues, including sponsoring major legislation during his time in the state legislature. He also has a reputation for being a straight-talking politician, who is not afraid to speak his mind.

Implicit

    Headline: Democratic/Republican Candidate Speaks at Education Forum, Urging People in the Inner-City to "Work Harder!"

    1st paragraph: Same as control

    2nd paragraph: Same as control.

    3rd paragraph [manipulation]: Harris' speech focused largely on the role of inner-city parenting on improving educational outcomes. The Democrat/Republican told the audience, "Parents in the inner-city are responsible for their children failing to achieve in school. If inner-city parents would work harder, inner-city communities would be more successful! I'm tired of people in the inner-city blaming the government for problems that they created. People in the inner-city need to learn the value of hard work. Work harder!"

    Final paragraph: Same as control.

Explicit

    Headline: Democratic/Republican Candidate Speaks at Education Forum, Urging Black People to "Work Harder!"

    1st paragraph: Same as control.

    2nd paragraph: Same as control.

    3rd paragraph [manipulation]: Harris' speech focused largely on the role of Black parenting in improving educational outcomes. The Democrat/Republican told the audience, "Black parents are responsible for their children failing to achieve in school. If Black parents would work harder, inner-city communities would be more successful! I'm tired of Black people blaming the government for problems that they created. Black people need to learn the value of hard work. Work harder!"

    Final paragraph: Same as control.

TABLE 5.2 **Predictors of Support for Black Democratic Candidates (Baseline=Candidate in the Control Condition)**

	All respondents (1)	Democratic respondents (2)	Republican respondents (3)
Experimental conditions			
Implicit	3.85	5.07	4.11
	(3.37)	(5.08)	(4.63)
Explicit	7.85**	−0.01	11.14**
	(3.88)	(5.67)	(5.68)
Constant	43.37***	38.16	43.08
	(5.99)	(8.77)	(16.81)
N	434	166	198
R squared	0.02	0.10	0.06

Note: Standard errors are in parentheses. All models include controls for partisanship, ideology, gender, education, and region.

* $p < .10$; ** $p < .05$; *** $p < .01$ for a two-tailed test.

Therefore, an African American politician who publicly chastises African Americans either implicitly through the term "inner-city," or explicitly by referencing "black people," should be rewarded for speaking out against the group.

The first column of table 5.2 displays the results of an ordinary least squares regression model in which I estimate the effect of being exposed to the black Democratic candidate with either an implicit or an explicit message, relative to the black Democratic candidate in the control condition. Likelihood of voting for the fictitious candidate Michael Harris was coded on a scale from 0 to 100. The higher the number, the more likely respondents were to vote for the candidate. As indicated in table 5.2, on average, respondents were no more likely to vote for the black Democratic politician with the implicit message than they were the black Democratic politician in the control condition. However, when exposed to the black Democratic politician with the explicit message, support for the politician increases by nearly one-tenth of the scale ($p < .05$).

The second and third columns of table 5.2 display results similar to Model 1, but for Democratic and Republican respondents, respectively. Democratic respondents were less likely to vote for a black Democratic candidate who suggested that people in the inner city (implicit) needed to "learn the value of hard work," relative to the black Democratic candidate depicted in the control condition, but this difference was not statistically significant. Democratic respondents were also less likely to vote for the black Democratic candidate in the explicit condition, relative to the black Democratic candidate in the control condition, but again this difference was not statistically significant. In other words, among Democratic respondents, support for the black Democratic candidate was virtually identical across the implicit, explicit, and control conditions.

Support among Democratic respondents for the black Democratic candidates across all three conditions was relatively lukewarm. A message that emphasizes hard work and personal responsibility as the solution to poor educational achievement is not likely to resonate with Democratic respondents, many of whom prefer structural solutions and government intervention.[9] Nevertheless, conventional wisdom suggests that a politician who openly peddles stereotypes of *African Americans* as "blaming the government for problems that they created" would fare *worse* among Democratic voters than a politician who speaks more generally about *people* "blaming the government for problems that they created." In other words, given the Democratic Party's reputation for racial liberalism and "political correctness," we might expect that a candidate, even if he is a black Democrat, would lose electoral support from Democratic voters for employing a personal responsibility message directed specifically at blacks, relative to a more general personal responsibility message. However, as table 5.2 indicates, no such loss of support occurred.

Republican respondents, on the other hand, were more receptive to the personal responsibility message in the explicit condition than they were to the general message in the control condition. Exposure to the black Democratic politician in the explicit condition was associated with an eleven-point increase in voting for the candidate, relative to the black Democratic candidate in the control condition ($p < .05$). On the other hand, exposure to the black Democratic politician with the implicit message was not associated with a statistically significant increase in electoral support for the candidate. Openly mentioning that black people in particular needed to work harder increased support for the candidate among Republicans, relative to the black Democratic candidate who said that people in general needed to work harder, and even relative to the black Democratic candidate who said that people in the inner city need to work harder. Thus, black Democratic politicians who engage in personal responsibility rhetoric directed specifically and explicitly at African Americans do not lose support from white Democratic voters and *gain* support among white Republican voters.[10]

The results thus far indicate that there are political gains for black Democratic politicians who explicitly call upon black people to "work harder." It is important, however, to explore whether these gains are afforded to other types of politicians, or just to black Democratic politicians specifically. Therefore, I also test the efficacy of this type of racial distancing for black Republican candidates, white Democratic candidates, and of course, white Republican candidates. As table 5.3 indicates, in the aggregate, the coefficients associated with the implicit and explicit messages from the black Republican politician are negative, but not statistically significant. In other words, voters do not exhibit a preference for a personal responsibility message that is implicitly or explicitly directed at blacks, relative to a black Republican who offers a general personal responsibility message.

When we limit the analysis to Democratic voters, we see that Democratic voters were also no more likely to vote for a black Republican politician with an implicit or explicit racial appeal, relative to the black Republican in the control condition. As was the case with their reaction to the black Democratic treatments, Democratic respondents did not punish the black Republican politician with the explicit message. Instead, they were equally lukewarm to the black Republican in the implicit, explicit, and control conditions. Among Republican respondents, however, there is more support for a black Republican politician who explicitly calls upon black people to work harder, relative to the black Republican politician in the control condition. Similar to their reaction to the messages from black Democratic politicians, Republican respondents were more likely to vote for the black Republican candidate with an explicit message, relative to the black Republican candidate in the control condition. Exposure to a black Republican candidate with an explicit message was associated with an increase in the likelihood of voting for the candidate by roughly 5 percentage points among Republican respondents, relative to the control condition. These results are perhaps to be expected, given that personal responsibility rhetoric is generally popular among Republican voters. Yet it is still worth noting that black politicians, Democrats and Republicans alike, who called upon black people specifically to work harder fared better electorally among Republican voters than those black politicians who emphasized the need for either "people in the inner-city" or "people" more generally to work harder. There was something especially appealing to the white Republican voters in the sample about a black politician who openly called upon *black*

TABLE 5.3 **Predictors of Support for Black Republican Candidates
(Baseline=Candidate in the Control Condition)**

	All respondents (1)	Democratic respondents (2)	Republican respondents (3)
Experimental conditions			
Implicit	−5.63	−5.74	−4.75
	(−3.41)	(5.59)	(4.59)
Explicit	−0.49	−0.64	5.68*
	(3.23)	(5.85)	(3.44)
Constant	17.94	13.62	79.58
	(6.00)	(9.91)	(12.58)
N	440	176	178
R squared	0.40	0.19	0.08

Note: Standard errors are in parentheses. All models include controls for partisanship, ideology, gender, education, and region.
* $p < .10$; ** $p < .05$; *** $p < .01$ for a two-tailed test.

people to "work harder." At the same time white Democratic voters did not make a distinction between the three types of messages when the politician was a black Republican, which is similar to their reaction to the messages from the black Democratic politician.

It is unclear, however, whether white politicians will experience an electoral boost among Republican voters, similar to their black counterparts, when they direct personal responsibility messages explicitly at blacks. In other words, is *any* message that tells black people to work harder popular? Or is there something especially powerful about a black politician telling black people to work harder? It is also unclear whether Democrats will be as forgiving of this behavior from white politicians as they were of black politicians. Presented in table 5.4 and table 5.5 are the results for white Democratic politicians and white Republican politicians, respectively. These results suggest that black politicians are uniquely rewarded by Republican voters for explicitly espousing personal responsibility messages to blacks, and that their white counterparts do not experience a similar electoral boost. While black politicians were rewarded by Republican voters for openly referring to the need for black people to "learn the value of hard work," white politicians generally lost support for those explicit statements. White politicians, regardless of their partisanship, were never rewarded for their use of an explicit message at levels that attained statistical significance, even among Republican respondents. Furthermore, Democratic voters were far less

TABLE 5.4 **Predictors of Support for White Democratic Candidates**
(Baseline=Candidate in the Control Condition)

	All respondents (1)	Democratic respondents (2)	Republican respondents (3)
Experimental conditions			
Implicit	4.80	–9.65	14.39***
	(4.43)	(7.39)	(5.31)
Explicit	–7.39	–22.51***	8.93
	(4.77)	(6.57)	(7.47)
Constant	38.97***	42.42**	75.40
	(11.45)	(18.56)	(17.56)
N	443	175	188
R squared	0.07	0.12	0.11

Note: Standard errors are in parentheses. All models include controls for partisanship, ideology, gender, education, and region.
* $p < .10$; ** $p < .05$; *** $p < .01$ for a two-tailed test.

forgiving of messages that were implicitly or explicitly directed at blacks when the messenger was white as opposed to African American.

When we examine white Democratic politicians specifically, the results displayed in table 5.4 indicate that among Democratic respondents, exposure to the white Democratic politician with an explicit message was associated with a decrease in voting for the candidate by roughly one-fifth of the scale, relative to exposure to the white Democratic politician in the control condition ($p < .01$). Among Democratic voters, it was "beyond the pale" for a white Democratic politician to espouse an explicit message directed at African Americans. The coefficient associated with the implicit message was also negative but falls short of traditional levels of statistical significance. This suggests that for white Democratic politicians, implicit messaging may have some political utility.

Among Republican respondents, exposure to the white Democratic politician with either an implicit or explicit message was associated with an increase in electoral support, relative to the white Democratic politician in the control condition. This suggests that Republican respondents react positively to counter-stereotypical behavior by white Democratic politicians. Exposure to the white Democrat with an implicit message was associated with an increase of 14 percentage points in willingness to vote for the white Democratic politician (p < .05). In other words, among Republican respondents, support for the white Democratic politician increased notably, simply by saying, "People in the inner city need to work harder," instead of "People need to work harder." Similarly, exposure to a message from a white Democratic politician saying, "Black people need to work harder," instead of "People need to work harder," was associated with an increase in electoral support of approximately 9 percentage points among Republican respondents, but this increase falls short of traditional levels of statistical significance. Among Republican respondents, white Democratic politicians benefited from a degree of subtlety that their black counterparts were unable to capitalize on. These results also suggest that white Democrats can also capitalize on the use of negative stereotypes about African Americans. White Democrats, however, do not have the latitude that black politicians have to invoke these stereotypes explicitly.

Finally, table 5.5 displays the likelihood of voting for the candidate when he is depicted as a white Republican. As table 5.5 indicates, white Republican politicians were punished by Democratic respondents for both the implicit and the explicit messages, relative to the control message in which the candidate referred to "people" needing to learn the value of hard work. Among Democratic respondents, exposure to the white Republican candidate who was depicted as using an implicit message was associated with a decrease of about 4 percentage points in the likelihood of voting for the candidate ($p < .05$). The explicit message was associated with a decrease of almost 19 percentage points among

TABLE 5.5 **Predictors of Support for White Republican Candidates (Baseline=Candidate in the Control Condition)**

	All respondents (1)	Democratic respondents (2)	Republican respondents (3)
Experimental conditions			
Implicit	−8.53**	−3.57**	−7.47
	(3.66)	(5.98)	(5.29)
Explicit	−15.23***	−18.54***	−9.03*
	(3.24)	(3.96)	(5.42)
Constant	17.45	26.98***	51. 99
	(5.12)	(6.24)	(18.58)
N	436	175	167
R squared	0.48	0.33	0.08

Note: Standard errors are in parentheses. All models include controls for partisanship, ideology, gender, education, and region.

$*p < .10$; $**p < .05$; $***p < .01$ for a two-tailed test.

Democratic respondents ($p < .01$). Personal responsibility messages are generally less likely to resonate with Democratic voters. Still, it is worth noting that when a white Republican politician espoused personal responsibility messages that implicated blacks, either implicitly or explicitly, they lost electoral support from Democratic respondents, relative to a message that called upon people in general to work harder. This reaction mimics the outcry that we tend to see when white Republican politicians invoke negative racial stereotypes about blacks, even when those messages are implicit or what Representative Barbara Lee (D-CA) referred to as "thinly-veiled."[11]

Among Republican respondents, the white Republican candidate with an explicit message was also less popular than the white Republican candidate depicted in the control condition. Exposure to the white Republican with the explicit message was associated with a statistically discernible decrease of 9 percentage points in electoral support, even among white Republican respondents ($p < .05$). On the other hand, the white Republican politician who referred to "people in the inner-city" needing to work harder did not lose electoral support at a statistically discernible difference. The results for the white Republican politician and the white Democratic politician support previous research in racial priming, which suggests that explicit appeals will ultimately be penalized, but the very same message delivered implicitly will not be. The differential results for the black and white politicians, however, suggest that we have likely ignored the ways in which black politicians capitalize upon the invocation of negative stereotypes about blacks.

Again, these results stand in stark contrast to the results for black politicians. Openly calling upon black people to work harder was never associated with a statistically discernible increase in electoral support for white politicians. Black politicians, however, were rewarded among Republican voters when they explicitly called upon black people to "learn the value of hard work." Voters' reactions to implicit messages also differed by the race of the politician. Black politicians never obtained a statistically significant boost for an implicit message, relative to the control condition, suggesting that subtle messages may not be sufficient for black politicians to disrupt the stereotype of them being beholden to their black constituents. Black candidates, therefore, may be incentivized to "go explicit" to garner electoral support, especially if they are not punished by white Democratic voters— and are rewarded by white Republican voters.

On the other hand, the white Democratic politician received an electoral boost from Republican voters for messages either implicitly or explicitly directed at blacks, although the explicit message fell just short of statistical significance. Specifically, the white Democratic politician experienced an increase in electoral support among Republican voters of 14 percentage points by simply referencing the need for "people in the inner-city" to learn the value of hard work, rather than "people" needing to learn the value of hard work. The fact that the white Democratic politician was not penalized by white Republican respondents suggests that this is not merely a matter of voters not punishing an in-group conversation among African Americans. Even when an out-group member, in this case, a white Democratic politician, invoked negative stereotypes about African Americans, on average white Republican respondents did not penalize the politician. In fact, the white Democratic politician was rewarded for a message that implicitly and counter-stereotypically invoked negative stereotypes about blacks. These results are supported by examples from real-world politics in which white Democrats such as President Bill Clinton have racially distanced themselves from African Americans.[12] Conversely, white Republican politicians never experienced an increase in electoral support for either an implicit or an explicit message that targeted blacks. Many voters likely perceived those appeals as consistent with their expectations for white Republican politicians as racially insensitive and thus reacted negatively to those messages. These results suggest that there is a "shared norm of racial equality" leading to a prohibition on explicit appeals that is most strongly enforced when the politician is white and Republican.

Evidence from the open-ended questions on the survey also suggests that the norm of equality is most heavily enforced when the politician is a white Republican. I used text analysis software to assess whether certain words were more likely to appear in the responses about what people disliked about the candidate, conditional on whether they saw the explicit appeal from a black Democrat, white Democrat, black Republican, or white Republican. When asked what they disliked about the politician, the idea that he was racist was a charge that was leveled at all of the politicians in the explicit conditions. In other words, at least some respondents perceived the explicit message as a norm violation, regardless of whether the politician making the appeal was black or white, Democrat or Republican. The charge of racism, however, was most likely to be leveled at the white Republican, relative to the other conditions. This difference was statistically significant when compared to the explicit conditions where the politician was depicted as a black Democrat or as a black Republican ($p < .01$). This difference in frequency, however, falls just short of statistical significance when compared to the white Democrat with the explicit message ($p < .103$), even though voters were twice as likely to mention that they thought the white Republican was racist compared to the white Democrat.

The white Republican politician was the only politician who in the aggregate experienced a statistically discernible loss of support when he explicitly called upon black people to work harder, which indicates that white Republicans are more likely to be penalized when making explicit racialized appeals. Again, I report these results to highlight the ways in which a candidate's race and partisanship can either facilitate or hinder their use of different types of racial appeals. Since previous work has devoted so much attention to the use of negative racial appeals by white Republican politicians, we have tended to overlook the ways in which other types of politicians are not held accountable for their use of racialized rhetoric, and in some cases can even capitalize on this use of racialized rhetoric. According to the racial priming hypothesis, candidates who use negative explicit appeals should receive less electoral support than candidates who use negative implicit appeals, because virtually all Americans, regardless of ideology or partisanship, are committed to the norm of racial equality. As Mendelberg (2001, 18) notes, "The norm of racial equality has become descriptive and injunctive, endorsed by nearly every American."

Testing the Racial Priming Hypothesis—Study 1

As we saw in the previous section, black politicians actually received more electoral support from Republican voters when they explicitly called upon black people to work harder. The white Democratic politician also received more support from Republican voters when his message was implicit. The previous analyses, however, did not offer a direct test of the racial priming hypothesis because I examined voters' reactions to the various appeals by the partisanship of the respondents, rather than by their levels of negative attitudes about blacks. Examining whether implicit appeals are more effective than explicit appeals across various levels of voters' negative attitudes about blacks is a more direct test of the racial priming hypothesis. Therefore, in this section, I explore the relationship between negative stereotype endorsement of blacks and voters' reactions to implicit versus explicit messages by candidate race.[13]

There have been very few tests of the racial priming hypothesis in the context of a black messenger (for an exception, see White 2007). And to my knowledge, we are yet to vary the race and party of the messenger in tests of the racial priming hypothesis. The source cue literature, however, indicates that people's response to a message can be influenced by the race and partisanship of the messenger (Kuklinski and Hurley 1994). Therefore, I hypothesize that a white candidate with an explicit message will lose electoral support from whites with positive attitudes about blacks, but whites with negative attitudes about blacks will be more likely to support a white candidate with an explicit message. When the candidate is depicted as black, whites with pro-black or neutral attitudes will not punish the candidate, while whites who express negative attitudes about blacks will become more supportive of a black candidate with an explicit message. The more anti-black respondents are, the more likely they will be to vote for a candidate with an explicit appeal, regardless of the race of the candidate. Although the theory of racial priming predicts that awareness of the racial content results in a lack of a priming effect for explicit racial appeals, I hypothesize that awareness of the racial content makes anti-black voters *more* likely than voters who do not express anti-black attitudes to support a candidate with an explicit racial appeal. Explicit appeals underscore the negative racial stereotypes to which voters with anti-black attitudes ascribe, and thus it is quite possible that an explicit appeal will garner support from voters with anti-black attitudes. However, since whites with anti-black attitudes have likely been underrepresented in previous racial priming studies, we may have overlooked the potential for explicit appeals to activate the racial predispositions of whites with high levels of anti-black attitudes.

Figure 5.1 presents the predicted probability of likely vote for the Democratic candidate, by the race of candidate, as a function of whether the respondent thinks that blacks are on average lazier than whites. Likely vote was coded from 0 to 100. The left panel displays those respondents who perceived blacks as more hardworking than whites (pro-black), the middle panel displays those respondents who perceive blacks and whites as equally hardworking (neutral), and the right panel displays those respondents who think that whites are more hardworking than blacks (anti-black).[14] As indicated in figure 5.1, contrary to the racial priming hypothesis, among much of the sample, exposure to the explicit message was actually associated with *increased* support for the black Democratic politician, relative to the control condition.

Respondents who think that blacks and whites are equally hardworking were no less likely to vote for the black Democratic candidate when his message was explicit.[15] Among respondents who think that whites are on average more hardworking than blacks, they were *more* likely to vote for the black Democratic candidate when he said that "black people need to learn the value of hard work," relative to when he said that "people need to learn the value of hard work" ($p < .05$). The racial priming hypothesis, however, predicts that exposure to a messenger with an explicit message should *not* be associated with an activation of voters' negative racial predispositions. If anything, exposure to an explicit appeal should be associated with a loss in electoral support.

The results for respondents who think that blacks are more hardworking than whites, however, are more in line with the expectations of the racial priming hypothesis. Pro-black respondents were less likely to vote for the black Democratic politician with the explicit message, relative to the black Democratic candidate in the control condition, which is what the racial priming hypothesis would predict ($p < .05$). If whites with liberal racial attitudes or pro-black attitudes are more likely to enforce the norm of racial equality than racially conservative whites, or even those whites who view blacks and whites as equally hardworking, then it suggests that the norm of equality is not as fully embraced as we may have once expected.[16] This is especially troubling, given that whites with pro-black racial attitudes are a small fraction of the population.

As figure 5.1 also indicates, when the politician is depicted as a white Democrat, the results are markedly different than when the politician is depicted as a black Democrat. Among those respondents who see blacks and whites as equally hardworking, there is drop-off in support for the white Democrat with an explicit appeal, relative to the control condition. Recall, however, that when the politician was depicted as a black Democrat, respondents who saw blacks and whites as equally hardworking, did not punish the black Democrat with an explicit message, relative to the black Democrat in the control condition. The loss in electoral support among neutral respondents, for the white Democratic politician, is what the racial priming hypothesis would predict, which again underscores how the racial priming hypothesis seems to be confirmed when the messenger is white, but not when the messenger is black with the identical message. Pro-black respondents were also less likely to

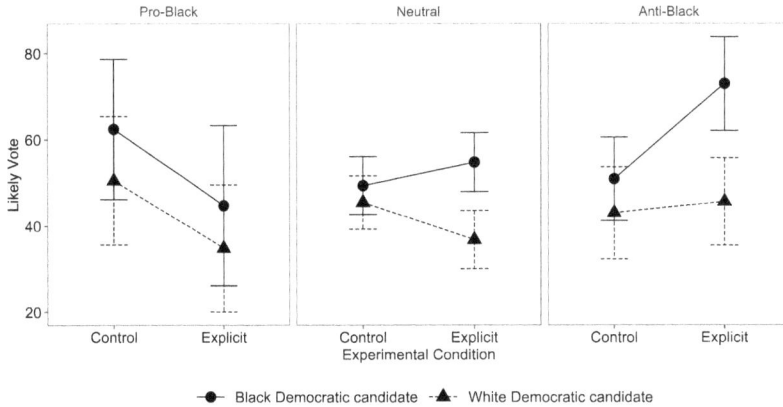

FIGURE 5.1. Predicted Probability of Voting for the Democratic Candidate as a Function of Negative Stereotype Endorsement
Source: 2018 YouGov Study
Note: The points represent the predicted probability of voting for the candidate by the race of the candidate and the type of message across the different levels of negative stereotype endorsement. 95 percent confidence intervals. Estimates from the full model appear in table A.5.1 in the appendix.

vote for the white Democratic politician with the explicit message, relative to the control condition, which is again what the racial priming hypothesis would predict.[17] It is worth noting, however, that those respondents who were anti-black or who thought blacks were less hardworking than whites were *more* likely to support the white Democratic politician with the explicit message, relative to when his message was race-neutral (control condition), which runs contrary to the expectations of the racial priming hypothesis. As figure 5.1 indicates, however, this increase in electoral support for the white Democratic politician with the explicit message was nowhere near as great as the boost in electoral support for the black Democratic politician with the identical message.

Next, figure 5.2 displays the results of a model in which I interact the type of message (control vs. explicit) with the race of the candidate (black or white) as a function of respondents' negative racial attitudes about blacks. It is very similar to figure 5.1, except that the candidates are Republicans, as opposed to figure 5.1, where the candidates are Democrats. As indicated in figure 5.2, among pro-black respondents, there is a sharp drop-off in electoral support for the candidate with an explicit message, regardless of whether the politician is depicted as a black or white Republican ($p < .01$). When the black Republican goes from a message that says, "People need to work harder" to saying,

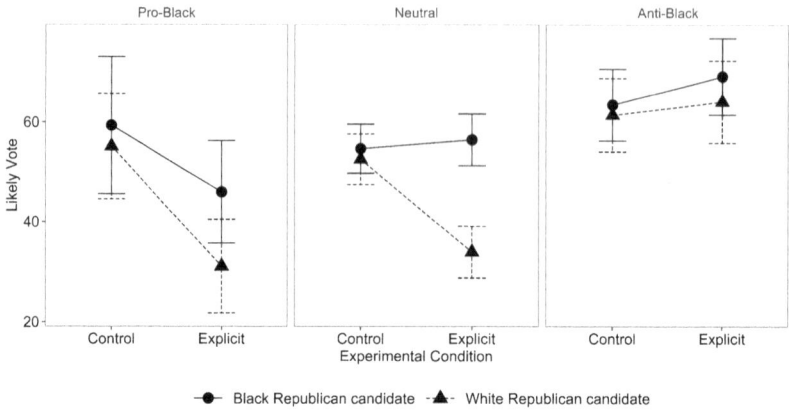

FIGURE 5.2. Predicted Probability of Voting for the Republican Candidate as a Function of Negative Stereotype Endorsement
Source: 2018 YouGov Study
Note: The points represent the predicted probability of voting for the candidate by the race of the candidate and the type of message across the different levels of negative stereotype endorsement. 95 percent confidence intervals. Estimates from the full model appear in table A.5.2 in the appendix.

"Black people need to work harder," the likelihood of voting for the candidate drops by about 13 percentage points, as opposed to a decrease of about 24 percentage points for the same change in messaging for the white Republican candidate. Also of note is that the white Republican politician with an explicit message receives, on average, 6 percentage points less in vote support, relative to the black Republican with the identical message. Support for the candidate in either condition is notably low, but we still see evidence that black politicians have more latitude than their white counterparts to invoke negative stereotypes about blacks, even when the politicians are both Republicans.

Neutral and anti-black respondents also respond differently to an explicit message from the white Republican politician, relative to the identical message from the black Republican. Among neutral respondents, the likelihood of voting for a white Republican with an explicit message is more than 20 percentage points less than the likelihood of voting for the black Republican with the same message ($p < .01$). The white Republican in the control condition also receives far more electoral support among the neutral respondents, relative to the white Republican with the explicit message ($p < .01$), which is what the racial priming hypothesis would predict. When the candidate is a black Republican with an explicit message, however, neutral voters are no less likely to vote for the candidate, relative to the black Republican in the control condition. When it comes to anti-black respondents, both the black and white Republican politicians with the explicit messages, if anything, receive *more* support, relative to the messages in the control condition. We once again see evidence that black politicians who invoke negative stereotypes about other black people can actually benefit from drawing attention to race explicitly. The same is also true for white Republican politicians.[18] Contrary to the racial priming hypothesis, respondents with negative racial attitudes toward African Americans are generally unperturbed by explicit racial rhetoric, regardless of the race of the candidate. Since racially conservative whites have likely been underrepresented in earlier racial priming studies, we may have underestimated white racial conservatives' receptivity to explicit racial appeals.

Testing the Racial Priming Hypothesis—Study 2

In this section, I use Study 2 to also test the racial priming hypothesis. Study 2 relies on a nationally representative sample of 399 whites from a 2 x 2 factorial design Internet-based survey experiment conducted in June 2011.[19] The median respondent in Study 2 was fifty-two years old, with some college, and a household income between $60,000 and $74,999. Forty-four percent of respondents identified as Democrats, and 52 percent as Republicans. All participants read a mock Internet news article involving a recent speech about education, delivered by a fictitious Democratic candidate for the U.S. House of Representatives named Greg Davis.

As indicated in table 5.6, the experimental design of Study 2 is very similar to the experimental design of Study 1, discussed in the previous section. In Study 2, respondents were randomly assigned one of four treatment conditions in which Davis's race was manipulated (black or white), and the type of appeal was manipulated (implicit, explicit). Each treatment condition included two photos—one of the candidate and one of a black audience. The photograph of the candidate accompanying the article was used to cue the candidate's race (black or white). The candidate is depicted as calling for a need to reform the public education system, but the reason varies by condition. In the explicit version, black parents are held responsible for "black students falling behind." Furthermore, "black parents" are admonished to "start parenting," and "stop blaming the government," which plays on stereotypes of African

TABLE 5.6 **Experimental Manipulations in Study 2**

Appeal	Headline	Quotes	Photos
Implicit	On Campaign Trail Candidate Says, "It's Parents' Fault Kids Are Falling Behind"	"Parents are responsible for their children failing to achieve in school." "Government can't force a kid to pick up a book or finish their homework. I'm tired of people blaming the government for problems when it's their own fault that they have fallen behind." "Some students are falling behind." "It's unacceptable! Parents need to start parenting."	First photo: Black or white candidate Second photo: Black audience
Explicit	On Campaign Trail Candidate Says, "It's Black Parents' Fault Kids Are Falling Behind"	"Black parents are responsible for their children failing to achieve in school." "Government can't force a kid to pick up a book or finish their homework. I'm tired of black people blaming the government for problems when it's their own fault that they have fallen behind." "Black students are falling behind." "It's unacceptable! Black parents need to start parenting."	First photo: Black or white candidate Second photo: Black audience

Americans as lazy and as dependent on assistance from the government. Conversely, in the implicit version, "parents" are held responsible for "students falling behind" with no mention of race. Although there is no mention of race in the implicit version, race is implied, because the article is accompanied by a photo of an exclusively black audience. Therefore, the photo of the black audience acts as a useful symbol for connecting failing students with beliefs respondents may have about black parenting and black culture, without actually ever mentioning stereotypes about black parenting. As the work of other scholars (Gamson 1992; Mendelberg 2001; Nelson and Kinder 1996) suggests, visual cues can also be important for conveying messages regarding which considerations citizens should draw upon. This occurs because visual images act as useful symbols for connecting "the issue with deeper values, principles, beliefs, and emotions that the individual may not even consciously recognize as directly relevant" (Nelson and Kinder 1996, 1073).

All respondents answered questions in the pre-test questionnaire about their partisanship, ideology, and racial attitudes.[20] To avoid any priming effects from the pre-test questionnaire, there was a lag of three to seven days between the first and second waves of the study. During the second wave of the study, subjects received the experimental treatment (mock news article) and the post-treatment questionnaire. After reading the article, participants were asked a series of questions, including how likely they were to vote for Greg Davis and whether they perceived the candidate to be liberal or conservative. Finally, all subjects were thoroughly debriefed after completion of the study so that they understood the article they read was fictitious and that "Greg Davis" was not actually running for the U.S. House of Representatives.

It is worth noting, however, that Study 2 differed from Study 1 in a few dimensions. In Study 1, I manipulated the race and the partisanship of the politician, such that there was a black Democratic politician, a black Republican politician, a white Democratic politician, and a white Republican politician, whereas in Study 2, the politician is either a black Democrat or a white Democrat. Also, the implicit and explicit messages in Study 1 of "working harder" might be more directly relevant to stereotypes of black people lacking work ethic, whereas the message in Study 2 of "Black parents need to start parenting" may be less relevant to some of the dominant stereotypes about black people and their purported lack of work. The idea that "black parents need to start parenting," however, is by no means benign, and also plays into stereotypes of black dysfunction and pathology.

Another difference is that Study 2 did not have a control condition. Therefore, in the analyses for Study 2, I can make comparisons only between the implicit and explicit messages and cannot compare these messages to a control condition. Finally, the data collection for these two studies is separated by almost seven years. Not only is there a difference in time, but the political environments in which the data were collected are starkly different. The time between the two studies is bookended by the end of the first term of the nation's first black president on one end, and on the other end, the first term of President Donald Trump, who bucked many of the traditional norms around campaigning, including the norm of not openly and categorically referencing groups in a negative manner. Yet in spite of the differences between the two studies, similar patterns emerge across them.

Figure 5.3 displays the predicted probability of voting for the candidate with an implicit message versus an explicit message, by the race of the candidate (black or white), as a function of the respondents' level of racial resentment.[21] On the left panel of the figure are those respondents

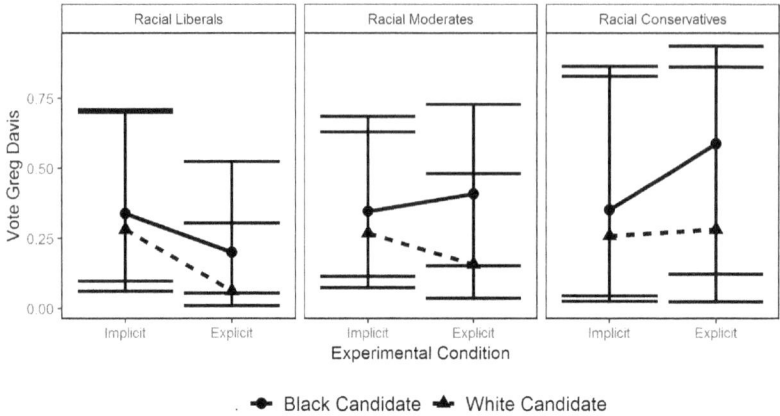

FIGURE 5.3. Likelihood of Voting for the Candidate as a Function of Racial Resentment
Source: 2011 GfK Study
Note: The points represent the predicted probability of voting for the candidate by the race of the candidate and the type of message. 95 percent confidence intervals. Estimates from the full model appear in table A.5.3 in the appendix.

whose racial resentment score is below the midpoint of the scale (racial liberals), while on the right panel are those respondents whose racial resentment scores are above the midpoint of the scale (racial conservatives). As indicated in figure 5.3, racial liberals were less likely to vote for the white Democratic politician with the explicit appeal, relative to the white Democratic politician with the implicit appeal ($p < .05$). Therefore, racial liberals enforced the norm of racial equality when the politician was depicted as a white Democrat, as predicted by the racial priming hypothesis. When the politician is depicted as a black Democrat, exposure to a black Democrat with an explicit message is associated with a small decline in support among racial liberals, but this difference is not statistically significant. Thus, these findings contradict the racial priming hypothesis, which suggests that explicit appeals are always less effective than implicit appeals in generating electoral support. Instead, these results are more consistent with a source credibility hypothesis, or the notion that white racial liberals think that black political elites have more credibility to speak on matters of race than white politicians—even if the messages are disparaging and play to negative stereotypes of the black community. Since previous studies testing the efficacy of negative explicit appeals have not varied the race of the source cue, scholars have been unaware of the contingent nature of the rejection of explicit racial appeals.

The results for white racial conservatives are also contrary to what the racial priming hypothesis would predict. White racial conservatives became more supportive of the politician with an explicit as opposed to implicit message, regardless of whether the Democratic politicians were white or black. In short, the most racially resentful respondents liked a message that explicitly told black parents to "start parenting," as opposed to a message directed at "parents in the inner city."[22] It is worth noting that the confidence intervals around the point estimates in Figure 5.3 are relatively wide, which may be a consequence of the small sample size. Nevertheless, the results are in the expected direction and are similar to the results presented in Study 1.

Across two different studies, separated by several years, a consistent finding is that black politicians are rewarded by both Republican respondents and racially resentful respondents for explicit appeals, regardless of whether the black candidate is a Democrat or a Republican. Therefore, even if one is skeptical that white Republicans and racially resentful whites will vote for a black *Democrat*, these results highlight that at the very least, black Republicans can be advantaged by this type of messaging, gaining support among the racially resentful and Republicans, while not losing support from racial liberals or Democrats. Explicit racial appeals are not universally rejected, which suggests that the norm of equality is not nearly as injunctive as previously thought. As revealed in figure 5.3, white racial liberals are less likely to punish white candidates with explicit racial messages than they are to punish black politicians with an identical message. Whites who are high on racial resentment, on the other hand, actually become more supportive of a black candidate when their message is explicit.[23]

Why Do Explicit Appeals Work Better for Black Politicians Than for Their White Counterparts?

Thus far we have seen that black politicians with explicit racial messages are able to gain more electoral support than similarly situated white politicians. Black politicians with explicit messages also fare better among racially conservative whites than black politicians with implicit messages. One reason why black politicians who espouse explicit racial messages fare better than the conventional thinking on explicit appeals suggests may be because an explicit message from a black politician forcefully disrupts the stereotype of a black politician as liberal.

Previous research indicates that black politicians are perceived as more liberal than similarly situated white politicians (Jacobsmeier 2015; Sigelman et al. 1995). The perception of black candidates as liberal likely works to their detriment, because as McIlwain and Caliendo (2011) argue, "liberal" is a racial codeword applied disproportionately to black politicians, often by their white opponents, serving as a proxy for "radical" or "extremist." Therefore, a negative explicit appeal delivered by a black candidate may translate into more electoral support for black candidates from white voters, because a negative explicit appeal sends the message to white voters that a black politician is more conservative than their perception of the stereotypical black politician.

Relying on data from Study 2, I estimated a logistic regression model in which I predicted respondents' perception of the candidate's ideology as a function of the race of the candidate (black or white) and the message (implicit or explicit).[24] As indicated in figure 5.4, white respondents exposed to the black candidate with the explicit appeal were more likely to think that the candidate was conservative, relative to white respondents exposed to the black candidate with the implicit appeal ($p < .05$). The likelihood of perceiving the candidate as conservative was 24 percent when respondents were exposed to the black candidate with the implicit appeal, as opposed to 36 percent when respondents were exposed to the black candidate with the explicit appeal. In other words, a black candidate with an explicit appeal depresses the perception that the candidate is liberal. Interestingly, the type of appeal did not alter white respondents' perception of the white candidates' ideology. White respon-

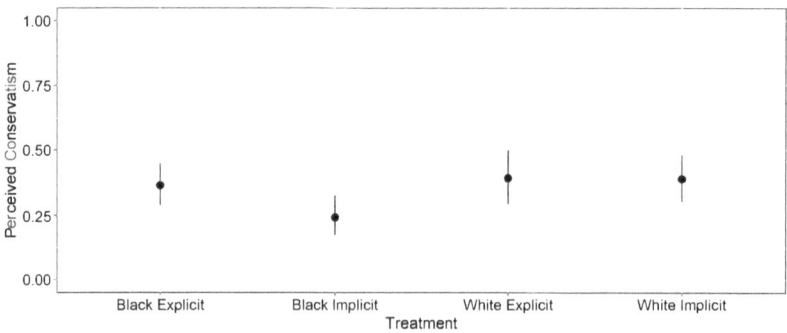

FIGURE 5.4. Predicted Probability of Perceiving the Candidate as Conservative
Source: 2011 GfK Study
Note: The points represent the predicted probability of thinking the candidate is conservative by the race of the candidate and the type of message. Estimates from the full model appear in table A.5.4 in the appendix.

dents' perceptions of the white candidates' ideology is equivalent, as the likelihood of perceiving them as conservative was 39 percent, regardless of whether the message was explicit or implicit. In short, a black Democrat with an implicit appeal was perceived as far more liberal than his white counterpart. Espousing an explicit racial message, however, dampened white voters' perception of the black Democrat as liberal. Although not pictured here, respondents who were exposed to the black candidate with the explicit message as opposed to the implicit message were also more likely to think that the candidate was hardworking.[25]

Downstream Consequences of Explicit Messaging: Support for Policy

Proponents of personal responsibility messages directed at black communities argue that exhortations to take personal responsibility at their worst do no harm. In other words, perhaps there is nothing problematic with directing personal responsibility messages at a community that is more likely to be at the worst end of many key indicators of well-being, including unemployment, homeownership, and graduation rates. Framing racial disparities, however, as a problem that is simply solved by black people working harder has downstream consequences, such as diminished support for government intervention to address racial disparities. Black politicians are perceived to be especially credible on matters of race, particularly when they speak against their perceived group interest (Nelson, Sanbonmatsu, and McClerking 2007). Therefore, an explicit appeal that calls upon black people to work harder, espoused by a black candidate, is likely to be more influential than a black politician with an implicit appeal. I expect that white Americans will be more likely to support decreased federal spending to address racial disparities when they are exposed to a black candidate with an explicit appeal. A negative explicit appeal that frames racial disparities as the inevitable result of pathological behavior by blacks is in effect arguing that government spending to reduce racial disparities is a waste of money. Therefore, respondents who are exposed to the black candidate with the explicit appeal should be likely to support reducing spending to address racial disparities. Specifically, I anticipate that respondents who were exposed to the black candidate with the explicit appeal will be more supportive of decreasing federal spending to reduce racial disparities in education.

Relying on data from Study 2, I estimated a logistic regression model to predict support for federal spending to reduce the achievement gap,

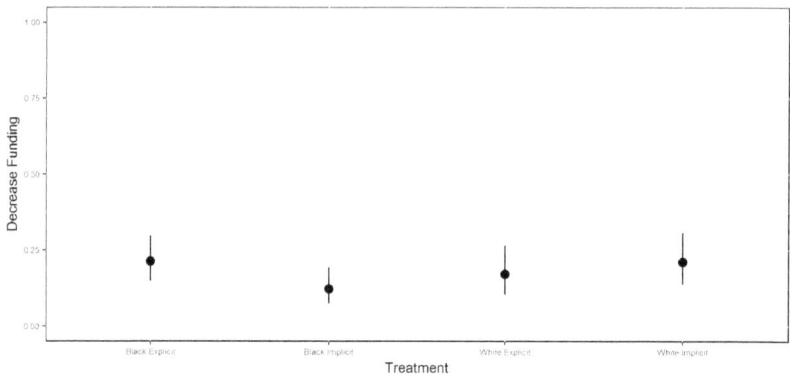

FIGURE 5.5. Respondents' Support for Decreasing Funding to Reduce the Racial Achievement Gap
Source: 2011 GfK Study
Note: The points represent the predicted probability of respondent wanting to decrease funding to reduce the racial achievement gap by the race of the candidate and the type of message. Estimates from the full model appear in table A.5.4 in the appendix.

or black-white disparities in education.[26] As indicated in figure 5.5, the explicit appeal from the black candidate was far more likely to depress support for spending to reduce racial disparities in education than the implicit appeal from the black candidate ($p < .05$). Exposure to the black candidate with the explicit appeal was associated with a 27 percent chance that respondents would support a decrease in funding, as opposed to a 17 percent chance among those respondents exposed to the black candidate with the implicit appeal.[27] This difference between respondents' reaction to the implicit versus explicit appeal is not observed when the candidate is depicted as a white Democrat.

Concluding Remarks

Despite the premise that negative explicit appeals about blacks are rejected across the ideological spectrum, the results of this study indicate that is not actually the case. I have demonstrated that voters' reactions to explicit racial appeals may be more complex and more consequential than previously thought. However, since previous research has tested the implicit/explicit model almost exclusively in the context of white Republican source cues, scholars have overlooked the nuance and caveats associated with the theory of racial priming.

I tested the implicit/explicit model separately for black and white candidates and found that contrary to the theory of racial priming, explicit appeals were not universally rejected by white Americans. Instead, only those whites with positive attitudes toward blacks (a minority of the sample) punished black candidates with an explicit appeal, regardless of whether the candidate was a Democrat or a Republican. Whites with anti-black attitudes remained relatively unperturbed in the face of explicit racial appeals, when the candidate was black, and even in some instances when he was white.

The fact that the racial liberals in the sample largely drove white Americans' punishment of the explicit appeal from white candidates also raises questions about the nature of the samples that have been used to test the racial priming hypothesis. Many of the seminal racial priming studies were conducted at a time when access to high-quality representative samples was prohibitively expensive, which resulted in many of these studies relying on convenience samples of college students and nonstudent samples from college towns. However, the level of negative attitudes toward blacks may be higher in the general population than in convenience samples. Thus, the reliance on convenience samples may have resulted in an inflated perception of the inefficacy of negative explicit appeals.

Although sampling differences have likely contributed to an inflated perception of the inefficacy of explicit appeals, admittedly, there may be other reasons why my study indicates a utility of explicit appeals that has not been demonstrated in previous research. For one, the racial landscape has changed since many of the seminal racial priming studies were conducted, most notably through the election of our nation's first black president. It is plausible that after Obama's election, the impact of race became so chronically high that subtlety was no longer a necessary condition for racial attitudes to be primed (Tesler and Sears 2010). Furthermore, for many Americans, Obama's election may have indicated that racism was no longer a problem in the United States (Kaiser et al. 2009), and thus there was no need for "political correctness," or the need to abide by the norm of equality. This made them more willing to openly support a candidate who uses a negative explicit appeal than they would have been prior to Obama's election. Unfortunately, it is not possible to definitively determine the degree to which these potential explanations may have altered our conclusions about racial priming and the effectiveness of negative explicit racial appeals. Still, it is worth noting that one study was fielded pre-Trump and one study was fielded post-Trump, yet the receptivity to explicit racial appeals was remarkably similar across the two studies. In other words, voter willingness to support politicians who use explicit appeals is not something that only came about during the age of Trump.

The present study should give pause to scholars who think that explicit appeals are universally rejected, because the results indicate that appeals that openly denigrate African Americans are *accepted* by wide swaths of the population. Furthermore, those respondents who had the most negative attitudes were not just willing to accept these messages when the messenger was black but were also receptive to these appeals when the messenger was white. In other words, this is not simply a matter of the message being acceptable because it was a member of the in-group delivering the message. Aside from the implications for the theory of racial priming, this study has implications for campaigning and candidate behavior. The fact that the black candidate with the explicit appeal was not punished as severely as his white counterpart by white racial liberals, and was not punished at all by white racial moderates and conservatives, suggests that parties who are looking to appeal to racially conservative whites (who are typically the majority of whites in nationally representative samples) may field candidates of color who espouse racially conservative messages without fear of generating a backlash. Examples of this phenomenon abound in the American context, including Herman Cain, Ben Carson, Mia Love, and even President Obama.

Two other implications from this chapter merit specific attention. First, white respondents exposed to the black candidate with an explicit appeal thought that the candidate was far more conservative than the black candidate with the implicit appeal. Being perceived as more conservative by white voters is likely to be especially beneficial for black politicians, who are interested in attracting white electoral support. Second, negative explicit racial appeals about blacks may have the consequence of depressing support for spending to address racial disparities. White respondents who were exposed to the black candidate who made an explicit appeal were less likely to support increased spending to reduce racial disparities in education than white respondents who were exposed to the black candidates who made an implicit appeal. Thus, explicit racial rhetoric not only has electoral consequences, but also affects the way in which we define public policy problems and ultimately the solutions citizens support to address those problems. However, since previous research has focused on white Republican source cues, we have known very little about the policy consequences of explicit rhetoric from black politicians.

Also of note is that explanations of racial priming that fail to account for the race of the source cue may provide a more sanguine view of the state of race relations and African American representation than is presently warranted. The politicians whom we might assume to best represent black interests (black politicians) may be incentivized to disparage other blacks when trying to appeal to racially moderate to racially conservative whites, while the citizens who are presumed to be allies of African Americans (white Democrats) are unperturbed by negative racial appeals when the messenger is black. Furthermore, in some instances, even white Democratic politicians were able to capitalize on negative stereotypes about blacks, when those stereotypes were invoked implicitly. Thus, political progress for African Americans may be more tenuous than previously thought. Future racial priming research must take into account the role of source cue characteristics in citizens' information processing. Our understanding of racial priming would also greatly benefit from more scholarly attention to inter- and intragroup differences in receptivity to different racial appeals. Without a more nuanced understanding of who is allowed to use different types of racial appeals, and how voters respond to these appeals, we are to likely underestimate the role of race in elite communication, and thus overestimate the degree to which racial progress has been made.

In chapter 6, I use a survey experiment to test whether the racial and partisan characteristics of a politician facilitate or hinder their use of subtle racial imagery to signal that they will not disrupt the racial status quo. Specifically, I test whether a subtle association with white imagery helps politicians to effectively signal that they will not disrupt the racial status quo. Or do black politicians in particular have to resort to more explicit forms of racial distancing to overcome the perception that they will favor blacks over whites? Also, does an association with black imagery, even if it is innocuous and counter-stereotypical in nature, hinder some politicians' ability to overcome the perception that they will favor blacks over whites?

CHAPTER SIX

Racial Distancing and Racial Imagery

During the summer of 2016, Speaker of the House, Paul Ryan, posted a selfie with House Republican interns to social media, accompanied by the caption "I think this sets the record for the most number of Capitol Hill interns in a single selfie."[1] For Ryan, the most notable feature of the photograph was that he managed to fit so many people into a single frame. However, for many people on social media, the photograph was remarkable for another reason—the young interns in the Speaker's photograph were overwhelmingly white. After Speaker Ryan posted the photograph, the picture went viral on the Internet and was widely ridiculed for the lack of racial diversity in the photo, accompanied by hashtags such as #InternsSoWhite or #GOPSoWhite. The most direct rebuke of the Ryan photo came from House Democrats, who posted their own intern selfies to highlight the party's relative diversity. The selfies from House Democrats included captions, such as "The picture of the Democratic interns looks a lot different than the #speakerselfie," accompanied by the hashtag #Diversity.[2]

The "selfie incident" trended for just a few days and was mostly forgotten. However, this incident speaks to the larger issue of the racial composition of the two major parties, as well as the demographic imagery that is associated with each party. The Democratic and Republican parties are increasingly aligned along racial lines, with racial and ethnic minorities constituting only 11 percent of registered Republican voters, compared to the Democratic Party, where racial and ethnic minorities make up about 40 percent of registered voters.[3] The reputations of the two parties on matters of race are also starkly different, with the Republican Party having a reputation for looking out for the interests of whites, while the Democratic Party has a reputation for being substantively and visually associated with racial and ethnic minorities.

It is unclear, however, whether the Democratic Party's relative diversity is perceived as a strength by many white American voters. The Democratic Party's association with African Americans and African American interests has been cited as an explanation for the partisan realignment in the latter half of the twentieth century (Carmines and Stimson 1989). The close affiliation between African Americans and the Democratic Party has also been cited as an explanation for the defection of so-called Reagan Democrats to the Republican Party. More recently, in some circles, Hillary Clinton's stunning loss in 2016 was attributed to her attention to "identity politics," presumably at the expense of the concerns of working-class white voters (Lilla 2016). Therefore, it is unclear whether the Democratic Party leadership *consistently* perceives their party's racial diversity as a strength. Despite House Democrats' celebration of diversity within their ranks in response to Speaker Ryan's selfie, it is well documented that the Democratic Party has at times tried to downplay their support from or association with voters of color (Hutchings, Walton, and Benjamin 2010; Walton 2000; Frymer 1999; Kinder and Sanders 1996), even though the party is dependent on the votes of racial and ethnic minorities—especially African Americans.

In 2008, for example, at a rally in Detroit for then presidential candidate Barack Obama, two Muslim women were reportedly barred from sitting behind the podium. According to the women, campaign volunteers did not want one of the women to appear on television or in photographs with the candidate because she was wearing a hijab: "Because of the political climate, and what's going on in the world, and what's going on with Muslim Americans, it's not good for [her friend] to be seen on TV or associated with Obama" (Smith 2008).

More recently, during the 2017 Virginia gubernatorial race, photographs of the Democratic candidate for lieutenant governor, Justin Fairfax, who is African American, were omitted from some of the campaign fliers of his running mate, Ralph Northam, who is white. This omission was viewed by some people as an attempt to distance the Democratic Party from their association with African Americans. The fliers were a small fraction of the total number of campaign fliers issued by the campaign and were targeting members of the Laborers' International Union of North America. The Northam campaign maintained that Fairfax's photograph was removed because Fairfax's opposition to a proposed pipeline was unpopular with members of the union. Yet there is evidence to suggest that at least some people thought that the omission of the Fairfax photo was because of the candidate's race. Quentin James, founder of Collective PAC, a political action committee that supports black candidates, said of the incident, "It reeks of subtle racism" (Nirappil 2017). It is worth noting, however, that Fairfax did not call the incident racist, instead referring to it as "a mistake" (Nirrapil 2017).

While the Democratic Party has seemingly made efforts at different junctures to distance the party from an association with African Americans, the Republican Party, on the other hand, has made efforts to visually, although perhaps not substantively, associate their party with African Americans. African Americans have been overrepresented at the Republican National Convention and other high-profile Republican events, relative to their representation in the actual Republican delegation, presumably as a means of making the party appear more diverse and welcoming to people of color (Hutchings et al. 2004; Philpot 2007). An association with African Americans helps dispel the perception, at least among some voters, that the Republican Party is hostile to people of color. On the other hand, for the Democratic Party, an association with African Americans tends to reinforce the perception that the party favors the interests of blacks at the expense of whites. Thus, both major parties appear to be strategic about their visual association with African Americans, albeit with different goals in mind.

I hypothesize that the demographic composition of the constituent groups pictured in a campaign mailer, even if rather innocuous, should influence voters' perception of the candidate, specifically with respect to racial issues. American public opinion is group-centric (Nelson and Kinder 1996), such that individuals often make sense of the world by associating themselves with groups and treating the interests of that group as their own (Achen and Bartels 2016; Converse 1964; Tajfel 1981). Since most of the citizenry does not exhibit coherent ideological constraint, they rely on "visible social groupings" (Converse 1964)—Democrats or Republicans, as well as blacks versus whites—to make their political judgments. Therefore, group-centrism functions as an efficient heuristic (Nisbett and Ross 1980; Popkin 1991).

Furthermore, some previous research has demonstrated that the mere presence of a racial or ethnic minority on the ballot activates racial resentment (McConnaughy et al. 2010; Petrow 2010). Studies have found that even positive coverage of an African American, such as President Obama, can lead to a racialized response from white voters. For example, Tesler and Sears (2010) found that as Obama's candidacy grew in salience, the influence of anti-black attitudes on whites' opinions grew. Also, Andersen and Junn (2010) found that during Obama's 2004 U.S. Senate race more highly racialized framings of Obama that highlighted his racial identity and his connection with African Americans were associated with more unfavorable evaluations from white voters, relative to more deracialized framings. Other work has also shown that opposition to Obama among white Americans was significantly driven by anti-black attitudes (Kinder and Dale-Riddle 2012).

Alternatively, some research suggests that counter-stereotypical messages, cues, and information about blacks should either dampen negative racial predispositions (Valentino, Hutchings, and White 2002) or not prime racial resentment at all (Mendelberg 2001; Nelson and Kinder 1996). Central to these accounts is the negative stereotypical depiction of blacks as a condition for the activation of group sentiment (Nelson and Kinder 1996; Valentino, Hutchings, and White 2002). In fact, research has found that an implicit racial message works "because it uses *negative* images of the target group" (Mendelberg 2008, 110; emphasis added). Outside of the experimental context, positive coverage of blacks has also been associated with dampening racial priming. For example, positive coverage of figures such as President Obama has been found to weaken racial animus (Goldman and Mutz 2014). Similarly, racial attitudes were not found to be significant predictors of public opinion about Colin Powell (Kinder and McConnaughy 2006). Positive performance information is also likely to weaken racial animosity as a force in whites' opinion of black mayors (Hajnal 2007). In short, some studies suggest that counter-stereotypical images of blacks neutralize the effect of racial resentment, while other studies suggest that the mere presence of African Americans can activate racial resentment.

Therefore, I am interested in the following questions: Are white Democratic and black candidates penalized for the use of African American images in their advertisements, even absent the use of racially coded language? Or are some candidates rewarded for their use of white images? Can an association with counter-stereotypical black imagery, or white imagery for that matter, help black politicians overcome the perception that they will favor blacks over whites? Similarly, can an association with black imagery help Republican politicians overcome their reputation for looking out for the interests of whites? And when a candidate is surrounded by images of whites, does that serve as an implicit cue? Finally, do voters make substantive inferences about a candidate's issue positions based on the racial composition of their campaign materials?

In this chapter, I answer these questions by exploring voters' reactions to campaign mailers that have varying degrees of demographic diversity. I also consider how those reactions are conditioned by the race and the partisanship of the candidate. The racial and partisan characteristics of the politicians are considered simultaneously, which very few studies have done. As Weaver (2012, 171) indicates, "Prior studies have . . . avoided party labels because of their potential to 'swamp' the results." The results of the present study underscore the importance of studying race and partisanship cues simultaneously, because I find that voters draw a very different meaning when a candidate is associated with images of black people, depending on the race and partisanship of the politician. Thus, this chapter also helps us understand why for some politicians subtle or implicit cues are effective, while for others they are ineffective.

To foreshadow my results, I find that the effects of being associated with counter-stereotypical images of blacks are far more negative for white Democratic candidates than they are for white Republican candidates. White Democratic candidates whose advertisements included black supporters lost the support of white voters, unlike their similarly situated white Republican counterparts. White Democratic candidates were also significantly more likely to be perceived as liberal, supporting affirmative action, and favoring blacks over whites when the mailers included images of African Americans. In fact, when the candidate was a white Democrat, the inclusion of images of African Americans was associated with a racial priming effect. In other words, even *counter-stereotypical* black images in the campaign mailer of a white Democratic politician made race salient, such that there was an increase in the weight that voters gave to their negative racial predispositions about blacks. An association with black imagery might make white Democratic politicians more susceptible to a racial priming effect, because of the conflicting nature of the racial and partisan cues associated with white Democrats. Recall from chapter 2 that when asked whether they thought different types of candidates would "favor blacks over whites," "whites over blacks," or "treat both groups the same," white Democratic politicians were closest to a rating of "treat both groups the same." Perhaps this perception of evenhandedness on the part of white Democratic politicians also made it more likely that perceptions of them could be altered by the mere inclusion of black imagery. In other words, voters' perceptions of white Republicans and black Democrats, for example, were far more crystallized, and thus less likely to be altered by an association with black imagery.

For black politicians of either party, voters' perception of black candidates as favoring blacks over whites or supporting affirmative action did not change when they included black images, relative to a mailer with all white images. In short, for black politicians, implicit or subtle cues, such as the inclusion of white images, may not be sufficient to overcome voters' stereotype of black politicians as preoccupied with minority interests. Black candidates' efforts to counter the uncertainty around their candidacies are often ignored by white voters (Hajnal 2007). Therefore, a subtle racial cue, such as an association with white imagery, is not enough to overcome the perception that a black candidate would be preoccupied with the interests of blacks, regardless of the black candidate's party affiliation. Also, contrary to the findings for the white Democratic politician, the inclusion of black images in the campaign mailer of a black candidate was not associated with a racial priming effect. I argue that the very presence of a black candidate already makes race salient such that it is virtually impossible to increase the weight that voters give to their negative racial predispositions about blacks.

White Republican politicians, on the other hand, have such an established reputation for looking out for the interests of whites that a visual association with blacks is not sufficient in most instances to dampen the perception that they will look out for the interests of whites. As Philpot (2007) has shown, efforts on the part of the Republican Party to diversify are often met with skepticism and perceived as "cheap talk." Partisan stereotypes in particular are especially difficult to alter (Rahn 1993; Arceneaux 2008). As Fiske and Taylor (1991, 50) note, "Well-developed schemas generally resist change and can even persist in the face of disconfirming evidence." One implication of this resistance to change is that citizens absorb stereotype-consistent information more readily than inconsistent information (Fiske and Taylor 1991). Thus, a white Democratic candidate associated with black imagery is more readily absorbed, because that information is consistent with voters' stereotype of the Democratic Party. Conversely, a white Republican candidate who is associated with even exclusively black images is less likely to be absorbed, and thus unlikely to prime racial resentment. Because of the party's stance on racial matters, a white Republican candidate who is associated with black images is stereotype-inconsistent and does not provide a credible threat to the racial status quo. I expect that white Democratic candidates confirming that partisan stereotype will be judged harshly by voters who do not like black representation, while white Republican candidates cutting against their party's pro-white stereotype will be disbelieved, and their signal dismissed by every type of voter, whether Democrat or Republican. Visuals showing black constituents with white Democratic candidates fall on fertile ground, because many whites fear that exact possibility.

I used a nationally diverse sample of 600 non-Hispanic white Americans in July 2012 to test my predictions about the impact of subtle racial imagery on voters' perceptions of various types of politicians. The survey was fielded by YouGov.[4] The sample skews slightly female, as females account for 52 percent of respondents. In addition, 41 percent of the sample identified as Democrats, and 49 percent as Republicans. The remaining 10 percent of the sample identified as Independents. The average age of the sample was fifty-two years old, and the geographic location of the respondents was relatively balanced, with 18 percent of respondents residing in the Northeast, 21 percent in the West, 23 percent in the Midwest, and 35 percent in the South. Thirty-one percent of the sample held a bachelor's degree or higher, and the median annual household income was $60,000–$69,999.

Respondents were first asked to answer a series of pre-treatment questions concerning their demographic characteristics, party affiliation, and racial resentment. Several distracter questions were also included to minimize the possibility that racial resentment was primed during the pre-treatment phase.[5] Subsequently, all participants viewed a mock campaign mailer from a candidate named Greg Davis who was running for the U.S. Senate. Participants were told that they were evaluating the mailer to provide feedback to the candidate and his staff. The respondents were unaware that the candidate and the campaign mailer were fictitious until they were debriefed at the end of the study.

As indicated in table 6.1, respondents were randomly assigned one of twelve treatment conditions (campaign mailers). Each mailer features six photos—one of the candidate, and five photos of constituent groups (homeowners, senior citizens, students, small-business owners, and health-care workers). The partisanship of the candidate (Democrat

TABLE 6.1 **Experimental Conditions in Campaign Mailer Study**

Treatment	Candidate race	Candidate party affiliation	Racial composition of photos
White Democratic candidate w/ whites	White	Democrat	Five white photos
White Democratic candidate w/ mixed group	White	Democrat	Three white photos, two black photos
White Democratic candidate w/ blacks	White	Democrat	Five black photos
White Republican w/ whites	White	Republican	Five white photos
White Republican w/ mixed group	White	Republican	Three white photos, two black photos
White Republican w/ blacks	White	Republican	Five black photos
Black Democratic candidate w/ whites	Black	Democrat	Five white photos
Black Democratic candidate w/ mixed group	Black	Democrat	Three white photos, two black photos
Black Democratic candidate w/ blacks	Black	Democrat	Five black photos
Black Republican candidate w/ whites	Black	Republican	Five white photos
Black Republican w/ mixed group	Black	Republican	Three white photos, two black photos
Black Republican w/ whites	Black	Republican	Five white photos

or Republican), the race of the candidate (black or white), as well as the racial composition of the constituent groups pictured, were all manipulated. The racial composition of the constituent groups pictured was altered such that the mailer included five photos of African Americans, five photos of whites, or three photos of whites and two photos of blacks (mixed condition). Varying the presence of African Americans in the fictitious campaign mailer enables us to measure the degree of influence of counter-stereotypical African American images. If, for example, there are detrimental consequences for candidates associated with the "mixed condition" (two black images and three white images), then this suggests that the mere presence of black images has negative consequences for some candidates, and not just when voters receive the overwhelming cue of all black images. Varying the presence of black images also helps allay any concerns about external validity that might arise from the condition in which all five of the images picture African Americans.

Another aspect of the experiment that was designed to mimic real-world conditions was the vagueness of the message, as it is well established that parties have an incentive to be vague (Downs 1957). This vague language also ensured that subjects were responding to the candidate and not specific policy positions. The mailer read, "In the United States Senate, I'll be fighting to make a difference for YOU. A vote for Greg Davis on Tuesday, November 8th, means a vote for: homeowner-ship for families, high quality healthcare, investing in small business, protecting senior citizens, educating our children." Also, each of these statements was paired with a picture of a relevant group (e.g., senior cit-izens, children), and the mailer did not include any racially coded lan-guage. Photos of blacks and photos of whites were selected so as to be comparable in terms of age, attractiveness, and setting. Immediately af-ter reviewing the mailer, subjects were asked a battery of questions, in-cluding questions about their likelihood of voting for the candidate and their perceptions of various candidate traits. It is worth noting that I used photographs that depicted an intact two-parent family in a middle-class neighborhood, a young female medical professional with a stetho-scope around her neck, people in professional attire in a business setting, a senior citizen couple, and a smiling boy actively engaged in the learn-ing process in a classroom setting. These images do not portray blacks violating traditional American values, but instead blacks "playing by the rules." Thus, according to the conventional wisdom on racial priming, there is little reason to expect that these positive images of blacks would activate racial resentment.

The Impact of Demographic Diversity on Voter Perceptions of Candidates

First, I checked whether the manipulation worked as intended by see-ing whether respondents were able to accurately identify the content of the campaign mailer. Respondents were given a list of four statements about the mailer and asked to check as many statements as they believed to be true.[6] The results of the manipulation check indicate that the ma-nipulation worked as intended, as the percentage of correct responses ranged from 91 to 99 percent. I subsequently examined the distribution of responses for the four variables of interest and found that they were all normally distributed. These variables of interest were measured to gauge respondents' perception of the type of policy the candidate would enact if elected.

I began by estimating a series of ordered logistic regression models in which the dependent variables include the likelihood of voting for the candidate, the perception that the candidate would support the policy of affirmative action for blacks in the workplace, the perception that if elected the candidate would favor blacks over whites, and the perception that the candidate was liberal. I chose these specific variables because I wanted to test whether the mere presence of black images was associated with the perception that the candidate was more liberal on racial issues. I also wanted to test whether even counter-stereotypical images of black people could foster negative outcomes for a candidate, depending on her race or partisanship. I estimated these models for all of the conditions displayed in table 6.1. The results for each of the models are displayed in tables located in the appendix to this chapter. However, for ease of interpretation I have plotted the predicted probabilities associated with the various models. All of the models control for education, gender, income, partisanship, and residing in the South.[7]

Figure 6.1 displays the predicted probability of "likely vote" for the candidate, as a function of the varying levels of demographic diversity in the mailers. "Whites" refers to the version of the mailer with only white images, "Mixed" refers to the version with three white images and two black images, and "Blacks" refers to the version of the mailer with only images of African Americans. As indicated in figure 6.1, the "likely vote" for the white Democratic candidate whose campaign mailer includes only images of whites is not especially high, given that the predicted probability of "likely vote" for the candidate in that condition is 0.45. The aim here, however, is not to estimate the absolute levels of support for candidates, but rather to examine whether that support is altered by a visual association with African Americans.

Figure 6.1 indicates that the inclusion of black images, even though these images are counter-stereotypical, is associated with a decrease in support for the white Democratic candidate. People who were exposed to the mailer of the white Democratic candidate with all black images were on average 17 percentage points less willing to vote for the candidate, relative to the white Democrat with all white images ($p < .05$), while exposure to the white Democrat in the mixed condition was associated with a decrease of 11 percentage points in willingness to vote for the candidate, relative to the baseline candidate ($p < .10$). Simply including *positive* images of blacks in the mailer decreased support for a white Democratic candidate, relative to a white Democratic candidate whose campaign mailer included exclusively white images.

When we examine the results for the white Republican candidate,

Probability of Voting

White Democratic Candidate

Whites   Mixed   Blacks

Black Democratic Candidate

Whites   Mixed   Blacks

White Republican Candidate

Whites   Mixed   Blacks

Black Republican Candidate

Whites   Mixed   Blacks

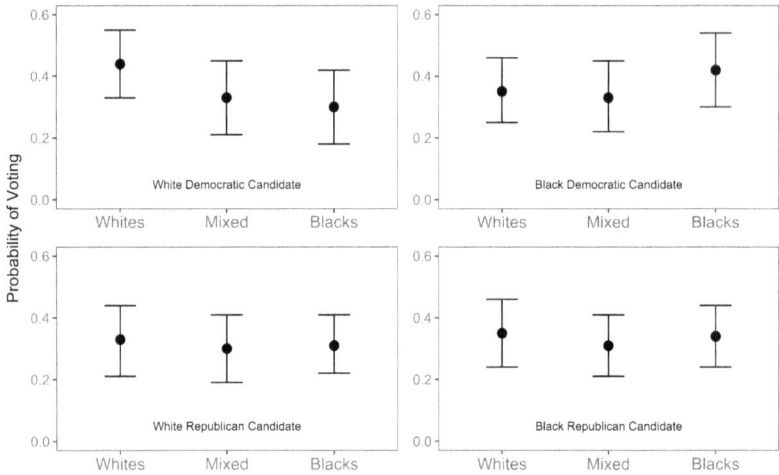

FIGURE 6.1. Effect of Black Inclusion on Likely Vote for the Candidate
Source: 2012 YouGov Study
Note: The points represent the predicted probability of voting for the candidate by the race and partisanship of the candidate across different levels of black inclusion. "Whites" denotes the campaign mailer with five white images, "Blacks" denotes the campaign mailer with five black images, and "Mixed" denotes the campaign mailer with three white images and two black images. 95 percent confidence intervals. Estimates from the full model appear in table A.6.1 in the appendix.

however, increasing demographic diversity is not associated with a decline in electoral support for the candidate. Since the white Democratic conditions and the white Republican conditions are equivalent in all dimensions, save for the difference in the partisan cue, any difference in the results can be attributed to the partisanship of the candidate. While the predicted probability of being "likely to vote" for the white Republican candidate whose campaign mailer included all white images was 0.33, the "likely vote" for the candidate declined by only 3 percentage points in the mixed condition and 1 percentage point in the all black images condition. Thus, an association with black images was not harmful to the electoral chances of white Republican candidates.

Next, I test whether the inclusion of white images in a campaign mailer, as opposed to black images, is associated with more favorable electoral outcomes for black politicians. I also test whether the partisan cue of Republican attenuates the potentially negative consequences of being associated with images of blacks as opposed to whites when the politician is African American. As indicated in figure 6.1, altering the racial imagery in a black candidate's campaign mailer was not associated with a statistically significant change in respondents' willingness to say that they were "likely to vote" for the candidate. There was a 35 percent chance of respondents saying that they were likely to vote for the black Democratic candidate whose campaign mailer included all white images, compared to a decrease of 2 percentage points in the mixed condition and an increase of 7 percentage points in the all black condition. None of these differences attained traditional levels of statistical significance. Thus, the subtle inclusion of white Americans in the mailer was not associated with a change in electoral support for the black Democratic candidate, unlike his white co-partisan. Similarly, the predicted probability of voting for the black Republican candidate whose campaign mailer included exclusively white images was 0.35, whereas the likelihood of voting for the black Republican candidate decreased by 3 percentage points in the mixed condition and 1 percentage point in the all black images condition. None of these differences attained traditional levels of statistical significance. At least on the metric of electoral support, only the white Democratic politician experienced a loss in electoral support when the mailer included images of African Americans. I suspect that voters' perceptions of white Republican politicians and black politicians of either major party are so crystallized that altering the racial imagery had little to no impact.

I also examine the relationship between black inclusion and the perception that the candidate would support affirmative action (figure 6.2). The results indicate that the white Democratic candidate whose mailer included images of African Americans was also more likely to be perceived as supporting affirmative action, relative to the white Democratic candidate whose campaign mailer included only images of whites.

There was a 4 percent chance that voters perceived a white Democratic candidate with all white images as supportive of affirmative action. This low percentage is not especially surprising, given that the campaign mailer does not make any mention of affirmative action or any other race-related policies for that matter. However, when a white Democratic candidate's campaign mailer includes images of African Americans— even when black images are the minority of images—the perception that the candidate will support affirmative action jumps by 16 percentage points ($p < .01$). Similarly, when the white Democratic candidate is associated with all black images in the campaign mailer, the perception that the candidate favors affirmative action increases by 20 percentage points. Again, the results are substantively quite large, considering that the mailer does not include any language about affirmative action.

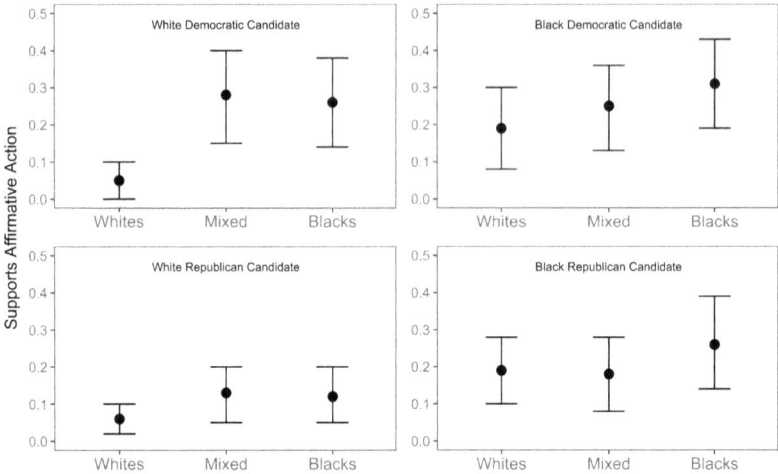

FIGURE 6.2.   Effect of Black Inclusion on the Perception the Candidate Will Support Affirmative Action

Source: 2012 YouGov Study

Note: The points represent the predicted probability of thinking the candidate will support affirmative action by the race and partisanship of the candidate across different levels of black inclusion. "Whites" denotes the campaign mailer with five white images, "Blacks" denotes the campaign mailer with five black images, and "Mixed" denotes the campaign mailer with three white images and two black images. 95 percent confidence intervals. Estimates from the full model appear in table A.6.2 in the appendix.

Furthermore, they are particularly striking when considering that in the mixed condition, only two of the five images are of blacks.

The presence of black imagery was also associated with an increase in the perception that a white Republican candidate would support affirmative action. A white Republican candidate whose campaign mailer included only images of whites had a 7 percent chance of being perceived as supportive of affirmative action for blacks in the workplace. The perception that a white Republican candidate would support affirmative action for blacks in the workplace roughly doubled when the mailer included images of blacks. Regardless of whether respondents were exposed to a white Republican candidate in the mixed condition (two black images and three white images) or to the white Republican candidate condition in which all five of the images were black, the perception that the candidate would support affirmative action was 6 percentage points higher than the white Republican candidate with all white images ($p < .05$).

However, these results are dwarfed by the results for the white Democratic versions of the treatments, where the predicted probability of thinking the candidate would support affirmative action was 24 percent when the mailer included exclusively black images. In other words, even though the impression that a white Republican candidate would be in favor of affirmative action doubled when black images were included in the campaign mailer, even at its highest (13 percent), the perception that a white Republican politician would support affirmative action was still notably lower—in fact, roughly half that of a white Democratic politician ($p < .05$). This observation underscores the point that voters draw very different inferences from a white Republican candidate who is associated with images of blacks than they do from his white Democratic counterpart.

There is also evidence to suggest that the inclusion of white images in the mailer dampened the perception that the black Democratic candidate would support affirmative action. When the black Democratic candidate's campaign mailer included only images of whites, there was a 19 percent chance that voters thought the candidate would support affirmative action.[8] In the mixed condition, the perception that the black Democratic candidate would support affirmative action increased by 5 percentage points, but this was not statistically distinguishable from the condition with all white images. However, when the black Democratic candidate was associated with all black images, the perception that the candidate would support affirmative action was notably higher, with an increase of 12 percentage points ($p < .10$). Also of note is that a black Democratic candidate was automatically more likely to be presumed as supporting affirmative action, relative to his white Democratic counterpart. The white Democrat with all white images was associated with a 4 percent chance of thinking that the candidate would support affirmative action, compared to 19 percent for his black Democratic counterpart whose campaign mailer included the identical imagery, save for the imagery of the candidate himself ($p < .05$).

Similarly, voters' perception of a black Republican's likelihood to support affirmative action was not altered by the inclusion of white images, as the differences between the black Republican candidate whose mailer included black images and the black Republican politician with exclusively white images did not attain traditional levels of statistical significance. Respondents were no more likely to think that a black Republican politician supported affirmative action when his campaign mailer included all black images as opposed to all white images. Voters' perceptions of black Republican candidates in this dimension look much more similar to voters' perceptions of black Democratic candidates than they do to perceptions of their white Republican counterparts. There was a 20 percent chance that voters would think that the black Republican politicians whose campaign mailer included all white images would support affirmative action for blacks in the workplace, as opposed to 6 percent for the white Republican equivalent, 4 percent for the white Democratic equivalent, and 19 percent for the black Democratic equivalent. Thus, regardless of party, black candidates whose campaign mailers include all white images are generally perceived as more likely to support affirmative action than their white counterparts.

Also relevant to my argument are the results regarding the perception that the candidate will favor blacks over whites. Racial distancing theory is based in part on the premise that many whites oppose candidates who are perceived as disrupting the racial status quo or favoring blacks at the expense of whites. Figure 6.3 indicates that even very subtle racial imagery influences voters' perceptions of a politician's advocacy for a certain group. For example, there was only a 3 percent likelihood of perceiving a white Democratic politician whose mailer includes exclusively white

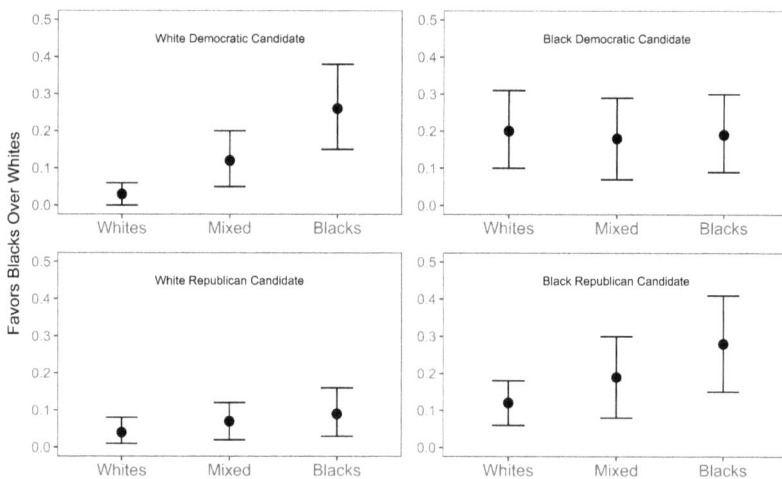

FIGURE 6.3. Effect of Black Inclusion on the Perception the Candidate Will Favor Blacks over Whites

Source: 2012 YouGov Study

Note: The points represent the predicted probability of thinking the candidate will "favor blacks over whites" by the race and partisanship of the candidate across different levels of black inclusion. "Whites" denotes the campaign mailer with five white images, "Blacks" denotes the campaign mailer with five black images, and "Mixed" denotes the campaign mailer with three white images and two black images. 95 percent confidence intervals. Estimates from the full model appear in table A.6.3 in the appendix.

images as favoring blacks over whites. This perception increases remarkably when African Americans are included in the mailer. Exposure to the white Democratic candidate with all black images and the white Democratic candidate with mixed images was associated, respectively, with a 24 percentage point increase and a 9 percentage point increase in the perception that the candidate would favor blacks over whites, relative to the white Democratic candidate whos Ye mailer included only images of whites ($p < .01$). The fact that the mere inclusion of black images in the mailer altered people's perception of a white Democratic politician's position on racial issues suggests that for some whites, when it comes to white Democratic candidates, an association with blacks is equated with racial liberalism.

Also of note are the results associated with the perception that the white Republican candidate would favor blacks over whites. Exposure to the white Republican candidate in the mixed condition was associated with a 3 percentage point increase in the perception that the candidate would favor blacks over whites ($p < .10$), while exposure to the white Republican candidate with all black images was associated with a 4 percentage point increase in the same perception ($p < .05$), relative to the white Republican candidate with all white images. The magnitude of these effects is much smaller than the magnitude of the effects associated with the white Democratic candidates in the identical conditions ($p < .01$). Once again, the results suggest that the racial cue of African American images accompanying white Democratic candidates is associated with the perception that the candidates are far more liberal on racial matters than their Republican counterparts.

The inclusion of white images as opposed to black images was not associated with a change in the assessment that a black Democratic candidate would favor blacks over whites. Black Democrats associated with white images were just as likely to be perceived as favoring blacks over whites, relative to the black Democratic candidate whose campaign mailer included all black images. Thus, it was difficult for black Democratic candidates to alter voters' perception that they would favor blacks over whites through the implicit cue of including white imagery. The black Democratic candidate whose campaign mailer included images of only white people was associated with a 35 percent chance of thinking that the candidate would favor blacks over whites, which was higher than the perception for similarly situated white Democratic, white Republican, and black Republican politicians. The perception that the black

Democratic candidate would favor blacks over whites decreased by only 2 percentage points in the mixed condition and 1 percentage point in the condition with all black images. None of these differences attained traditional levels of statistical significance. In short, including white racial imagery as opposed to black racial imagery in the campaign mailer was associated with very little change in voters' perception of and support for the black Democratic candidate.

The inclusion of images of whites as opposed to images of blacks, however, was associated with a change in the perception that a black Republican candidate would favor blacks over whites. There was a 12 percent chance that a black Republican candidate would be perceived as favoring blacks over whites when the mailer included exclusively white images, but this perception increased by 14 percentage points when the mailer included only images of African Americans. Recall that for the equivalent condition for a white Republican politician, there was only a 9 percent chance that the candidate would be perceived as favoring blacks over whites ($p < .10$). Therefore, for black Republican candidates, despite the partisan stereotype of the Republican Party looking out for the interests of whites, the inclusion of black images increases the perception that a black Republican candidate would look out for the interests of blacks, more than it does for his white co-partisan. In short, black candidates, regardless of party, did little to alter voters' perception that they would be looking out for black interests, in spite of altering the racial imagery included in their campaign mailers. On the other hand, white Democratic candidates were generally penalized for an association with blacks. In the case of white Republican candidates, an inclusion of black imagery increased the perception that they might be liberal on racial matters, but nowhere near the increase in that perception for the white Democratic conditions.

Finally, I examine whether the inclusion of black images also increases the perception that a candidate is liberal. These results are displayed in figure 6.4. The pattern of results is similar to the other candidate traits. Once again, we see the most consequential results for the white Democratic politician. Any inclusion of black images in the mailer increases the perception that the candidate is liberal by a magnitude of at least 15 percentage points ($p < .01$). For the black Democratic politician, the inclusion of black images in the mailer also increases the perception of candidate liberalism, but these differences are not statistically significant. The inclusion of black imagery in the Republican versions of

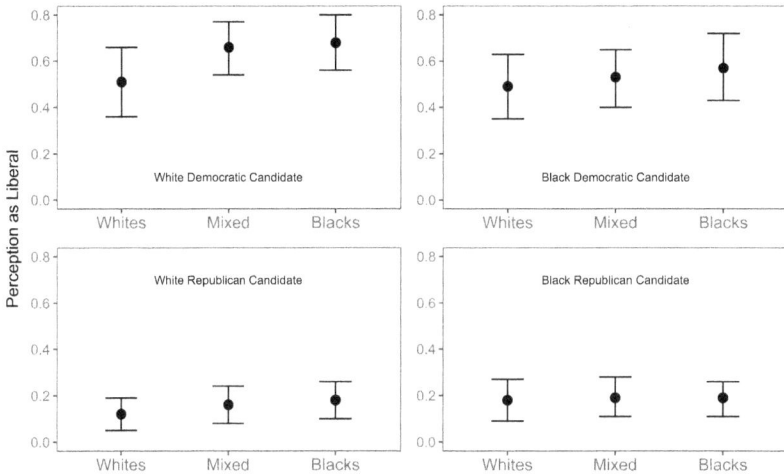

FIGURE 6.4. Effect of Black Inclusion on the Perception the Candidate Is Conservative
Source: 2012 YouGov Study
Note: The points represent the predicted probability of thinking the candidate is conservative by the race and partisanship of the candidate across different levels of black inclusion. "Whites" denotes the campaign mailer with five white images, "Blacks" denotes the campaign mailer with five black images, and "Mixed" denotes the campaign mailer with three white images and two black images. 95 percent confidence intervals. Estimates from the full model appear in table A.6.4 in the appendix.

the treatments did very little to increase the perception that the politicians were liberal. Even in the case of the black Republican, the inclusion of black imagery was not associated with the perception that the politician was liberal.

In short, across four different dependent variables, the inclusion of black imagery had different outcomes depending on the race and partisanship of the politician in question. The most consistent finding was that the inclusion of black imagery seemed to change voters' perceptions of white Democrats, whereas perceptions of black politicians were not altered by changes in the demographic diversity of their campaign mailers. The inclusion of counter-stereotypical images of African Americans did, however, alter perceptions of white Republican candidates at times, but the change in perception was nowhere near as great as it was for their Democratic counterparts. The impact of these images was also less consistent for white Republican candidates. Furthermore, unlike white Democratic candidates associated with blacks, white Republican candidates associated with counter-stereotypical images of blacks did not lose vote support, relative to the white Republican candidate whose mailer included only images of whites. These results indicate that an association with black images is not wholly detrimental. An association of a white Democratic candidate with black images, even if those images are counter-stereotypical, signals a threat to the racial status quo, whereas for white Republican politicians, an association with black images does not signal a credible threat. Finally, in the case of African American politicians, both Democrats and Republicans alike, subtly altering the racial imagery was typically not associated with a change in the perception of the candidates.

Priming Racial Resentment

Thus far, I have presented the main effects of being exposed to treatments that included counter-stereotypical images of blacks, relative to treatments that featured whites exclusively. More relevant for the racial priming hypothesis, however, is whether the presence of counter-stereotypical images of African Americans *primes* racial resentment, such that respondents bring their racial predispositions to bear on their likelihood of voting for the candidate. Accordingly, I estimated a series of ordered logistic regression models for each type of candidate (white Democrat, white Republican, black Democrat, black Republican), in which I interacted *racial resentment* with exposure to the two treatments in which the campaign mailer included images of African Americans.[9]

For ease of interpretation, I also plot the predicted probability of respondents' willingness to say that they would be "likely to vote" for the candidate, conditional on respondents' level of racial resentment, holding all other variables at their means. Figure 6.5 displays the conditional effect of racial resentment on the "likely to vote" option for the candidates depicted in the various conditions. Racial resentment is plotted along the x axis, with the center of the axis representing the average level of racial resentment for the sample.[10] Along the x axis, I have also denoted respondents who were one standard deviation above (racial conservatives) or below (racial liberals) the average level of racial resentment for the sample. Along the y axis, I have plotted the predicted probability of respondents saying that they were "likely to vote" for the candidate in question.

As indicated in figure 6.5, the slope of the line representing the interaction between racial resentment and exposure to the white Democratic candidate with all white images is virtually zero. Thus, racial resentment

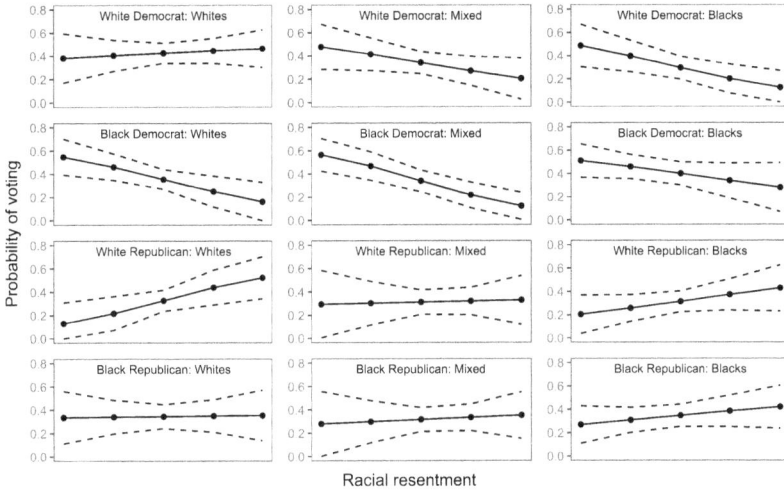

FIGURE 6.5. Effect of Black Inclusion on Likely Vote as a Function of Racial Resentment
Source: 2012 YouGov Study
Note: The points represent the predicted probability of voting for the candidate by the race and partisanship of the candidate across different levels of black inclusion as a function of racial resentment. "Whites" denotes the campaign mailer with five white images, "Blacks" denotes the campaign mailer with five black images, and "Mixed" denotes the campaign mailer with three white images and two black images. 95 percent confidence intervals. Estimates from the full model appear in table A.6.5 in the appendix.

was not primed when respondents were exposed to the white Democratic candidate with all white images. However, a different story emerges for the white Democratic candidates who were associated with black images. As figure 6.5 indicates, as racial resentment increases, the less willing respondents are to say that they are "likely to vote" for the white Democratic candidate when his campaign mailer includes images of African Americans, even though those images are counter-stereotypical. More importantly, for our purposes, as more black people were included in the campaign mailer of the white Democratic candidate, racially resentful voters were less likely to vote for the candidate.

Take, for example, a respondent whose racial resentment score was at the mean for the sample, or about 0.61. A racial resentment score of 0.61 indicates that the respondent is racially conservative, but by no means the most racially conservative in the sample, as about 25 percent of the sample had racial resentment scores of 0.75 or higher. When the white Democratic mailer included all white images, the likelihood of a respondent with an average level of racial resentment stating that they were "likely" to vote for the candidate was about 43 percent. Of course, this

is not an overwhelming level of support, but the aim here is not to measure absolute levels of support, but rather to see how support varies with
the demographic composition of the mailer. Thus, it is worth noting that
when the mailer of the white Democratic candidate included three white
images and two black images, support for the candidate among respondents with an average level of racial resentment declined by 9 percentage
points to 34 percent, and even lower to 29 percent when the mailer included all black images. In other words, moving from an association with
all white images to all black images lowered support for the white Democratic candidate by about 15 percent of the scale ($p < .01$). As the number of black images in the mailer increased, the likelihood of the average
respondent stating that they were "likely to vote" for the white Democratic candidate decreased. The mere presence of black images was associated with a large and statistically discernible racial priming effect.
In short, while neither stereotypical nor paired with racially coded language, images of blacks still primed racial resentment.

I also hypothesized that when the campaign mailer of a white Republican candidate included counter-stereotypical images of blacks, exposure to the mailer would not be associated with a racial priming effect,
relative to a white Republican candidate associated with only white images. Therefore, figure 6.5 also presents the predicted probability of respondents choosing the "likely to vote" option for the white Republican
candidate for the three versions of the campaign mailer (all black images, all white images, mixed condition). The baseline condition is the
white Republican with all whites, which enables us to test whether a racial priming effect is associated with the presence of counter-stereotypic
black images paired with a white Republican candidate, relative to a
white Republican candidate with exclusively white images.

As indicated in figure 6.5, the consequences of being associated with
counter-stereotypical black images are very different for the white Republican candidates than for their Democratic counterparts, despite the
partisan cue of Republican versus Democrat being the only thing that
differs between the two conditions. The inclusion of black images on the
campaign mailer of a white Republican is not associated with a decrease
in electoral support for a white Republican candidate. Relative to white
Republican politicians, white Democratic politicians are more likely
to be perceived as looking out for the interests of blacks, which likely
means that voters perceive an association of a white Democratic politi-

cian with black images as a credible threat. A Democratic politician as-sociated with blacks—even if those images are counter-stereotypical—is more likely to activate negative racial attitudes toward African Amer-icans than the very same images associated with a white Republican politician.

The results displayed in figure 6.5 also indicate a lack of a racial prim-ing effect for black Democratic politicians. As racial resentment in-creased among respondents, the more unwilling they were to vote for a black Democratic politician, but this unwillingness to vote for the black Democratic politician was not contingent on the demographic composi-tion of the people pictured in the mailer. In other words, racially resent-ful respondents were no less likely to vote for a Democratic politician when the campaign mailer included images of blacks as opposed to the campaign mailer having exclusively white images.

Similarly, for black Republican politicians, there is no evidence of a racial priming effect when the campaign mailer included images of Af-rican Americans as opposed to images of whites. As figure 6.5 indicates, the slope of the lines associated with the different black Republican con-ditions are relatively flat, or equal to zero. Thus, changing the demo-graphic composition of the campaign mailer did nothing to alter voters' willingness to support the Republican candidate. Support for the black Republican candidate, regardless of the racial composition of the mailer, was also relatively consistent across the different levels of racial resent-ment. Racially resentful whites were about as likely to vote for the black Republican candidate as were their racially liberal counterparts.

In short, the results from this experiment highlight the difficulties that black politicians encounter when trying to alter some white Amer-icans' perceptions of them through the use of subtle racial signals. Ex-cluding black images from the campaign mailers did not provide suffi-cient information to alter the perception that the black candidates would favor blacks over whites or support affirmative action, relative to black candidates who included exclusively black images in their mailers. Simi-larly, white Republican politicians were also unable to alter voters' per-ception of them by changing the demographic composition of their cam-paign mailers. White Democratic politicians, however, were penalized when their campaign mailers included images of blacks as opposed to whites. Thus, voters' perceptions of some types of politicians are more malleable than others. Voters appear to have a solidified impression of black candidates and white Republican candidates, such that an association with subtle visual imagery was not sufficient to alter voters' perceptions of either type of candidate.

Of course, it is worth noting that this experiment featured fictitious candidates in a low-information context, which may raise some concerns about external validity. The aim of this study, however, was not to completely replicate the real electoral environment. Instead, this study serves as a useful experiment regarding the penalties that some candidates might experience for even very subtle associations with African Americans. The experiment also helps inform our thinking about the incentives that different types of candidates have to "distance" themselves from African Americans—even if only visually or symbolically. If in fact a mere visual association with African Americans has negative electoral consequences for white Democratic candidates, then it is likely that a more substantive association with black interests might also result in a lack of support for white Democratic candidates from racially moderate and racially conservative whites. It is not hard to imagine a scenario, for example, where a Republican candidate might try to associate her white Democratic opponent with negative, stereotypical imagery of African Americans. If counter-stereotypical portrayals of African Americans as business professionals, two-parent families, and senior citizens are associated with a loss of electoral support, then what should we make of efforts to associate Democratic politicians with black criminals and welfare recipients? It is probable that more stereotypical imagery might be associated with an even larger racial priming effect when paired with a white Democratic politician.

Concluding Remarks

In this chapter I conducted a series of tests to examine whether counter-stereotypical images of blacks prime racial resentment. I demonstrated that white Democratic candidates who are associated with images of blacks as opposed to whites receive less electoral support from racially resentful voters, precisely because these white Democratic candidates are perceived as more likely to favor blacks over whites. I argued that this perception is because the Democratic Party already has a reputation for representing black interests (presumably at the expense of whites). In short, the mere visual association of a white Democratic candidate with seemingly innocuous, counter-stereotypical images of blacks causes racial interests to compete at the ballot box. However, for black candidates, regardless of party, it is very difficult to alter the perception that they will favor blacks over whites. Therefore, the inclusion or exclusion of even innocuous, counter-stereotypical imagery of blacks does very little to alter voters' perceptions of black politicians in a low-information context. Finally, white Republican politicians can solidify their reputation for looking out for the interests of whites over blacks by associating themselves with exclusively white images, while an association with black imagery does little to hurt white Republican politicians' "brand" of looking out for the interests of whites. I also found that it is much easier to prime racial resentment than previously thought, because counter-stereotypical images of blacks make group interests salient, regardless of whether African American images were in the minority or the majority. Exposure to white Democratic candidates who were paired with counter-stereotypical images of blacks was associated with a racial priming effect on likely vote.

Aside from the racial priming effect, the results also indicate a main effect for counter-stereotypical images of blacks paired with a white Democratic candidate. The mere presence of African American images in the mailer of a white Democratic candidate was associated with a loss in electoral support, and an increase in the perception that the candidate would support affirmative action and favor blacks over whites. Although the campaign mailer did not include any references to racial policies, black images—seemingly in common cause with a white Democratic candidate—were used as a cue for the candidate's stances on racial policy.

Also of note is that the negative electoral consequences for white Democratic candidates associated with blacks are not just about racial animus toward African Americans. If in fact candidates were being punished simply because respondents disliked blacks, then the partisanship of the candidate should be inconsequential. Instead, I demonstrated that the magnitude of the racial priming effect was greater for white Democratic candidates associated with blacks than it was for white Republicans associated with blacks—and statistically significant. I argue that these results highlight the need to devote more attention to the study of partisanship and racial cues simultaneously, as well as the role of group interests in accounts of racial priming.

Thus, these results have implications for the theory of electoral capture (Frymer 1999), which argues that candidates from both the Democratic and the Republican parties have shied away from courting African American voters for fear of alienating working-class and middle-class whites, who not only express resentment toward African Americans but also make up the bulk of swing voters in national elections. The results of my study demonstrate that the fear of alienating white Americans is not unfounded, as there are negative electoral consequences for white Democratic candidates who are associated with African Americans. This study empirically demonstrates what scholars have long suspected to be true—racially resentful whites penalize the Democratic Party—at least white Democrats— for association with African Americans, whereas white Republicans are not penalized for a visual association with African Americans. Democratic Party leaders may in fact be correct in their assumption that "their victory is threatened by their association with large numbers of African American voters. This leads them to minimize the *public appearance* of their candidates with these voters" (Frymer 1999, 121; emphasis added).

These results suggest the need for more research about the potential of counter-stereotypical cues to prime racial resentment, because according to the theory of racial priming, there is no reason to expect that positive images, depicting African Americans as working hard and "playing by the rules," would result in a racial priming effect. Scholars of racial resentment define the construct as something that is "preoccupied with the moral character of African Americans" (Kinder and Sanders 1996, 105–6); it is something that is activated "when issues are framed in ways that draw attention to the moral qualifications of the intended beneficiaries" (Nelson and Kinder 1996, 1072). However, the results of this study indicate that the role of negative stereotypes in racial priming may have been previously overstated, as it appears that negative stereotypes are a sufficient, but not a necessary, condition for racial resentment to be activated. Although there were no depictions of African American criminality, poverty, or drug use, I found that depictions of blacks as homeowners, small-business owners, and so on were still able to activate racial resentment. I demonstrate that when these images were paired with white Democratic candidates, some whites were less inclined to support white Democratic candidates. The apparent concern here is not with the behavior of blacks, or even the dislike of the group. Instead, these results suggest a concern with white Democratic politicians governing on behalf of this group—even when the latter are depicted counter-stereotypically.

It is worth noting that it has been ten to twenty years since much of the seminal work on racial priming was published. Despite the election of the nation's first black president, racial attitudes continue to play a pivotal role in vote choice and perceptions of candidates. Racial predispositions can be activated when groups' interests are made salient through partisan cues. Scholars have long posited race as the underlying determinant of partisan division (Huckfeldt and Kohlfeld 1989; Frymer 1999), and the results discussed in this chapter indicate that citizens support candidates in large part based on their perception of a party's reputation with respect to race. Finally, the fact that black politicians were unable to alter voters' perceptions, even when they included exclusively white imagery, supports the findings from the previous chapter. In chapter 5, we saw that black politicians typically did not benefit from implicit appeals. Instead, it seems that they were most likely to alter voters' perceptions when they engaged in explicit appeals. The findings from this chapter are yet another example of a more subtle or implicit appeal not working for black politicians in the way such appeals seem to work for white politicians.

CHAPTER SEVEN

Conclusion

For many Americans, one of the most puzzling elements of the 2016 election was the millions of white American voters who voted for Barack Obama in 2012 but switched to Donald Trump in 2016. Trump voters who previously voted for Obama have been the subject of intense fascination, and some might even argue, preoccupation. The underlying thought process driving this fascination is the idea that if white Americans voted for an African American president (in some cases twice), then surely, they could not be motivated by negative racial attitudes in their decision to vote for Donald Trump. How could people who voted for a candidate who rose to national prominence with a speech at the 2004 Democratic National Convention, in which he famously said, "There is no black America, there is no white America,"[1] subsequently cast a vote for someone who launched his campaign by saying, "When Mexico sends its people, they're not sending their best. . . . They're bringing drugs. They're bringing crime. They're rapists . . ."?[2]

While I am not in the position to definitively explain why people who voted for Obama in 2012 voted for Trump in 2016, what I can say is that these seemingly disparate outcomes are supported by my theory of racial distancing. The theory of racial distancing predicts that racially conservative whites and racially moderate whites will prefer candidates who indicate that they will not disrupt the racial status quo, or that they will not favor their racial and ethnic minority constituents. Such a candidate could be white, but she could also be a person of color. She could be a Republican, but she could also be a Democrat. Racial distancing helps black politicians and white Democratic politicians disrupt the stereotype of being beholden to racial and ethnic minorities, while racial distancing helps white Republican politicians reinforce their reputation for keeping intact the existing racial hierarchy. I argue that both Obama and Trump utilized a strategy of racial distancing whereby they conveyed to racially moderate and racially conservative whites that they would not disrupt the racial status quo. The *racial status quo* is characterized by racial inequality, with whites at the top of the hierarchy, including white dominance in political, social, and economic institutions.

Essentially, I am arguing that many white Americans are willing to vote for *a black candidate*, but they are not necessarily willing to vote for the candidate who *champions black interests*. If you accept that premise, then it becomes a lot easier to understand how someone could vote for Obama in 2012 and Trump in 2016. By no means am I saying that the behavior of President Obama was equivalent to that of President Donald Trump. I argue, however, that despite his message of racial unity, Barack Obama also engaged in a strategy of racial distancing, in which he distanced himself from stereotypes of black politicians as preoccupied with black interests. He also distanced himself from stereotypes of African Americans as not sufficiently committed to values of self-reliance and individualism by chastising African Americans for lacking in those areas. Initially this argument may seem controversial. It is, however, supported by evidence, which I will discuss in the following section.

Summary of Findings

Racial distancing theory argues that candidates across the racial and political spectrum use negative racial appeals about racial and ethnic minorities—often African Americans, but increasingly other marginalized groups, such as Latinos, immigrants, and Muslims—because these appeals are an effective way of communicating to racially moderate to racially conservative whites—the overwhelming majority of whites—that they will not disrupt the racial status quo. However, the electoral incentives, constraints, and considerations that candidates face when appealing to negative racial attitudes are largely influenced by the candidates' race, and, to a lesser degree, their partisanship. Scholarly and popular attention has tended to focus on white Republican politicians making appeals to prejudice while ignoring the incentives that also exist for white Democratic candidates, and black candidates from either major party, to appeal to negative racial attitudes about blacks for political gain.

The theory of racial distancing predicts that racially moderate and racially conservative whites will prefer candidates who indicate that they will not disrupt the racial status quo, or that they will not favor their racial and ethnic minority constituents. In the case of black politicians, this may also include distinguishing themselves from the "old guard" of black politicians, whom many white Americans perceive as preoccupied with race. Attempts to distinguish themselves from the old guard of black politicians may involve chastising other African Americans for their purported lack of work ethic, but it can also entail emphasizing their own personal work ethic and commitment to individualism.

When it comes to distancing themselves racially, however, politicians face a balancing act—on the one hand, they must indicate to a large fraction of white voters that they will maintain the racial status quo, but they must also not appear to be blatantly racist or racially insensitive. Most white Americans do not want to be seen as racist, nor do they want to be associated with a candidate who is perceived as racist. Since some racial and partisan groups are more likely to be thought of as beholden to certain demographic groups than others, the extent to which a candidate can credibly signal that she carries no special obligation to racial and ethnic minority voters without being perceived as racist is influenced foremost by the candidate's race and then her partisanship. Much of this theory and its predictions were discussed at length in chapters 1 and 2.

In chapter 2, I also provided empirical evidence of racialized partisan stereotypes, or the idea that a candidate's race either enhances or tempers the stereotypes associated with her party and the personal responsibility rhetoric it directs at African American and Latino audiences, relative to majority-white audiences. The results of a survey experiment on the CCES indicated that, on average, white respondents were more likely to rate white Republican politicians as favoring whites over blacks, whereas black Democratic and black Republican politicians were more likely to be rated as favoring blacks over whites. On the other hand, white Democratic politicians were closest to the perception of treating blacks and whites the same. I suspect that this is due to the conflicting nature of their racial and partisan cues. For white Democratic politicians, their racial group membership is more likely to be associated with racial conservatism, whereas their partisan membership is associated with racial liberalism, thus sending conflicting signals.

Obviously black Democrats, white Democrats, black Republicans, and white Republicans do not represent an exhaustive list of the types of politicians active in American politics. The aim here, however, was to get an understanding of how white Americans perceive white Republican politicians, since white Republican politicians have tended to be the dominant focus of discussions about negative appeals by politicians. The results indicate that white Republican politicians are uniquely perceived as protecting the interests of whites, which has implications for our study of race and politics—namely, that any studies that rely implicitly or explicitly on white Republican source cues have to take into consideration that the interpretation of a negative racial appeal delivered by a white Republican politician is likely to be viewed more harshly than an equivalent appeal by other types of politicians. In other words, if we rely on Republican source cues to test theories about the penalties associated with different types of negative racial appeals, we are likely overstating the penalties associated with invoking negative stereotypes about African Americans.

Subsequently in chapter 3, I focused on the 2008 presidential campaign of Barack Obama and his first term in office as a means of understanding how a prominent black Democrat engaged in a strategy of racial distancing. I demonstrated that Obama was more likely to direct personal responsibility rhetoric at African American and Latino audiences, relative to majority-white audiences. I also found that during the 2008 presidential campaign, Obama's television ads were more likely to include references to the racialized issues of welfare and crime, relative to John McCain, and relative to the two previous Democratic presidential nominees combined. To be fair, ads about welfare and crime represent a very small fraction of the total number of ads aired during the campaign, but it is still interesting that Obama's campaign featured more ads about policies for which black Democratic politicians arguably have a reputational disadvantage, at least among racially moderate and racially conservative white Americans.

In chapter 4, I discussed other examples of black politicians who have engaged in racial distancing. I focused my discussion on black politicians, not because racial distancing is a phenomenon that is limited to African American politicians, but because African American politicians are the most understudied example of this phenomenon. Again, the theory of racial distancing argues that politicians across the racial and political spectrum who are pursuing *white* electoral support are incentivized to engage in a strategy of racial distancing. I also provide evidence from a survey experiment that suggests that racially moderate and racially conservative whites were more receptive to a message from

a black Democrat that implicitly or explicitly invoked negative stereotypes about blacks, relative to a deracialized message that emphasized
universalism. Racial liberals, on the other hand, did not penalize a message from a black Democratic politician that either implicity or explicitly invoked negative stereotypes of African Americans, even relative to
a message emphasizing universalism. This experiment, however, was not
without its problems. It was difficult to keep the tone consistent across
the different treatment conditions. In other words, it was challenging to
create a treatment that emphasized universalism and racial neutrality,
while also creating parallel treatments that either implicitly or explicitly
invoked negative stereotypes about blacks.

Therefore, chapter 5 provides similar evidence from survey experiments in which the messaging was arguably more tightly controlled than
it was in the experiment from chapter 4. Specifically, in one study I find
that whites with anti-black attitudes were again more likely to vote for
a black candidate, Democrat or Republican, when he said that "black
people need to work harder," rather than when the message referenced
that "people need to work harder." Therefore, there was something especially appealing to a nontrivial fraction of whites about a personal responsibility message directed specifically at blacks. In other words, this
is not a matter of voters being more supportive of politicians who endorse the widely held American belief of hard work. Instead, many voters were more receptive to a message that explicitly emphasized the
need for black people to work harder, which speaks to the deeply held
nature of stereotypes about black work ethic. Furthermore, respondents
who endorsed anti-black stereotypes were also more likely to vote for
any candidate, black or white, Democrat or Republican, when they said
that "black people need to work harder," relative to saying that "people
need to work harder." On the other hand, respondents who perceived
blacks and whites as equally hardworking were no less likely to vote for
a black candidate with an explicit appeal, relative to the black candidate
in the control condition, which suggests that there is little to no penalty
for a black candidate who makes an explicit appeal. A second study in
chapter 5 largely confirmed previous findings: we saw that any punishment that politicians received for using a message that invoked negative stereotypes about blacks was largely driven by the racial liberals in
the sample. Still, racial liberals were far more likely to penalize a white
Democrat with a message that explicitly criticized blacks, relative to the
identical message from a black Democrat. At first glance, the disparate

findings for black and white politicians with explicit appeals might seem like voters withholding penalties from black politicians for what is simply an in-group conversation with fellow co-ethnics—a conversation in which a white politician should not engage. This, in fact, might explain the behavior of racial liberals and racial moderates in the sample, but the fact that racial conservatives were more supportive of candidates with explicit appeals, regardless of the race of the messenger, suggests that this is not simply about white politicians being penalized relative to their black counterparts. Among those whites who held the most negative attitudes about blacks, I consistently found that they were unperturbed by negative racial appeals that openly or explicitly invoked negative stereotypes about blacks' work ethic or parenting, regardless of whether the person espousing the message was black or white.

Subsequently, chapter 6 showed that black politicians' attempts to racially distance in a more subtle manner, by associating themselves with exclusively white imagery, did very little to diminish perceptions that they would pursue racially liberal policies. On the other hand, white Republican politicians who associated themselves with more black imagery also did very little to alter voters' perceptions of their racial conservatism. These results speak to the sticky nature of voters' perceptions of different types of candidates. Interestingly, white Democrats were most likely to benefit from a more subtle association with white imagery. These findings are similar to results from chapter 5, where I found that white Democratic politicians were most likely to benefit from using a message that implicitly invoked negative stereotypes about blacks. White Democratic politicians seem to benefit from a degree of subtlety that is unavailable to black Democratic or Republican politicians. The book concludes with this final chapter, where I summarize the findings and discuss the implications of these findings for American politics.

Racial Distancing beyond Black and White

Although my theory of racial distancing focuses primarily on distancing efforts related to African Americans, it is worth noting that there is also a practice of politicians appealing to voters' animus toward other groups. As the population of the United States becomes more racially and religiously diverse, Latinos and Muslims have become more salient in the political discourse (Perez 2015). Thus, politicians are increasingly likely to indicate that they will not disrupt the racial status quo, by distancing from these groups as well. During the 2016 presidential campaign, for example, Trump frequently invoked negative stereotypes about these groups. On numerous occasions he called for a categorical ban on Muslims entering the United States. He also announced his very decision to run for president with a speech that invoked stereotypes about Mexican people. Although Trump's comments were criticized in some circles as racist, he continued to inject race into his campaign with language that frequently targeted immigrants, Latinos, and Muslims —a strategy that likely helped mobilize his base of racial conservatives.

If many white voters perceive Latinos, Muslims, and immigrants as a threat, politicians from these groups may also be incentivized to engage in counter-stereotypical behavior to disrupt the stereotype that they themselves will be beholden to their group. For example, during the 2016 Republican presidential primaries, Ted Cruz and Marco Rubio, both of whom are Cuban American senators, attacked each other's stances on immigration, arguably in an attempt to make the other look weak on immigration. Presumably, these two candidates may have been more susceptible to the charge that they would be weak on immigration, because of their status as the children of Cuban immigrants, and the fact that Cruz himself is also an immigrant. Rubio was also vulnerable on immigration because he had previously worked on a bipartisan effort to create "a path to citizenship" for undocumented immigrants.

Cruz's campaign, for example, aired a television ad before the South Carolina primary comparing Rubio's comments on immigration to very similar statements by Obama: "Rubio got to Washington and wrote the bill giving amnesty to illegals using Obama's talking points," a narrator says ominously in the spot. "Marco Rubio burned us once. He shouldn't get the chance to sell us out again."[3] Although his ideas received less attention than President Trump's plan for a border wall, Cruz also supported building a border wall between the United States and Mexico and called for tougher restrictions on immigration from countries with large Muslim populations. He also called for police to "step up activity in Muslim neighborhoods."[4] Rubio, on the other hand, characterized Cruz as too moderate on immigration, saying, "he [Ted Cruz] is a supporter of legalizing people that are in this country illegally."[5] Although these exchanges are admittedly milder than some of the other examples of racial distancing, the behavior of the two Cuban American senators suggests that they may have wanted to shore up their credentials on this policy issue not only because it is important to the Republican base, but also because it is an issue on which they might be perceived as likely to be too moderate because of their ethnic background.

Interestingly, Cruz's and Rubio's stances on immigration were noticeably more conservative than those of some of the other Republican candidates for president, including Jeb Bush. In a two-party system that is largely divided along racial lines, candidates of color—even Republican candidates—may feel pressured to establish their racial conservatism credentials. Yet they also have more latitude to make racially inflammatory comments without generating backlash. Since racial and ethnic minorities are presumed to be preoccupied with the interests of other people of color, even when racial and ethnic minority candidates make negative comments about other people of color, they face less scrutiny and backlash.

Racial Distancing in 2020 and Beyond

After sweeping midterm losses in 2010 and 2014, the Democratic Party issued a postmortem report, pointedly noting that it needed to figure out ways to win over more Southern white voters. Although an appeal to Southern white voters does not necessarily have to entail an appeal to racial conservatism, research indicates that many white Southerners left the Democratic Party precisely because of the party's reputation for looking out for the interests of racial and ethnic minorities (Carmines and Stimson 1989). More recently, Trump's ability to outperform Clinton among white voters across demographic categories, but especially among working-class whites, has renewed the party's interest in courting the votes of white Americans. Pointing to these recent electoral losses, several Democratic Party elites have called for the party to abandon identity politics and go "back to the center" (Penn and Stein 2017; Lilla 2016). Ironically, these calls to abandon identity politics and focus on appeals to working-class whites ignore the fact that appealing to working-class whites is also identity politics (Jardina 2019).

Columbia University professor Mark Lilla, for example, has been a prominent voice calling for the Democratic Party to abandon identity politics. He blames Hillary Clinton's defeat on Clinton's appeals to identity: "Every time Hillary Clinton went out on the stump, she would call out to various groups, to women, to Latinos, to African Americans, to immigrants. She left out about 40 percent of the country in doing that, and she lost people: 51 percent of American women voted for Donald Trump."[6] In a similar vein, Democratic congresswoman Debbie Dingell said, "We've [Democrats] become this identity politics. The Women's Caucus, the Black Caucus, the Hispanic Caucus. We've lost the sense of 'we,' that our strength comes in community."[7] Related comments from 2016 presidential candidate Bernie Sanders after the election also seem to eschew "identity politics": "One of the struggles you're going to be seeing in the Democratic Party is whether we go beyond identity politics."[8] Thus, a common thread in the comments of Lilla, Dingell, and Sanders is the idea that appeals to the identities of racial and ethnic minorities are bad for the Democratic Party's brand.

Calls for the abandonment of identity politics suggest that there may be a renewed focus on appeals that signal that the Democratic Party will not be preoccupied with the interests of racial and ethnic minorities. Historically, risk-averse party leaders who have been interested in making the party appear more "centrist" have gone to great lengths to distance the party from African Americans (Frymer 1999). Previous manifestations of this behavior include the Democratic Party's efforts to reach out to "Reagan Democrats" and to rebrand the party as the "New Democrats," after high-profile presidential election losses in 1980, 1984, and 1988. In the wake of the Democrats' defeat in 2016, history is likely to repeat itself with similar efforts. Many Democratic Party elites perceive the party's association with racial and ethnic minorities as a liability. Therefore, we may see behavior from the Democratic Party that signals that the party will not disrupt the racial status quo. These efforts may include appeals that play to negative stereotypes of racial and ethnic minorities, or more subtle efforts to trespass on and "own" racialized issues that have typically been "owned" by the Republican Party, such as welfare and crime.

Yet, how do we reconcile the Democratic Party's concern with appealing to working-class whites with a 2020 Democratic presidential primary field in which the party seems increasingly drawn to the left? Contenders for the Democratic presidential nomination, for example, are being asked to state where they stand on racial issues like reparations for slavery for African Americans. Some politicians, such as Senators Elizabeth Warren (D-MA) and Kirsten Gillibrand (D-NY), have even launched their candidacies with explicit discussions of racial inequalities and racial justice, while Senator Cory Booker (D-NJ) has introduced a bill to the Senate that would study reparations. It is worth noting, however, that the Democratic primary electorate looks very different from the general election electorate, which is older, whiter, and more racially conservative. In other words, messages that might work in the Democratic primaries might not be sufficient to garner support from white Americans in the general election. Secondly, previous research indicates that there is a wide gap between white Democratic voters and their black counterparts, with white Democrats being far more conservative on racial policy issues than African Americans (Hutchings 2009). Therefore, it remains to be seen whether white Democratic voters will be supportive of these racially liberal stances from Democratic presidential candidates. I hypothesize that the candidate who wins the plurality of white American votes in the 2020 general election is likely a candidate who has sufficiently demonstrated that he is not beholden to racial and ethnic minorities.

The results discussed throughout this book indicate that many white Americans are quite comfortable with politicians who make explicit appeals, and this is not a phenomenon that simply arose as part of a Trump run for president. One of the most consistent findings of this book is that racial conservatives and racial moderates were actually not perturbed by openly racial appeals. Research in political science has long established that through the *democratic* electoral process, attitudes of prejudice, to the extent that they are widely shared, can be activated and subsequently linked to important political choices. This book builds upon that work by demonstrating that these attitudes of prejudice can be exploited by the politicians whom we would least expect to make appeals to racial prejudice—black politicians and white Democrats. The results discussed throughout the book also demonstrate that across time and across studies, white Americans are more receptive to messages that openly disparage blacks, contrary to what some previous research suggested. White racial liberals, in some instances, were no more likely to withdraw electoral support from a black candidate with an explicit appeal than they were from a black candidate with an implicit appeal. Conversely, white racial conservatives became remarkably *more* supportive of candidates who espoused explicit racial messages, especially when the messenger was black. The prohibition on explicit racial appeals was most consistently applied when the messenger was white and Republican. Thus, both major parties may be incentivized to field candidates of color who can espouse racially conservative messages, with less fear of generating a backlash than their white counterparts.

For many politicians and pundits, the election of President Donald Trump seemed to herald a new era in American politics, marked by racial vitriol and openly racist appeals. A focus on President Trump, or even Republican politicians more generally, however, obscures the ways in which a wider range of politicians also exploits racial animus for political gain. In short, the political strategy of distancing from racial and ethnic minorities is arguably more pervasive than previously thought. Focusing on Trump also obscures the fact that many Americans have been comfortable with explicit racial appeals since long before 2016. Evidence in this book dating as far back as 2011 indicates that many white racial moderates and racial conservatives were actually quite comfortable with a candidate who espoused openly negative messages about African Americans.[9] This finding was true whether the candidate making the appeal was white or African American. Not only were racially moderate and racially conservative whites unperturbed, but in some instances, they were actually *more* supportive of candidates, especially black candidates, who made these types of appeals. At the same time, racially liberal whites were far less likely to punish a black candidate with an explicit racial appeal than a white candidate with an identical message.

Two additional factors in the discussion of racial distancing merit specific attention. First, the findings of this book are troubling for American politics, specifically for norms around racial discourse. The results indicate that politicians receive more electoral support from a significant fraction of whites when they invoke stereotypes about blacks. These findings likely also apply to other marginalized groups, and reveal a political discourse in which many white Americans will be receptive to messages that at the very least suggest that some groups are more in need of personal responsibility. At the very worst, the findings suggest that politicians are rewarded for keeping the racial hierarchy intact.

Secondly, I would be remiss if I did not mention that by no means are politicians *forced* to engage in a strategy of racial distancing. The Democrats, in particular, could devote attention to messages that would mobilize and energize voters of color, rather than focusing on an increasingly elusive racially moderate to racially conservative white voter. Hajnal and Lee (2011), for example, provide ample evidence of the two major parties' failure to mobilize voters of color. It remains to be seen whether this strategy will be pursued in the near future. As of now, discussions of electability suggest that some Democratic voters and party leaders are worried about nominating a presidential candidate who is perceived as too far outside the mainstream, and this likely extends to racial matters as well.

Both major parties are interested in appealing to white voters—the majority of whom are moderate or conservative on matters of race. Republican politicians are therefore incentivized to invoke race to highlight their reputational advantage among whites for maintaining and enforcing the racial hierarchy. Conversely, Democrats—especially Democratic politicians of color—are incentivized to invoke race to help overcome the perception among some white voters that they will be beholden to racial and ethnic minorities. The implications of this trend among politicians of both parties are troubling for our democracy. In short, a strategy of exclusion rather than inclusion is associated with more electoral support from many white Americans, even as the country becomes ever more racially, ethnically, and religiously diverse.

Appendix

Likelihood of Voting for the Candidate as a Function of Racial Resentment (Baseline=Deracialized Condition)

	Likely vote
Implicit	−3.34
	(8.04)
Explicit	−6.14
	(7.73)
Racial resentment	−29.99***
	(10.29)
Implicit/Racial resentment	29.62**
	(13.21)
Explicit/Racial resentment	39.04***
	(12.52)
Education	−1.65
	(4.39)
Ideology	2.76
	(6.58)
Partisanship	−12.48**
	(4.86)
Gender	−4.16
	(2.50)
Region	0.58
	(1.22)
Age	0.20**
	(0.07)
Constant	66.03***
	(9.46)
N	508
R squared	0.13

Source: 2016 GfK Deracialization Study.

Note: Standard errors in parentheses. All variables coded 0 to 1, with higher values indicating more support for the variable in question. Entries are coefficients from an OLS model that includes controls for education, ideology, partisan identification, gender, region (residence in the South), and age. All explanatory variables are coded from 0 to 1, with 1 being the highest value.

*** $p < .01$; ** $p < .05$; * $p < .10$ for a two-tailed test.

TABLE A.4.2 **Likelihood of Voting for the Candidate as a Function of Negative Stereotype Endorsement (Baseline=Deracialized Condition)**

	Likely vote
Implicit	10.17
	(7.56)
Explicit	8.78
	(6.95)
Negative stereotype endorsement	−3.01
	(7.36)
Implicit/Negative stereotype endorsement	6.45
	(11.33)
Explicit/Negative stereotype endorsement	13.11
	(10.16)
Education	0.31
	(4.37)
Ideology	−2.39
	(6.41)
Partisanship	−11.31**
	(4.73)
Gender	−2.91
	(2.54)
Region	1.39
	(1.27)
Age	0.22***
	(0.07)
Constant	46.91***
	(8.78)
N	502
R squared	0.12

Source: 2016 GfK Deracialization Study.

Note: Standard errors in parentheses. All variables coded 0 to 1, with higher values indicating more support for the variable in question. Entries are coefficients from an OLS model that includes controls for education, ideology, partisan identification, gender, region (residence in the South), and age. All explanatory variables are coded from 0 to 1, with 1 being the highest value.

*** $p < .01$; ** $p < .05$; * $p < .10$ for a two-tailed test.

TABLE A.5.1 **Effects of Democratic Candidate Race and Message Type by Negative Stereotype Endorsement on Likely Vote**

	Likely vote
Black Democratic candidate	5.97
	(8.36)
Explicit	−17.41*
	(9.40)
Black Democratic candidate/Explicit	2.57
	(12.75)
Negative stereotype endorsement	−7.01
	(9.94)
Black Democratic candidate/Negative stereotype endorsement	0.03
	(12.46)
Explicit/Negative stereotype endorsement	19.26
	(14.05)
Black Democratic candidate/Explicit/ Negative stereotype endorsement	18.68
	(18.75)
Education	1.03
	(3.30)
Ideology	6.60
	(9.00)
Partisanship	4.39
	(6.17)
Gender	−3.15
	(3.19)
Region	0.86
	(3.28)
Age	0.04
	(0.11)
Constant	42.48***
	(10.89)
N	548
R squared	0.10

Source: 2018 YouGov Study.

Note: Standard errors in parentheses. All variables coded 0 to 1, with higher values indicating more support for the variable in question. Entries are coefficients from an OLS model that includes controls for education, ideology, partisan identification, gender, region (residence in the South), and age. All explanatory variables are coded from 0 to 1, with 1 being the highest value.

*** $p < .01$; ** $p < .05$; * $p < .10$ for a two-tailed test.

TABLE A.5.2 **Effects of Republican Candidate Race and Message Type by Negative Stereotype Endorsement on Likely Vote**

	Likely vote
Black Republican candidate	1.46
	(8.03)
Explicit	−28.26***
	(7.64)
Black Republican candidate/Explicit	21.63**
	(9.61)
Negative stereotype endorsement	8.83
	(8.91)
Black Republican candidate/Negative stereotype endorsement	0.86
	(12.09)
Explicit/Negative stereotype endorsement	26.13**
	(10.90)
Black Republican candidate/Explicit/Negative stereotype endorsement	−12.37
	(14.74)
Education	3.77
	(2.31)
Ideology	40.88***
	(5.45)
Partisanship	30.64***
	(4.76)
Gender	−3.33
	(2.15)
Region	−2.93
	(2.34)
Age	0.14
	(0.07)
Constant	8.96
	(9.07)
N	550
R squared	0.58

Source: 2018 YouGov Study.

Note: Standard errors in parentheses. All variables coded 0 to 1, with higher values indicating more support for the variable in question. Entries are coefficients from an OLS model that includes controls for education, ideology, partisan identification, gender, region (residence in the South), and age. All explanatory variables are coded from 0 to 1, with 1 being the highest value.

*** $p < .01$; ** $p < .05$; * $p < .10$ for a two-tailed test.

TABLE A.5.3 **Likelihood of Voting for the Candidate as a Function of Racial Resentment (Baseline=Explicit Condition)**

	Likely vote for black Democratic candidate	Likely vote for white Democratic candidate
Black implicit	1.28 (1.15)	—
White implicit		2.41** (1.10)
Racial resentment	2.32 (1.78)	2.37* (1.31)
Black implicit/Racial resentment	−2.24 (1.88)	—
White implicit/Racial resentment	—	−2.52 (1.57)
Education	0.97* (0.56)	−0.19 (0.51)
Ideology	−1.54* (1.10)	1.24 (0.79)
Partisanship	0.23 (0.80)	−0.42 (0.58)
Gender	0.24 (0.37)	−0.73** (0.33)
Region	0.37 (0.42)	−0.18 (0.33)
Age	−0.01 (0.01)	−0.01 (0.01)
Cut 1	−0.87 (1.13)	1.17 (1.42)
Cut 2	1.32 (1.18)	2.97 (1.43)
Log likelihood	−185.79	−158.69
N	184	169

Source: 2011 GfK Study.

Note: Standard errors in parentheses. All variables coded 0 to 1, with higher values indicating more support for the variable in question. Entries are ordered logit coefficients from a model that includes controls for education, ideology, partisan identification, gender, region (residence in the South), and age. All explanatory variables are coded from 0 to 1, with 1 being the highest value.

*** $p < .01$; ** $p < .05$; * $p < .10$ for a two-tailed test.

TABLE A.5.4 **Respondents' Support for Decreasing Funding to Reduce the Racial Achievement Gap (Baseline=Implicit Condition)**

	Perception that funding to help black students achieve should be reduced (Black candidate)	Perception that funding to help black students achieve should be reduced (White candidate)
Black explicit	0.67* (0.35)	—
White explicit	—	−0.27 (0.38)
Education	−0.67 (0.53)	−0.21 (0.58)
Ideology	0.50 (1.06)	1.37 (1.06)
Partisanship	2.46** (0.72)	1.46** (0.58)
Gender	0.40 (0.36)	1.03*** (0.36)
Region	0.41 (0.41)	−0.27 (0.40)
Age	−0.02 (0.01)	0.00 (0.01)
Cut 1	−0.47 (0.72)	0.44 (0.90)
Cut 2	2.68 (0.74)	3.17 (0.97)
N	188	168

Source: 2011 GFK Study.

Note: Standard errors in parentheses. All variables coded 0 to 1, with higher values indicating more support for the variable in question. Entries are ordered logit coefficients from a model that includes controls for education, ideology, partisan identification, gender, region (residence in the South), and age. All explanatory variables are coded from 0 to 1, with 1 being the highest value.

*** $p < .01$; ** $p < .05$; * $p < .10$ for a two-tailed test.

Effect of Black Inclusion on Likely Vote for Candidate

	White Democratic candidate	Black Democratic candidate	White Republican candidate	Black Republican candidate
Candidate w/ mixed group	−0.54*	−0.11	−0.15	−0.15
	(0.35)	(0.35)	(0.37)	(0.38)
Candidate w/ all blacks	−0.82**	0.29	−0.10	−0.01
	(0.38)	(0.35)	(0.35)	(0.35)
Education	−0.92*	1.36***	−0.04	0.68*
	(0.57)	(0.49)	(0.56)	(0.48)
Gender	−0.70**	−0.54**	0.12	0.17
	(0.33)	(0.31)	(0.29)	(0.29)
Partisanship	−2.85***	−2.73***	2.66***	1.47***
	(0.49)	(0.54)	(0.50)	(0.43)
Income	0.09**	−0.03	−0.01	0.04
	(0.05)	(0.04)	(0.04)	(0.04)
Region	0.11	−0.64**	−0.14	−0.10
	(0.32)	(0.32)	(0.33)	(0.34)
Cut 1	−3.18	−3.25	−0.37	−0.08
	(0.62)	(0.64)	(0.50)	(0.51)
Cut 2	−1.34	−1.00	1.82	1.83
	(0.57)	(0.58)	(0.54)	(0.52)
Cut 3	1.73	2.17	4.61	4.23
	(0.63)	(0.63)	(0.70)	(0.62)
Log likelihood	−184.07	−179.17	−194.34	−203.19
N	173	175	178	172

Source: 2012 YouGov Campaign Mailer Study.

Note: Standard errors in parentheses. All variables coded 0 to 1, with higher values indicating more support for the variable in question. Entries are ordered logit coefficients from a model that includes controls for education, gender, partisan identification, income, and region (residence in the South). All explanatory variables are coded from 0 to 1, with 1 being the highest value.

*** $p < .01$; ** $p < .05$; * $p < .10$ for a one-tailed test.

TABLE A.6.2 **Effect of Black Inclusion on Perception That Candidate Will Support Affirmative Action**

	White Democratic candidate	Black Democratic candidate	White Republican candidate	Black Republican candidate
Candidate w/ mixed group	2.05***	0.31	0.78**	−0.18
	(0.66)	(0.49)	(0.40)	(0.41)
Candidate w/ all blacks	2.21***	0.64*	0.75**	0.35
	(0.61)	(0.47)	(0.41)	(0.40)
Education	1.56**	0.46	−0.66	−0.70
	(0.69)	(0.61)	(0.60)	(0.55)
Gender	0.30	0.22	−0.62**	−0.15
	(0.40)	(0.37)	(0.35)	(0.37)
Partisanship	1.63***	0.71*	0.75*	1.62***
	(0.58)	(0.46)	(0.44)	(0.54)
Income	−0.17***	−0.05	−0.00	−0.05
	(0.05)	(0.05)	(0.04)	(0.04)
Region	−0.04	0.84**	0.04	−0.08
	(0.46)	(0.38)	(0.45)	(0.42)
Cut 1	−3.31	−4.36	−1.23	−2.65
	(0.85)	(1.34)	(0.51)	(0.54)
Cut 2	3.38	1.92	2.47	1.42
	(0.87)	(0.72)	(0.56)	(0.52)
Log likelihood	−81.53	−95.26	−133.54	−122.24
N	166	165	169	166

Source: 2012 YouGov Campaign Mailer Study.

Note: Standard errors in parentheses. All variables coded 0 to 1, with higher values indicating more support for the variable in question. Entries are ordered logit coefficients from a model that includes controls for education, gender, partisan identification, income, and region (residence in the South). All explanatory variables are coded from 0 to 1, with 1 being the highest value.

*** $p < .01$; ** $p < .05$; * $p < .10$ for a one-tailed test.

TABLE A.6.3 **Effect of Black Inclusion on Perception That Candidate Will Favor Blacks over Whites**

	White Democratic candidate	Black Democratic candidate	White Republican candidate	Black Republican candidate
Candidate w/ mixed group	1.41***	−0.15	0.57*	0.37
	(0.52)	(0.47)	(0.41)	(0.44)
Candidate w/ all blacks	2.39***	−0.04	0.76**	0.99**
	(0.52)	(0.47)	(0.41)	(0.42)
Education	0.40	−1.88**	−1.16**	0.00
	(0.65)	(0.84)	(0.62)	(0.60)
Gender	0.50	0.00	−0.25	−0.46
	(0.42)	(0.39)	(0.33)	(0.38)
Partisanship	2.27***	2.35***	1.70***	1.44***
	(0.59)	(0.52)	(0.49)	(0.54)
Income	−0.07	0.03	0.06*	−0.12***
	(0.06)	(0.06)	(0.04)	(0.04)
Region	−0.17	1.03**	−0.05	0.87**
	(0.39)	(0.45)	(0.38)	(0.43)
Cut 1	−0.51	−4.36	0.02	−2.91
	(0.65)	(0.92)	(0.63)	(0.61)
Cut 2	4.37	2.32	3.80	1.71
	(0.78)	(0.71)	(0.76)	(0.55)
Log likelihood	−106.24	−87.72	−134.48	−113.94
N	168	170	173	173

Source: 2012 YouGov Campaign Mailer Study.

Note: Standard errors in parentheses. All variables coded 0 to 1, with higher values indicating more support for the variable in question. Entries are ordered logit coefficients from a model that includes controls for education, gender, partisan identification, income, and region (residence in the South). All explanatory variables are coded from 0 to 1, with 1 being the highest value.

*** $p < .01$; ** $p < .05$; * $p < .10$ for a one-tailed test.

Effect of Black Inclusion on Perception That Candidate Is Conservative

	White Democratic candidate	Black Democratic candidate	White Republican candidate	Black Republican candidate
Candidate w/ mixed group	0.63*	0.15	0.32	0.07
	(0.40)	(0.38)	(0.39)	(0.38)
Candidate w/ all blacks	0.76**	0.36	0.47	0.03
	(0.42)	(0.42)	(0.36)	(0.36)
Education	1.32	1.12	−0.62	0.37
	(0.65)	(0.60)	(0.56)	(0.54)
Gender	0.87	0.57**	0.02	−0.05
	(0.36)	(0.33)	(0.31)	(0.30)
Partisanship	0.84**	1.64	0.14	0.73**
	(0.47)	(0.49)	(0.42)	(0.43)
Income	−0.04	0.03	0.06	−0.02
	(0.04)	(0.04)	(0.04)	(0.04)
Region	−0.22	−0.14	−0.47	−0.17
	(0.36)	(0.36)	(0.39)	(0.34)
Cut 1	−1.06	−0.86	0.50	−0.09
	(0.52)	(0.54)	(0.48)	(0.48)
Cut 2	1.00	1.92	2.26	1.84
	(0.55)	(0.56)	(0.50)	(0.50)
Log likelihood	−139.59	−137.14	−169.06	−179.42
N	169	168	171	173

Source: 2012 YouGov Campaign Mailer Study.

Note: Standard errors in parentheses. All variables coded 0 to 1, with higher values indicating more support for the variable in question. Entries are ordered logit coefficients from a model that includes controls for education, gender, partisan identification, income, and region (residence in the South). All explanatory variables are coded from 0 to 1, with 1 being the highest value.

*** $p < .01$; ** $p < .05$; * $p < .10$ for a one-tailed test.

TABLE A.6.5 **Effect of Black Inclusion on Likely Vote as a Function of Racial Resentment**

	White Democratic candidate	Black Democratic candidate	White Republican candidate	Black Republican candidate
Candidate w/ mixed group	2.08	0.48	2.65	−0.53
	(1.81)	(1.47)	(2.33)	(1.98)
Candidate w/ all blacks	2.58*	−0.97	1.40	−0.86
	(1.83)	(1.33)	(1.89)	(1.54)
Candidate w/ mixed group/ Racial resentment	−4.33*	−0.94	−4.52	0.59
	(2.88)	(2.44)	(3.60)	(2.96)
Candidate w/ all blacks/ Racial resentment	−5.68**	2.07	−2.42	1.45
	(2.94)	(2.37)	(3.06)	(2.48)
Racial resentment	1.01	−4.69**	4.90**	0.18
	(2.14)	(2.07)	(2.80)	(2.08)
Education	−0.84*	1.08**	0.24	0.67*
	(0.57)	(0.49)	(0.56)	(0.48)
Gender	−0.78**	−0.50*	0.04	0.17
	(0.34)	(0.31)	(0.29)	(0.29)
Partisanship	−2.49***	−2.08***	2.29***	1.26**
	(0.53)	(0.56)	(0.50)	(0.50)
Income	0.09**	−0.02	−0.01	0.05
	(0.05)	(0.04)	(0.04)	(0.04)
Region	0.10	−0.60**	−0.19	−0.11
	(0.33)	(0.32)	(0.34)	(0.34)
Cut 1	−2.43	−5.84	2.49	−0.06
	(1.43)	(1.30)	(1.78)	(1.40)
Cut 2	−0.52	−3.46	4.74	1.86
	(1.40)	(1.22)	(1.86)	(1.42)
Cut 3	2.60	−0.10	7.58	4.27
	(1.42)	(1.16)	(2.01)	(1.51)
Log likelihood	−179.81	−172.35	−191.31	−202.72
N	173	175	178	172

Source: 2012 YouGov Campaign Mailer Study.

Note: Standard errors in parentheses. All variables coded 0 to 1, with higher values indicating more support for the variable in question. Entries are ordered logit coefficients from a model that includes controls for education, gender, partisan identification, income, and region (residence in the South). All explanatory variables are coded from 0 to 1, with 1 being the highest value.

*** $p < .01$; ** $p < .05$; * $p < .10$ for a one-tailed test.

Acknowledgments

Wow! I cannot believe that this is finally finished. Of course, any researcher will tell you that "it" is never really finished, but you get the point. First things first—Thank you, Jesus. It was my Lord and Savior, Jesus Christ, who sustained me through the long, arduous process of writing this book, and I can honestly say that I would not have completed this book without Him. It feels kind of weird to write that in an academic context, but it's the truth.

Next, thank you to my family—especially my husband, Kwame, my daughter, Zadie, and my mom, Artilda. They put up with a lot during this process, but they each brightened the long days in their own special way. From home renovations gone amok to multiple moves, broken computers, and even a cancer scare, my family "held me down" throughout the process of writing this book and through the general ups and downs of life. Words cannot express how grateful I am for them and for their unwavering belief in me and my ability to complete this project. I also want to thank other members of my family, whose prayers, words of encouragement, and healthy distractions helped me along the way: Auntie Joyce, Uncle Allan, Uncle Fred, Aunt Enid, Ivan Stephens Jr., Dara Simmons, and Georgina Anderson.

A special debt of gratitude is also owed to my friends, many of whom are basically my family. Friends who either prayed for me or sent me encouraging texts and gifts throughout this process: Allison Anika, Ginette Azcona-Santana, Andrea Benjamin, LaToya Branch, Chinbo Chong, Jennifer Chudy (she read the entire thing!), Nyron Crawford, Vanessa Cruz Nichols, Menna Demessie, Michele Epstein, Keith Gibson, Andra Gillespie, Christina Greer, Shayla Griffin, Bai Linh Hoang, Ashley Jardina, Jackie Yu Johnson, Maria Johnson, Jennifer Maddox,

Dana Moorhead, Gbenga Olumolade, Monique Peters, Davin Phoenix (he read the entire thing!), Daniela Pineda, Melanye Price, Melynda Price, Helen Ray, Tonya Rice, Andre Rivera, Zawadi Rucks-Ahidiana, and Sophia Jordán Wallace. I am also thankful to all of the women from my BSF groups over the years.

As you can probably guess by now, I am blessed in many respects. One huge blessing is the opportunity to have studied race and politics at the University of Michigan. I am so grateful that I had the opportunity to learn and develop there. I am also thankful that I had the chance to join the ranks of the professional network, affectionately referred to as "The Michigan Mafia." Members of the Michigan Mafia read drafts of chapters, pointed me toward data sources, or gave feedback that helped me think about the narrative. Thank you to Antoine Banks, Allison Dale-Riddle, Marty Davidson, LaGina Gause, Hakeem Jefferson, Nathan Kalmoe, Michael Minta, Spencer Piston, Leanne Powner, Ismail White, and Princess Williams.

Some of the most formative people during my time at the University of Michigan included Nancy Burns, Richard Hall, Vincent Hutchings, Nicholas Valentino, and Hanes Walton Jr. I am especially thankful for Vince, who for some reason continues to take my calls. He is a wonderful mentor and friend. I could never repay him, so my only hope is that I can pay it forward.

My work has also benefited tremendously from my time at Princeton University. I am thankful to my colleagues at Princeton for offering feedback at various stages of the project, especially Chris Achen, Wendy Belcher, Rafaela Dancygier, Paul Frymer, Amaney Jamal, Tali Mendelberg, Markus Prior, Dara Strolovitch, Ali Valenzuela, and Omar Wasow. During his year at the Center for the Study of Democratic Politics, Jake Grumbach was also very helpful to me. I am also very appreciative of Jeremy Darrington, who was always willing to answer random questions about obscure sources of data.

Extremely talented graduate and undergraduate research assistants at Princeton University have also helped to bring this project to fruition. Thank you to Quinn Albaugh, Chaya Crowder, Risa Gelles-Watnick, June Hwang, Marcus Johnson, Naijia Liu, Natalie McGowen, Chinemelu Okafor, Andrew Proctor, Jessica Quinter, Tanika Raychaudhuri, Courtney Wax, and Ryan Zhang. Chaya deserves special gratitude for offering the right balance of levity and hard work. Sarah Chihaya, Tod Hamilton, Renita Miller, and Leslie Wingard are all friends I met at Princeton, but whose friendship is not confined to a particular place or institution—thank you for your support.

The manuscript conference sponsored by the Mamdouha S. Bobst Center at Princeton University was a game changer, enabling me to receive feedback on the manuscript from luminaries in the field, including Daniel Gillion, Leonie Huddy, Taeku Lee, and Michael Tesler. A special thanks also goes to Wendy Brill for her superb organizational skills. The manuscript also benefited from feedback that I received at presentations at Columbia University, Cornell University, the University of California at Berkeley, Northwestern University, The University of Pennsylvania, and the Center for the Study of Democratic Politics at Princeton.

Another game changer during the course of writing this book was the opportunity to spend a year at the Hutchins Center for African and African American Research at Harvard University. I am especially thankful to Skip Gates, Krishna Lewis, and Abby Wolf for allowing me to defer the fellowship for a year while I tended to the tasks of being a new mother.

I still cannot believe that this book is being published by my dream press—the University of Chicago Press. Thank you to Adam Berinsky, Susan Karani, Chuck Myers, Marian Rogers, and Alicia Sparrow for helping to make my dream a reality. Also, thank you to the anonymous reviewers, whose feedback made the book much better.

Finally, this project would not have been possible without the generous financial support of the University of Michigan Gerald R. Ford Presidential Fellowship, the Rackham Graduate School at the University of Michigan, the National Science Foundation's Time-sharing Experiments for the Social Sciences, the Alliances for Graduate Education and the Professoriate, the Center for the Study of Democratic Politics at Princeton University, the Princeton University Fund for Experimental Social Science, and the Princeton University Committee on Research in the Humanities and Social Sciences.

As you can see, there is no way that I could have done this on my own. I am thankful to everyone who has helped me on this journey. Any weaknesses of the manuscript can be attributed solely to me, but all of the strengths come from my wonderful community of family, friends, and colleagues. Thank you.

Notes

Chapter One

1. For a complete transcript of Obama's comments about Trayvon Martin and the acquittal of George Zimmerman, see "Remarks by the President on Trayvon Martin," July 19, 2013, https://obamawhitehouse.archives.gov/the-press-office/2013/07/19/remarks-president-trayvon-martin.

2. "Transcript: Obama's Remarks on Ferguson Grand Jury Decision," *Washington Post*, November 24, 2014, https://www.washingtonpost.com/politics/transcript-obamas-remarks-on-ferguson-grand-jury-decision/2014/11/24/afc3b38e-744f-11e4-bd1b-03009bd3e984_story.html?utm_term=.ca95f99a722e.

3. "Remarks by President Obama and Prime Minister Abe of Japan in Joint Press Conference," April 28, 2015, https://obamawhitehouse.archives.gov/the-press-office/2015/04/28/remarks-president-obama-and-prime-minister-abe-japan-joint-press-confere (emphasis added).

4. Bill Chappell, "Obama: 'No Sympathy' for Those Destroying Ferguson," NPR, November 26, 2014, https://www.npr.org/sections/thetwo-way/2014/11/25/366650380/obama-no-sympathy-for-those-destroying-ferguson.

5. Melissa Block, "The Racially Charged Meaning behind the Word 'Thug,'" *All Things Considered*, NPR, April 30, 2015.

6. Jennifer Ludden, "Baltimore Mayor Condemns Violent Protesters at Press Conference," *All Things Considered*, NPR, April 27, 2015, https://www.npr.org/2015/04/27/402661448/baltimore-mayor-condemns-violent-protesters-at-press-conference (emphasis added).

7. Erin Cox and Michael Dresser, "Gov. Larry Hogan Promises More Than 1,000 Additional Troops, Vows to Prevent Rioting," *Baltimore Sun*, April 28, 2015, https://www.baltimoresun.com/news/maryland/politics/blog/bal-hogan-in-baltimore-vows-to-bring-rioting-under-control-20150428-story.html (emphasis added).

8. Josh Levs, "Baltimore Councilman Tells CNN: 'Thug' Is New N-word."

CNN, April 29, 2015, https://www.cnn.com/2015/04/29/us/baltimore-riots-thug-n
-word/index.html.

9. Block, "The Word 'Thug.'"

10. Paul Schwartzman and Ovetta Wiggins, "In Baltimore, Questions about
Policing Ensnare Mayors Past and Present," *Washington Post*, April 28, 2015,
https://www.washingtonpost.com/local/md-politics/in-baltimore-a-political
-test-for-a-mayor--and-a-new-governor/2015/04/28/be3233c4-ed4d-11e4-a55f
-38924fca94f9_story.html?utm_term=.6c33304b69da.

11. McIlwain and Caliendo (2011) offer a broader theoretical account of race-
based appeals, but they reject the notion that candidates of color would use negative racial appeals about other people of color: "Put simply, we see very little evidence to suggest that minority candidates have any interest in appealing
to negative stereotypes, resentments, and prejudices associated with the racial
group to which they belong" (17).

12. I am not advocating this as a strategy, but it is evident that some black candidates have already embraced these types of appeals as a part of their electoral
tool kit.

13. "Cousin Pookie is a fictional, irresponsible, stand-in for anyone's black
relative, who[m] Obama has described as 'sitting on the couch.'" Nia-Malika
Henderson, "Cousin Pookie Is Back! And Yes, He Is Still Sitting on the Couch,"
Washington Post, October 20, 2014, https://www.washingtonpost.com/news/
the-fix/wp/2014/10/20/cousin-pookie-is-back-and-yes-he-is-still-sitting-on-the
-couch/?utm_term=.378f7ec9d245.

14. Henderson, "Cousin Pookie Is Back!"

15. "Obama's Father's Day Remarks," *New York Times*, June 15, 2008, https://
www.nytimes.com/2008/06/15/us/politics/15text-obama.html.

16. Julie Bosman, "Obama Sharply Assails Absent Black Fathers," *New York
Times*, June 16, 2008, https://www.nytimes.com/2008/06/16/us/politics/15cnd
-obama.html.

17. Frank James, "Obama's 'Stop Complaining' Order to Black Caucus Causes Stir," NPR, September 26, 2011, https://www.npr.org/sections/
itsallpolitics/2011/09/26/140802831/obama-stop-complaining-order-to-cbc-fires
-up-some-folks.

18. Sheryl Gay Stolberg, "Obama Speaks at N.A.A.C.P. Celebration," *New
York Times*, July 16, 2009, https://www.nytimes.com/2009/07/17/us/politics/
17obama.html.

19. Stolberg, "Obama Speaks at N.A.A.C.P. Celebration."

20. While on the campaign trail Obama often spoke about his admiration
for Reagan, which in and of itself was likely a racial signal. See also Robert G.
Kaiser, "On Welfare: Democrat Bullish, Republican Bearish (but Less Now),"
Washington Post, October 23, 1980, https://www.washingtonpost.com/archive/

politics/1980/10/23/on-welfare-democrat-bullish-republican-bearish-but-less
-now/d3c7899e-cd6b-461f-911d-718c86c2c6a9/?utm_term=.0795ab68f3ee.

21. "Obama Tells Black Fathers to Engage Their Kids," NBCNews.com, NBC Universal News Group, June 16, 2008, http://www.nbcnews.com/id/ 25176204/ns/politics-decision_08/t/obama-tells-black-fathers-engage-their-kids/ #.XUNAklB7nnQ.

22. Bosman, "Obama Sharply Assails Absent Black Fathers."

23. Although politicians may be incentivized to distance from a variety of minority groups, for the purposes of this book, I mainly focus on distancing from blacks. Black-white relations have long been at the center of American politics and are arguably the most salient racial divide in American politics. African Americans and whites are also the most polarized in terms of partisan affiliation and public opinion on matters of race. However, I do extend elements of racial distancing theory to other racial and ethnic cleavages, where appropriate. For example, I briefly examine signaling with respect to Latino communities.

24. "African American Senators," United States Senate, accessed February 27, 2019, https://www.senate.gov/pagelayout/history/h_multi_sections_and _teasers/Photo_Exhibit_African_American_Senators.htm.

25. "Fast Facts about American Governors," Center on the American Governor, Eagleton Institute of Politics, Rutgers University, New Brunswick, accessed February 27, 2019, http://governors.rutgers.edu/on-governors/us-governors/fast -facts-about-american-governors/.

26. Although, as some have noted, African American politicians are also less likely to run for office in majority-white jurisdictions, which also helps explain the low number of African Americans holding office in majority-white jurisdictions (Highton 2004). Other studies also suggest that the negative effect of race is largely dependent on electoral and candidate context.

27. By "racially liberal whites," I am referring to those white Americans who score below the midpoint of the racial resentment scale, a commonly used metric of white Americans' racial prejudice.

28. Author's calculations from the 2016 American National Election Study; "2016 Time Series Study," ANES | American National Election Studies, accessed March 1, 2019, https://electionstudies.org/project/2016-time-series-study/.

29. Author's calculations from the 2016 American National Election Study.

30. "Georgia 2018 Voter Poll Results," *Washington Post*, November 30, 2018, https://www.washingtonpost.com/graphics/2018/politics/voter-polls/georgia.html ?utm_term=.19d1b90e444c.

31. Author's calculations from the 2016 General Social Survey; "GSS General Social Survey 2016," GSS: The General Social Survey, NORC at the University of Chicago, accessed March 1, 2019, http://gss.norc.org/.

32. Author's calculations from the 2016 American National Election Study.

33. Author's calculations from the 2016 General Social Survey.

34. Ezra Klein, "Romney's Theory of the 'Taker Class,' and Why It Matters." *Washington Post*, September 17, 2012, https://www.washingtonpost.com/news/wonk/wp/2012/09/17/romneys-theory-of-the-taker-class-and-why-it-matters/?utm_term=.88d76cb09168.

35. Kamala Harris, "Attorney General Kamala D. Harris Inaugural Remarks," Office of the Attorney General, State of California Department of Justice, accessed March 1, 2019, https://oag.ca.gov/system/files/attachments/press_releases/n2021_final_speech.pdf.

36. A 2007 survey from Pew found that 61 percent of African Americans felt that the values of middle-class blacks and poor blacks had become more different for each other.

Chapter Two

1. *George Wallace: Settin' the Woods on Fire*, dir. Daniel McCabe and Paul Stekler, perf. Randy Quaid and Pat Buchanan, PBS, January 2000.

2. George Wallace, "Inaugural Address," January 14, 1963, Alabama Department of Archives and History, accessed August 26, 2019, http://digital.archives.alabama.gov/cdm/ref/collection/voices/id/2952.

3. *George Wallace: Settin' the Woods on Fire*.

4. The CCES is a collaborative research effort involving many different research teams, with each team developing a survey questionnaire for a nationally representative sample of approximately 1,000 respondents. All respondents answer a series of Common Content questions. Approximately 650 of the 1,000 respondents in my module were self-identified non-Hispanic whites.

5. Mendelberg (2001, 8) defines an appeal as "explicit" if it uses such words as "blacks," "race," or "racial" to express anti-black sentiment or to make racially stereotypical or derogatory statements.

6. Clinton publicly critiqued Jesse Jackson's Rainbow Coalition for inviting the rapper Sister Souljah to their convention. Souljah had made controversial statements in the past, including allegedly advocating black-on-white violence, of which Clinton was highly critical. Jackson critiqued Clinton for exploiting Souljah to make a headline.

7. This is at least in part driven by the fact that black politicians are increasingly pursuing office in majority-white jurisdictions, where they have to appeal to racially moderate to racially conservative white voters.

8. Since black politicians are overwhelmingly Democrats, it is less clear whether the public has established stereotypes about black Republican politicians. I am agnostic on this point.

9. Since "government aid to blacks" is fundamentally and unambiguously a policy about government spending, it is possible that support for this policy area more accurately rests on principles about the size of government than it does on attitudes about African Americans specifically. Nevertheless, it still enables us to see that for white Americans, the Republican Party is associated with the popular position on this question, while the Democratic Party is associated with the unpopular position.

10. I limit my discussion of the second tenet to black people specifically because societal repudiation of racist and xenophobic rhetoric directed at Latinos and Muslims has arguably not reached the level of repudiation associated with racist rhetoric directed at blacks. Some voters may feel less outraged about racist rhetoric directed at these groups than they would about similar rhetoric directed against blacks, especially given most black Americans' ties to chattel slavery and subjugation in the United States.

11. Even President Trump, who made racially comments throughout his campaign, did not invoke traditional racist rhetoric about African Americans. For example, he frequently referred to African Americans as "the blacks," and conflated "inner-city" with African American, but he never invoked traditional negative stereotypes about blacks as unintelligent, lazy, or sexually promiscuous.

12. Author calculations from the 1986–2016 American National Election Studies.

13. For example, based on my calculations from the 2016 American National Election Study, in 2016 only about 21 percent of white Americans supported "government aid to blacks," including a minority of white Democrats.

14. The order in which the racial groups were presented to the respondents was randomized.

Chapter Three

1. Chris Matthews, "Analyzing Obama's First Inaugural Address," *Hardball*, MSNBC, February 24, 2009.

2. "Third-wave" is a term used to refer to African American politicians who came of age after the civil rights movement. The approach of these politicians to politics is typically more moderate than earlier generations of African American politicians because their approach is not informed by the activist politics of the 1950s and 1960s.

3. There is no record of any poll asking the question of whether other candidates, such as Hillary Clinton or John McCain, would favor blacks over whites, which in and of itself suggests that Obama was more likely to be stereotyped as being beholden to racial and ethnic minorities, relative to his white counterparts.

4. Of course, without a comparison group, it is impossible to know how

much of this perception can be attributed to Obama's race, versus his partisan affiliation.

5. A more contemporary example of the latitude that white candidates may have to speak more publicly about race, relative to candidates of color, is found in the case of Robert Francis "Beto" O'Rourke, a white Democrat who is a 2020 presidential candidate. O'Rourke has made immigration a central part of his campaign, vocally supporting the Dream Act and a path to citizenship for un-documented immigrants. He has also called for the closing of private immigra-tion detention centers, denounced the militarization of immigration enforce-ment, and been a vocal critic of the proposed wall on the U.S.-Mexico border.

6. "Tavis to Michelle Obama: Thanks, but No Thanks," February 14, 2008, http://www.npr.org/blogs/newsandviews/2008/02/tavis_to_michelle_obama _thanks.html (emphasis added).

7. Hillary Clinton attended the event, while John McCain declined the invitation.

8. Paul Farhi, "Tavis Smiley Will Cut Ties with Joyner Radio Show," *Wash-ington Post*, April 12, 2008, http://www.washingtonpost.com/wp-dyn/content/ article/2008/04/11/AR2008041103056.html.

9. "Tavis Smiley Reportedly Quits Radio Show over Obama Hate," *Huffing-ton Post*, May, 25, 2011, http://www.huffingtonpost.com/2008/04/11/tavis-smiley -quits-radio_n_96246.html; Krissah Thompson, "Blacks at Odds over Scrutiny of President," *Washington Post*, April 6, 2009; Farhi, "Tavis Smiley Will Cut Ties with Joyner Radio Show"; Kelefah Sanneh, "What He Knows for Sure," *New Yorker*, August 4, 2008, https://www.newyorker.com/magazine/2008/08/04/ what-he-knows-for-sure.

10. "Race Over?," *Atlantic*, January/February 2009, https://www.theatlantic .com/magazine/archive/2009/01/race-over/307215/.

11. I also validated the WAP coding by reexamining all the ads that had been coded as a racial issue by the WAP content analysis team. Some ads that were classified as racial by WAP but did not meet my definition as racial were recoded by me. For example, they coded ads that mentioned "Medicare" as welfare ads, but Medicare ads did not meet my definition of welfare.

12. "Hands" also known as "White Hands" is a television ad that was aired during the 1990 North Carolina U.S. Senate race. The ad was sponsored by the campaign of the white Republican incumbent, Jesse Helms. "Hands" criticized Helms's African American opponent, Harvey Gantt, for being in favor of "ra-cial quotas."

13. The most prominent attack ad, "Know Enough," was not sponsored by the McCain campaign, but by a PAC called the American Issues Project. Obama's ad "What I Believe" was aired in response to "Know Enough" and makes the claim that "John McCain wants to scare you."

14. "Dignity," Barack Obama Political Advertisement, July 8, 2008, *Politi-*

cal Communication Lab, http://pcl.stanford.edu/campaigns/2008/?adv=Dignity
+-+Barack+Obama+-+Jun+30%2C+2008.

15. "Country I Love," Barack Obama Political Advertisement, June 19, 2008, *Political Communication Lab*, http://pcl.stanford.edu/campaigns/2008/?adv=Country+I+Love+-+Barack+Obama+-+Jun+19%2C+2008 (emphasis added).

16. A content analysis conducted by Hutchings et al. (2014) found that in their sample of television advertisements aired by the Obama campaign, 92 percent of the discernible faces in the Obama ads were white Americans, which far exceeds the share of the population (approximately 65 percent) or the general electorate (74 percent) that was comprised of non-Hispanic whites in 2008 (Abramson et al. 2009). This was also in stark contrast to the percentage of discernible white faces that Hutchings et al. found in the John McCain ads: only 67 percent.

17. Racial distancing theory generates vastly different hypotheses from those generated by the theories of racial priming, deracialization, and issue ownership. The theories of racial priming and issue ownership presume that only Republican candidates are incentivized to inject race into their campaigns by airing ads about implicitly racial topics such as welfare and crime. In the case of racial priming, the goal would be for Republican candidates to make negative racial predispositions about blacks relevant to white voters' decision calculus, whereas for issue ownership, the goal would be for Republicans to run on issues with respect to which their party has a reputational advantage. Deracialization predicts that Democratic candidates would not run ads about welfare or crime, to minimize the racial discourse in the campaign.

18. I also conducted a content analysis of television advertisements from the 2000 and 2004 presidential elections.

19. "Clinton and Obama Unite in Pleas to Blacks," *New York Times*, March 5, 2007, https://www.nytimes.com/2007/03/05/us/politics/05selma.html. For the full text of the speech, see Barack Obama, "Selma Voting Rights March Commemoration," https://americanrhetoric.com/speeches/barackobama/barackobamabrown chapel.htm.

20. Lynn Sweet, "Obama Tells Blacks: Shape Up," *Chicago Sun-Times*, February 29, 2008.

21. For the full text of this speech, see Barack Obama, "A More Perfect Union," March 18, 2008, https://www.npr.org/templates/story/story.php?storyId =88478467.

22. Number determined from author's content analysis of Obama speeches.

23. "Remarks by the President to the NAACP Centennial Convention," July 17, 2009, https://obamawhitehouse.archives.gov/the-press-office/remarks -president-naacp-centennial-convention-07162009.

24. "President Obama Delivers Morehouse College Commencement Address," May 20, 2013, https://obamawhitehouse.archives.gov/photos-and-video/

video/2013/05/20/president-obama-delivers-morehouse-college-commencement
-address.

25. Jackson made this comment to another guest during a break in an interview with Fox News on July 6, 2008.

26. "Obama's Father's Day Remarks."

27. Clarence Page, for example, has argued that the turning point in the 1992 presidential election came when Bill Clinton publicly criticized Jesse Jackson's Rainbow Coalition for giving a platform to rapper Sister Souljah, who had spoken favorably about blacks killing whites instead of each other. Although Jackson criticized Clinton for exploiting the occasion to make a headline, the critique from Jackson may have only helped further bolster Clinton's popularity among whites. Clarence Page, "Bill Clinton's Debt to Sista Souljah," *Chicago Tribune*, October 28, 1992.

28. Pew Research Center, "Gaffes Drove the Campaign Narrative Last Week," July 13, 2008, https://www.journalism.org/2008/07/11/pej-campaign -coverage-index-july-7-13-2008/.

29. For a full transcript of Obama's speech, see "Remarks by the President at the Congressional Black Caucus Foundation Annual Phoenix Awards Dinner," https://obamawhitehouse.archives.gov/the-press-office/2011/09/24/remarks -president-congressional-black-caucus-foundation-annual-phoenix-a.

30. James, "Obama's 'Stop Complaining'' Order."

31. When I was unable to find a comparable white audience speech, I used the most proximate presidential weekly address as a match.

32. This sample of speeches yielded similar results to the speeches that were matched on subject matter, timing, and audience size.

33. The intercoder reliability rating was 85 percent.

34. In order to have a sufficient sample size of speeches delivered to African American and Latino audiences, I analyzed speeches from both of Obama's presidential campaigns and during his two terms in office. The speeches were obtained from the American Presidency Project at the University of California, Santa Barbara. A total of fifty-three speeches were delivered to black/Latino audiences/affinity events. I excluded any speeches that were about foreign policy or fund-raising because the aim was to capture Obama's rhetoric to ordinary Americans in a domestic context.

35. A two-proportions z-test was performed to determine whether there was a significant difference between the occurrence of personal responsibility rhetoric in his speeches to blacks versus Latinos, and in his speeches to blacks versus whites.

36. Kathy Kiely and Jill Lawrence, "Clinton Makes Case for Wide Appeal," *USA Today*, May 8, 2008.

37. William J. Clinton, "News Conference," Columbia, SC, January 26, 2008, http://voices.washingtonpost.com/44/2008/01/for-bill-clinton-echoes-of-jac.html.

38. Newt Gingrich, "Town Hall," Plymouth, NH, January 5, 2012, https://abcnews.go.com/blogs/politics/2012/01/gingrichs-naacp-food-stamp-remarks-stir-controversy/.

39. Gingrich doubled down on his use of the term "food-stamp president" during a Republican primary debate in Myrtle Beach, South Carolina. One of the panelists was Juan Williams, an African American conservative commentator, who suggested that some people might find Gingrich's comments about the "food-stamp president" offensive. Gingrich's widely publicized response in which he derided "political correctness" was reported to have been met with the only standing ovation of the night. Gingrich also went on to use the exchange with Williams in a television ad that aired in South Carolina.

40. Rick Santorum, "Campaign Stop," Sioux City, IA, January 1, 2012, https://www.npr.org/sections/itsallpolitics/2012/01/03/144613385/santorum-explains-his-comments-about-black-people-and-entitlements.

41. PolitiFact and FactChecker.org gave the ad their most dishonest rating.

Chapter Four

1. The study design, however, does not make it possible to determine whether a message that invokes negative stereotypes about a group other than African Americans would produce similar results, relative to a deracialized message that emphasizes universalism.

2. Lauren Williams, "The Herman Cain Guide to Race and Politics," The Root, June 4, 2011, https://www.theroot.com/the-herman-cain-guide-to-race-and-politics-1790867947.

3. Williams, "The Herman Cain Guide to Race and Politics."

4. Kevin Liptak, "Cain: Racism Not Holding Anyone Back," CNN, October 9, 2011, http://politicalticker.blogs.cnn.com/2011/10/09/cain-racism-not-holding-anyone-back/.

5. Andrew Kaczynski, "Ben Carson: Racism in United States Is 'Mostly with the Progressive Movement,'" BuzzFeed News, October 9, 2015, https://www.buzzfeednews.com/article/andrewkaczynski/ben-carson-racism-in-united-states-is-mostly-with-the-progre.

6. Sean Sullivan, "Ben Carson: Obamacare Worst Thing 'since Slavery,'" *Washington Post*, October 11, 2013, https://www.washingtonpost.com/news/post-politics/wp/2013/10/11/ben-carson-obamacare-worst-thing-since-slavery/?utm_term=.e92383893367.

7. Justin W. Moyer, "Rupert Murdoch Longs for 'Real Black President,'" *Washington Post*, October 8, 2015, https://www.washingtonpost.com/news/morning-mix/wp/2015/10/08/rupert-murdoch-longs-for-real-black-president/?utm_term=.ff72bfa29fa3.

8. It is also a religious denomination that has a history of racial exclusion. African Americans were excluded from the Mormon priesthood until 1978.

9. Krissah Thompson, "Mia Love of Utah Hopes to Become the First Black Republican Woman in Congress," *Washington Post*, June 25, 2012, https://www .washingtonpost.com/politics/mia-love-of-utah-hopes-to-become-the-first-black -republican-woman-in-congress/2012/06/25/gJQAbUiq2V_story.html?utm _term=.ec8fd9488150.

10. Seth McLaughlin, "Minority Hopefuls Add Color to Monochrome GOP," *Washington Times,* October 5, 2010.

11. Jamie Weinstein, "The Second Battle of Boca Raton," *Weekly Standard*, December 16, 2009.

12. William E. Gibson, "Immigration Issue Could Sway Key Races in Florida," *Sun-Sentinel*, October 11, 2010.

13. It is worth noting that West's white *Democratic* opponent, Ron Klein, employed negative racial appeals as well. Klein made an effort to associate West with the racially tinged issue of crime, by associating West with the Outlaws, a motorcycle gang with ties to drug trafficking and prostitution. Klein's campaign pointed out that West was a contributor to *Wheels on the Road*, a publication that covers the Outlaws' Florida clubs. This connection appeared to be tenuous at best. While West's campaign disputed the charges, neither he nor his supporters decried the insinuation as racially motivated.

14. Josh Goodman, "Out of the Blue," Governing.com, September 30, 2007, https://www.governing.com/templates/gov_print_article?id=89056177.

15. Cynthia Burton, "Mayor John Street Again Apologizes," *Philadelphia Inquirer*, April 17, 2002.

16. "Michael Nutter—Speech at Mount Carmel Baptist Church," August 7, 2011, https://www.americanrhetoric.com/speeches/michaelnuttermountcarmel baptist.htm.

17. Peter Wallsten, "GOP Attack Ad Draws Heat for Racial Undertones," *Los Angeles Times,* October 24, 2006, https://www.latimes.com/archives/la-xpm -2006-oct-24-na-ford24-story.html.

18. Elisabeth Kauffman, "Campaign '06: The G.O.P. Gets Nervous in Tennessee," *Time*, October 20, 2006, http://content.time.com/time/nation/article/0 ,8599,1548892,00.html.

19. Kauffman, "Campaign '06."

20. AP Photo by Alex Brandon, Jackson, TN, November 7, 2006.

21. Ken Rudin, "Where Did Alabama's Artur Davis Go Wrong? Let Us Count the Ways," NPR, June 2, 2010, https://www.npr.org/sections/politicaljunkie/ 2010/06/02/127372010/how-did-alabama-s-artur-davis-go-wrong-let-us-count -the-ways.

22. Although African Americans constituted a significant minority of 34.5 percent of the county in 2000, they had been unable to elect a candidate

of their choice, which was typically the Democratic Party-at large candidate. According to the Department of Justice, "White bloc voting usually results in the defeat of candidates who are preferred by black voters," which is why the Department of Justice was advocating for the creation of single-member districts; David Firestone, "U.S. Sues Charleston County, S.C., Alleging Violation of Black Rights, *New York Times,* January 19, 2001, https://www.nytimes.com/2001/01/19/us/us-sues-charleston-county-sc-alleging-violation-of-black-voting-rights.html.

23. To achieve a representative sample, GfK uses random-digit sampling (RDD) methods. When a person agrees to participate, they are provided with free Internet access and are given the necessary hardware for as long as they remain in the GfK panel. Most research to date comparing this kind of sample with telephone RDD samples suggests they are representative, and some suggest that the data obtained via probability-based Internet surveys are more reliable than what is obtained by phone.

24. The problem is that we do not know whether there is something special about targeting blacks in particular, or if targeting any group would have yielded similar results.

25. The racial resentment scale has been validated as a measure of anti-black predispositions (Kinder and Sanders 1996; Tarman and Sears 2005) and has proved to be a powerful predictor of opposition to policies and candidates viewed as pro-black (Kinder and Sanders 1996; Mendelberg 2001; Valentino, Hutchings, and White 2002).

26. The order was randomized.

27. The median level of racial resentment for the sample was 0.56, and the mean was 0.57.

28. Thirty-one percent of the sample thought that whites were more hardworking than blacks, whereas 62 percent rated blacks and whites as equally hardworking. Only 7 percent rated blacks as more hardworking than whites.

Chapter Five

1. "Paul Ryan Clarifies 'Inarticulate Remarks' on Inner Cities," BBC, March 13, 2014, https://www.bbc.com/news/world-us-canada-26564949.

2. "Paul Ryan Clarifies 'Inarticulate Remarks.'"

3. Ta-Nehesi Coates, "The Secret Lives of Inner-City Black Males," *Atlantic,* March 18, 2014, https://www.theatlantic.com/politics/archive/2014/03/the-secret-lives-of-inner-city-black-males/284454/.

4. Jonathan Chait, "Barack Obama, Ta-Nehesi Coates, Poverty, and Culture," *New York* magazine, March 19, 2014, http://nymag.com/intelligencer/2014/03/obama-ta-nehisi-coates-poverty-and-culture.html.

5. John McWhorter, "It's about Time Obama Stuck Up for His 'Respectability Politics.'" *Washington Post*, May 14, 2015, https://www.washingtonpost.com/posteverything/wp/2015/05/14/its-about-time-obama-stuck-up-for-his-respectability-politics/?utm_term=.738ef2bcbc58.

6. The sample is selected in two stages. In the first stage, a traditional random sample is drawn. In the second stage, one or more participants from an opt-in Internet panel who match respondents selected from the first stage are selected using a propensity matching method. The goal of the second stage selection is to choose respondents who are as similar as possible to individuals selected from the probability sample in the first stage. The data are weighted to reflect the demographic composition of the United States.

7. Rhetoric about white Americans failing to work hard and take personal responsibility is absent from our political discourse, whereas the same cannot be said for rhetoric about African Americans needing to take personal responsibility.

8. The standard racial resentment battery was also asked of respondents in a second wave (one month after the first wave).

9. Republican respondents were more receptive to the personal responsibility message in the control condition, relative to Democratic respondents in the same condition, but not overwhelmingly so.

10. These results are similar to the results from the deracialization experiment discussed in chapter 4. Republican respondents are more receptive to a black Democratic candidate who explicitly peddles stereotypes of African Americans.

11. "Paul Ryan Clarifies 'Inarticulate Remarks.'"

12. Hutchings and Stephens 2008.

13. I also explore the relationship between respondents' racial resentment and respondents' reaction to implicit or explicit appeals by the race of the candidate. These results are reported in the appendix.

14. Twelve percent of the all-white sample is pro-black, 64 percent of the sample is neutral, and 24 percent is anti-black.

15. Some people who rated blacks and whites as equally hardworking may have done so because of social desirability concerns.

16. The confidence intervals around the estimates for the pro-black respondents are so wide, in part, because the percentage of respondents who expressed pro-black responses is fairly small (12 percent).

17. The results are similar when we look at vote support as a function of racial resentment. The magnitude and direction of the results are the same, but they do not always attain conventional levels of statistical significance.

18. The implicit appeals were never associated with an increase in electoral support for black Republican and black Democratic candidates. Only the white Democratic politician experienced a statistically significant uptick in support for

an implicit appeal, and that support was concentrated among those respondents who were anti-black.

19. The survey was conducted under the auspices of Time-Sharing Experiment for the Social Sciences (TESS). TESS provides high-quality survey data at an affordable cost by working with GfK (formerly Knowledge Networks), a survey firm that recruits panelists using traditional address-based and random-digit sampling (RDD) methods. See chapter 4, note 23.

20. In Study 2, I do not have a measure of respondents' endorsement of the negative stereotype of blacks as lazy, so I rely on the racial resentment scale.

21. There was no control condition in Study 2, so I compare the results for the implicit messages relative to the explicit messages.

22. I find similar results when I look at likely vote as a function of partisanship. Republican respondents were more supportive of the black Democratic politician with the explicit, as opposed to implicit, message.

23. Of course, it is worth noting that there is a fair degree of uncertainty in the estimates, which is due to the relatively small sample cell. However, the pattern of results is similar to the results from Study 1, and in accord with the theory of racial distancing.

24. Study 1 does not include this variable.

25. I do not find similar results when the candidate is depicted as white.

26. This question was not asked in Study 1.

27. I also examined support for education spending more generally, but support for education spending was unrelated to treatment condition. Thus, exposure to the black candidate with the explicit message affected spending related to *racial disparities* in education, and not education spending more generally.

Chapter Six

1. Kait Richmond, "Democrats' Diverse Interns Respond to Paul Ryan's #SpeakerSelfie," CNN, July 21, 2016, https://www.cnn.com/2016/07/21/politics/dc-intern-selfie/index.html.

2. Richmond, "Interns Respond to Paul Ryan's #SpeakerSelfie."

3. Pew Research Center, "Wide Gender Gap, Growing Educational Divide in Voters' Party Identification," March 20, 2018, https://www.people-press.org/2018/03/20/wide-gender-gap-growing-educational-divide-in-voters-party-identification/.

4. See chapter 5, note 6.

5. These included questions about income tax deductions and homeownership.

6. Respondents were asked whether the ad they viewed dealt with the environment, whether it showed a candidate wearing glasses, whether it dealt with the war in Afghanistan, and whether the candidate was African American.

7. Subsequent analyses all control for party identification, education, gender, income, and residence in the South. While statistical controls are often unnecessary when analyzing experimental designs with random assignment, it makes sense to include controls for variables that affect the dependent variable, as is the present case with the aforementioned demographic variables: (a) to guard against inadvertent failures of random assignment and (b) to reduce residual variance and increase statistical power (Field and Hole 2003).

8. The mailer did not include any language about affirmative action or any mention of racialized policies, so there is no reason to expect that exposure to the mailer would influence voters' perception of the candidate's position on affirmative action.

9. Racial resentment was measured with the standard four-item scale. The scale is comprised of four agree/disagree items listed above in chapter 2 (and revisited in chapter 4). The Cronbach's alpha for the scale is 0.88.

10. Racial resentment is coded from 0 to 1. Any values above 0.50 would be classified as racially resentful, whereas values below 0.50 are classified as not racially resentful. The average level of racial resentment for the sample was 0.60, which indicates that, on average, respondents were racially resentful. This is similar to the average level of racial resentment found in other studies, such as the American National Election Study.

Chapter Seven

1. Barack Obama, "Democratic National Convention Keynote Address," Boston, MA, 2004, http://www.americanrhetoric.com/speeches/convention2004/barackobama2004dnc.htm.

2. Quoted in Amber Phillips, "'They're Rapists': President Trump's Campaign Launch Speech Two Years Later, Annotated," *Washington Post*, June 16, 2017, https://www.washingtonpost.com/news/the-fix/wp/2017/06/16/theyre-rapists-presidents-trump-campaign-launch-speech-two-years-later-annotated/?utm_term=.e5d7194c6c45.

3. Cruz for President, "Sales Pitch," YouTube, February 17, 2016, www.youtube.com/watch?v=uKcQoFSVvGQ.

4. John Wildermuth and Hamed Aleaziz, "Cruz, Trump Intensify Anti-Muslim Rhetoric after Brussels Attacks," *San Francisco Chronicle*, March 22, 2016, https://www.sfchronicle.com/politics/article/Cruz-Trump-intensify-anti-Muslim-rhetoric-after-6974308.php.

5. Matt Flegenheimer, "Sharpening Attacks on Marco Rubio, Ted Cruz Urges New Immigration Limits," *New York Times*, November 13, 2015, https://www.nytimes.com/2015/11/14/us/politics/sharpening-attacks-on-marco-rubio-ted-cruz-urges-new-immigration-limits.html.

6. Lilla's language is imprecise because the majority of women actually voted for Clinton. The majority of *white* women voted for Trump.

7. Emily Jashinsky, "Michigan Democrat Debbie Dingell: 'I Don't Know Where I Belong' in the Party of Identity Politics," *Washington Examiner*, June 26, 2017, https://www.washingtonexaminer.com/michigan-democrat-debbie -dingell-i-dont-know-where-i-belong-in-the-party-of-identity-politics.

8. Jeff Stein, "Bernie Sanders: 'It Is Not Good Enough for Someone to Say, "I'm a Woman! Vote for Me!."'" *Vox*, November 21, 2016, https://www.vox.com/ policy-and-politics/2016/11/21/13699956/sanders-clinton-democratic-party.

9. Hutchings, Walton, and Benjamin (2010) also found with data that pre- dated the Obama era that some white Americans became *more* supportive of the Confederate flag when it was associated with the Ku Klux Klan.

Bibliography

Abrajano, Marisa, and Zoltan L. Hajnal. 2015. *White Backlash: Immigration, Race, and American Politics*. Princeton: Princeton University Press.

Abramson, Paul R., John H. Aldrich, and David W. Rohde. 2009. *Change and Continuity in the 2008 Elections*. Washington, DC: CQ Press.

Achen, Christopher H., and Larry M. Bartels. 2016. *Democracy for Realists*. Princeton: Princeton University Press.

Allport, Gordon Willard. 1954. *The Nature of Prejudice*. Oxford: Addison-Wesley.

Andersen, David, and Jane Junn. 2010. "Deracializing Obama: White Voters and the 2004 Illinois U.S. Senate Race." *American Politics Research* 38 (3): 443–70.

Arceneaux, Kevin. 2008. "Can Partisan Cues Diminish Democratic Accountability?" *Political Behavior* 30 (2): 139–60.

"The Ax-Man Cometh." 2008. *The Economist*, August 21, 2008.

Benjamin, Andrea. 2017. *Racial Coalition Building in Local Elections: Elite Cues and Cross-Ethnic Voting*. New York: Cambridge University Press.

Berinsky, Adam J. 2002. "Political Context and the Survey Response: The Dynamics of Racial Policy Opinion." *Journal of Politics* 64 (2): 567–84.

Blumer, Herbert. 1958. "Race Prejudice as a Sense of Group Position." *Pacific Sociological Review* 1 (1): 3–7.

Bobo, Lawrence, and James R. Kluegel. 1993. "Opposition to Race-Targeting: Self-Interest, Stratification Ideology, or Racial Attitudes?" *American Sociological Review* 58 (4): 443–64.

Bobo, Lawrence, and Mia Tuan. 2006. *Prejudice in Politics: Group Position, Public Opinion, and the Wisconsin Treaty Rights Dispute*.

Bonilla-Silva, Eduardo. 2010. *Racism without Racists: Color-Blind Racism and the Persistence of Racial Inequality in America*. 2nd ed. Lanham, MD: Rowman & Littlefield.

Campbell, Angus, Philip E. Converse, Warren E. Miller, and Donald Stokes. 1960. *The American Voter*. Chicago: University of Chicago Press.

Carmines, Edward G., and James A. Stimson. 1989. *Issue Evolution: Race and the Transformation of American Politics*. Princeton: Princeton University Press.

Carter, Niambi, and Pearl Ford Dowe. 2015. "The Racial Exceptionalism of Barack Obama." *Journal of African American Studies* 19 (2): 105–19.

Chong, Dennis, and Reuel Rogers. 2005. "Racial Solidarity and Political Participation." *Political Behavior* 17 (4): 347–74.

Citrin, Jack, Donald Phillip Green, and David O. Sears. 1990. "White Reactions to Black Candidates: When Does Race Matter?" *Public Opinion Quarterly* 54 (1):74–96.

Coates, Ta-Nehisi. 2013. "How the Obama Administration Talks to Black America." *Atlantic*, May 20, 2013.

Cohen, Cathy J. 1999. *The Boundaries of Blackness: AIDS and the Breakdown of Black Politics*. Chicago: University of Chicago Press.

Colby, Sandra L., and Jennifer M. Ortman. 2015. "Projections of the Size and Composition of the U.S. Population: 2014–2060." Washington, DC: U.S. Census Bureau.

Converse, Philip E. 1964. "The Nature of Belief Systems in Mass Publics." *Critical Review* 18 (January): 1–74.

Corn, David. 2012. "Romney Tells Millionaire Donors What He REALLY Thinks of Obama Voters." *Mother Jones*. September 17, 2012. https://www.motherjones.com/politics/2012/09/secret-video-romney-private-fundraiser/.

Craig, Maureen A., and Jennifer A. Richeson. 2014. "On the Precipice of a 'Majority-Minority' America." *Psychological Science* 25 (6): 1189–97.

Crandall, Christian S., and Amy Eshleman. 2003. "A Justification-Suppression Model of the Expression and Experience of Prejudice." *Psychological Bulletin* 129 (3): 414–46.

Dawson, Michael C. 1994. *Behind the Mule: Race and Class in African-American Politics*. Princeton: Princeton University Press.

———. 2001. *Black Visions: The Roots of Contemporary African-American Political Ideologies*. Chicago: University of Chicago Press.

DeSante, Christopher D. 2013. "Working Twice as Hard to Get Half as Far: Race, Work Ethic, and America's Deserving Poor." *American Journal of Political Science* 57 (2): 342–56.

Downs, Anthony. 1957. "An Economic Theory of Political Action in a Democracy." *Journal of Political Economy* 65 (2): 135–50.

Dupree, Cydney H., and Susan T. Fiske. 2019. "Self-Presentation in Interracial Settings: The Competence Downshift by White Liberals." *Journal of Personality and Social Psychology* 117 (3): 579–604.

Earnest, Josh. 2015. "Press Briefing by Press Secretary Josh Earnest, 4/29/15." Washington, DC: Office of the Press Secretary, The White House. https://

obamawhitehouse.archives.gov/the-press-office/2015/04/29/press-briefing
-press-secretary-josh-earnest-42915.

Ehrenfreund, Max. 2015. "What Social Science Tells Us about Racism in the Republican Party." *Washington Post*, December 11, 2015.

Ehrenstein, David. 2007. "Barack the 'Magic Negro': The Illinois Senator Lends Himself to White America's Idealized, Less-than-Real Black Man." *Los Angeles Times*, March 19, 2007.

Enos, Ryan D. 2014. "Causal Effect of Intergroup Contact on Exclusionary Attitudes." *Proceedings of the National Academy of Sciences* 111 (10): 3699–704.

Epstein, Ethan. 2013. "One Tough Nutter." *City Journal*, Spring 2013.

Feldman, Stanley, and Leonie Huddy. 2005. "Racial Resentment and White Opposition to Race-Conscious Programs: Principles or Prejudice?" *American Journal of Political Science* 49 (1): 168–83.

Field, Andy P., and Graham Hole. 2003. *How to Design and Report Experiments*. Thousand Oaks, CA: Sage.

Fields, Corey D. 2016. *Black Elephants in the Room: The Unexpected Politics of African American Republicans*. Oakland: University of California Press.

Fiske, Susan T., Hillary B. Bergsieker, Ann Marie Russell, and Lyle Williams. "Images of Black Americans: Then,'Them,' and Now,'Obama!'" *DuBois Review: Social Science Research on Race* 6 (1): 83–101.

Fiske, Susan T., and Shelley E. Taylor. 1991. *Social Cognition*. 1st ed. New York: McGraw-Hill.

Franklin, Sekou. 2010. "Situational Deracialization, Harold Ford, and the 2006 Senate Race in Tennessee." In *Whose Black Politics? Cases in Past-Racial Black Leadership*, edited by Andra Gillespie, 214–40. New York: Routledge.

Frymer, Paul. 1999. *Uneasy Alliances: Race and Party Competition in America*. Princeton: Princeton University Press.

Gaines, Kevin K. 1996. *Uplifting the Race: Black Leadership, Politics, and the Culture of the Twentieth Century*. Chapel Hill: University of North Carolina Press.

Gamson, William. 1992. *Talking Politics*. Cambridge: Cambridge University Press.

Gilens, Martin. 1999. *Why Americans Hate Welfare: Race, Media, and the Politics of Antipoverty Policy*. Chicago: University of Chicago Press.

Gillespie, Andra. 2010. *Whose Black Politics? Cases in Post-Racial Black Leadership*. New York: Routledge.

———. 2012. *The New Black Politician: Cory Booker, Newark, and Post-Racial America*. New York: New York University Press.

Gilliam, Franklin D., and Shanto Iyengar. 2000. "Prime Suspects: The Influence of Local Television News on the Viewing Public." *American Journal of Political Science* 44 (3): 560.

Gillion, Daniel Q. 2015. *Governing with Words: The Political Dialogue on Race, Public Policy, and Inequality in America*. New York: Cambridge University Press.

Glaude, Eddie S. 2016. *Democracy in Black: How Race Still Enslaves the American Soul*. New York: Crown.

Goffman, Erving. 1963. *Stigma*. Englewood Cliffs, NJ: Spectrum.

Goldman, Seth K., and Diana C. Mutz. 2014. *The Obama Effect: How the 2008 Campaign Changed White Racial Attitudes*. New York: Russell Sage Foundation.

Hajnal, Zoltan. 2007. *Changing White Attitudes Toward Black Leadership*. New York: Cambridge University Press.

Hajnal, Zoltan L., and Taeku Lee. 2011. *Why Americans Don't Join the Party: Race, Immigration, and the Failure (of Political Parties) to Engage the Electorate*. Princeton: Princeton University Press.

Hamilton, Charles. 1977. "Deracialization: Examination of a Political Strategy." *First World*, March/April 1977: 3–5.

Harris, Fredrick C. 2012. *The Price of the Ticket: Barack Obama and the Rise and Decline of Black Politics*. New York: Oxford University Press.

Harris-Lacewell, Melissa Victoria. 2004. *Barbershops, Bibles, and BET: Everyday Talk and Black Political Thought*. Princeton: Princeton University Press.

Helman, Scott. 2007. "Obama Shows an Ability to Transcend Race." *Boston Globe*, August 19, 2007.

Henderson, Lenneal J., Jr. 1996. "The Governance of Kurt Schmoke as Mayor of Baltimore." In *Race, Politics, and Governance in the United States*, edited by Huey Perry, 165–78. Gainesville: University Press of Florida.

Higginbotham, Evelyn Brooks. 1993. *Righteous Discontent: The Women's Movement in the Black Baptist Church, 1880–1920*. Cambridge, MA: Harvard University Press.

Highton, Benjamin. 2004. "White Voters and African American Candidates for Congress." *Political Behavior* 26 (1): 1–25.

Hillygus, D. Sunshine., and Todd G. Shields. 2008. *The Persuadable Voter: Wedge Issues in Presidential Campaigns*. Princeton: Princeton University Press.

Huber, Gregory A., and John Lapinski. 2006. "The 'Race Card' Revisited: Assessing Racial Priming in Policy Contests." *American Journal of Political Science* 50 (2): 421–40.

Huckfeldt, R. Robert., and C. W. Kohlfeld. 1989. *Race and the Decline of Class in American Politics*. Urbana: University of Illinois Press.

Huddy, Leonie, and Stanley Feldman. 2009. "On Assessing the Political Effects of Racial Prejudice." *Annual Review of Political Science* 12: 423–47.

Hurwitz, Jon, and Mark Peffley. 1998. *Perception and Prejudice*. New Haven: Yale University Press.

———. 2005. "Playing the Race Card in the Post-Willie Horton Era: The Impact of Racialized Code Words on Support for Punitive Crime Policy." *Public Opinion Quarterly* 69 (1): 99–112.

Hutchings, Vincent L. 2009. "Change or More of the Same?" *Public Opinion Quarterly* 73 (5): 917–42.

Hutchings, Vincent L., Vanessa Cruz Nichols, LaGina Gause, and Spencer Piston. 2014. "Whitewashing: How Obama Used Implicit Racial Cues as a Defense against Political Rumors." Paper presented at the Annual Meeting of the Midwest Political Science Association.

Hutchings, Vincent L., and LaFleur Stephens. 2008. "African-American Voters and the Presidential Nomination Process." In *The Making of the Presidential Candidates 2008*, edited by W. G. Mayer, 119–39. Lanham, MD: Rowman and Littlefield.

Hutchings, Vincent L., and Nicholas A. Valentino. 2004. "The Centrality of Race in American Politics." *Annual Review of Political Science* 7 (1): 383–408.

Hutchings, Vincent, Nicholas Valentino, Tasha Philpot, and Ismail White. 2004. "The Compassion Strategy: Race and the Gender Gap in Campaign 2000." *Public Opinion Quarterly* 68 (4): 512–41.

Hutchings, Vincent L., Hanes Walton, and Andrea Benjamin. 2010. "The Impact of Explicit Racial Cues on Gender Differences in Support for Confederate Symbols and Partisanship." *Journal of Politics* 72 (4): 1175–88.

Jacobsmeier, Matthew L. 2015. "From Black and White to Left and Right: Race, Perceptions of Candidates' Ideologies, and Voting Behavior in U.S. House Elections." *Political Behavior* 37 (3): 595–621.

Jardina, Ashley E. 2019. *White Identity Politics*. Cambridge: Cambridge University Press.

Jeffries, Judson L. 1999. "US Senator Edward W. Brooke and Governor L. Douglas Wilder Tell Political Scientists How Blacks Can Win High-Profile Statewide Office." *PS: Political Science & Politics* 32 (3): 583–87.

Jones, Jeffrey M. 2014. "U.S. Whites More Solidly Republican in Recent Years." Gallup, March 24, 2014. https://news.gallup.com/poll/168059/whites-solidly -republican-recent-years.aspx.

Jost, John T., Mahzarin R. Banaji, and Brian A. Nosek. 2004. "A Decade of System Justification Theory: Accumulated Evidence of Conscious and Unconscious Bolstering of the Status Quo." *Political Psychology* 25 (6): 881–919.

Judd, Dennis R., and Todd Swanstrom. 1994. *City Politics: Private Power and Public Policy*. New York: HarperCollins.

Kaiser, Cheryl R., Benjamin J. Drury, Kerry E. Spalding, Sapna Cheryan, and Laurie T. O'Brien. 2009. "The Ironic Consequences of Obama's Election: Decreased Support for Social Justice." *Journal of Experimental Social Psychology* 45 (3): 556–59.

Kelley, Harold H. 1973. "The Processes of Causal Attribution." *American Psychologist* 28 (2): 107–28.

Kim, Claire Jean. 2003. *Bitter Fruit: The Politics of Black-Korean Conflict in New York City.* New Haven: Yale University Press.

Kinder, Donald R., and Allison Dale-Riddle. 2012. *The End of Race? Obama, 2008, and Racial Politics in America.* New Haven: Yale University Press.

Kinder, Donald R., and Corinne McConnaughy. 2006. "Military Triumph, Racial Transcendence, and Colin Powell." *Public Opinion Quarterly* 70 (2): 139–65.

Kinder, Donald R., and Tali Mendelberg. 2000. "Individualism Reconsidered: Principles and Prejudice in Contemporary American Public Opinion on Race." In *Racialized Politics: Values, Ideology, and Prejudice in American Public Opinion*, edited by David Sears, Jim Sidanius, and Lawrence Bobo, 44–74. Chicago: University of Chicago Press.

Kinder, Donald R., and Lynn Sanders. 1996. *Divided by Color:Racial Politics and Democratic Ideals.* Chicago: University of Chicago Press.

Kinder, Donald R., and David O. Sears. 1981. "Prejudice and Politics: Symbolic Racism versus Racial Threats to the Good Life." *Journal of Personality and Social Psychology* 40 (3): 414–31.

Kinder, Donald R., and Nicholas Winter. 2001. "Exploring the Racial Divide: Blacks, Whites, and Opinion on National Policy." *American Journal of Political Science* 45 (2): 439–53.

King, Desmond S., and Rogers M. Smith. 2011. *Still a House Divided: Race and Politics in Obama's America.* Princeton: Princeton University Press.

Klein, Ezra. 2012. "The Unpersuaded." *New Yorker*, March 12, 2012.

Knoles, Lucia Z. 2006. "Racial Stereotypes of the Civil War Era." An American Antiquarian Society Online Resource. https://www.americanantiquarian .org/Freedmen/Intros/questions.html.

Krogstad, Jens Manuel. 2016. "2016 Electorate Will Be the Most Diverse in U.S. History." Pew Research Center, February 3, 2016. https://www.pewresearch .org/fact-tank/2016/02/03/2016-electorate-will-be-the-most-diverse-in-u-s -history/.

Kuklinski, James H., Michael D. Cobb, and Martin Gilens. 1997. "Racial Attitudes and the 'New South.'" *Journal of Politics* 59 (2): 323–49.

Kuklinski, James H., and Norman L Hurley. 1994. "On Hearing and Interpreting Political Messages: A Cautionary Tale of Citizen Cue-Taking." *Journal of Politics* 56 (3): 729–51.

Kunda, Ziva, and Paul Thagard. 1996. "Forming Impressions from Stereotypes, Traits, and Behaviors: A Parallel-Constraint-Satisfaction Theory." *Psychological Review* 103 (2): 284–308.

Lamont, Michele, and Crystal Fleming. 2005. "Everyday Antiracism: Competence and Religion in the Cultural Repertoire of the African-American Elite." *DuBois Review: Social Science Research on Race* 2 (1): 29–43.

Lee, Taeku. 2002. *Mobilizing Public Opinion: Black Insurgency and Racial Attitudes in the Civil Rights Era.* Chicago: University of Chicago Press.

Lerman, Amy E., and Meredith L. Sadin. 2014. "Stereotyping or Projection? How White and Black Voters Estimate Black Candidates' Ideology." *Political Psychology* 37 (2): 147–63.

Lilla, Mark. 2016. "The End of Identity Liberalism." *New York Times*, November 18, 2016.

Lopez, Ian Haney. 2014. *Dog Whistle Politics: How Coded Racial Appeals Have Reinvented Racism and Wrecked the Middle Class.* Oxford: Oxford University Press.

Lublin, David. 2018. "Eight White-Majority Districts Elected Black Members of Congress This Year: That's a Breakthrough." *Washington Post*, November 19, 2018.

Malcolm, Andrew H. 1983. "Victory Claimed for Washington in Chicago Vote." *Washington Post*, February 23, 1983.

Marable, Manning. 2009. "Racializing Obama: The Enigma of Post-Black Politics and Leadership." *Souls* 11 (1): 1–15.

Martin, Jonathan. 2015. "Ben Carson Appeals to Black Voters, but His Campaign Doesn't, Yet." *New York Times*, November 5, 2015.

McConnaughy, Corrine M., Ismail K. White, David L. Leal, and Jason P. Casellas. 2010. "A Latino on the Ballot: Explaining Coethnic Voting among Latinos and the Response of White Americans." *Journal of Politics* 72 (4): 1199–1211.

McCormick, Joseph, and Charles Jones. 1993. "The Conceptualization of Deracialization." In *Dilemmas in Black Politics*, edited by Georgia Persons, 66–84. New York: Harper Collins.

McDermott, Monika L. 1998. "Race and Gender Cues in Low-Information Elections." *Political Research Quarterly* 51 (4): 895–918.

McIlwain, Charlton D., and Stephen M. Caliendo. 2011. *Race Appeal.* Philadelphia: Temple University Press.

Mendelberg, Tali. 2001. *The Race Card: Campaign Strategy, Implicit Messages, and the Norm of Equality.* Princeton: Princeton University Press.

———. 2008. "Racial Priming Revived." *Perspectives on Politics* 6 (1): 109–23.

———. 2009. "Deliberation, Incivility, and Race." In *Democratization in America*, edited by Desmond King, Robert C. Lieberman, Gretchen Ritter, and Laurence Whitehead, 157–83. Baltimore: Johns Hopkins University Press.

Moskowitz, David, and Patrick Stoh. 1994. "Psychological Sources of Electoral Racism." *Political Psychology* 15 (2): 307–29.

Muhammad, Khalil G. *The Condemnation of Blackness.* Cambridge, MA: Harvard University Press, 2010.

Myrdal, Gunnar. 1944. *An American Dilemma.* New York: Harper and Row.

Nelson, Thomas E., and Donald R. Kinder. 1996. "Issue Frames and Group-Centrism in American Public Opinion." *Journal of Politics* 58 (4): 1055–78.

Nelson, Thomas E., Kira Sanbonmatsu, and Harwood K. McClerking. 2007. "Playing a Different Race Card: Examining the Limits of Elite Influence on Perceptions of Racism." *Journal of Politics* 69 (2): 416–29.

Nicholson, Stephen P. 2012. "Polarizing Cues." *American Journal of Political Science* 56 (1): 52–66.

Nirappil, Fenit. 2017. "Black Democrat Omitted from Some Democratic Campaign Fliers in Virginia." *Washington Post*, October 19, 2017.

Nisbett, Richard, and Lee Ross. 1980. *Human Inference: Strategies and Shortcomings of Social Judgment*. Englewood Cliffs, NJ: Prentice-Hall.

Olzak, Susan. 1990. "The Political Context of Competition: Lynching and Urban Racial Violence, 1882–1914." *Social Forces* 69 (2): 395–421.

O'Reilly, Kenneth. 1995. *Nixon's Piano: Presidents and Racial Politics from Washington to Clinton*. New York: Free Press.

Orey, Byron D., and Boris E Ricks. 2007. "A Systematic Analysis of the Deracialization Concept: A Systematic Analysis of the Deracialization Concept." *National Political Science Review* 11: 325–34.

Oskamp, Stuart, and P. Wesley Schultz. 2005. *Attitudes and Opinions*. Mahwah, NJ: Lawrence Erlbaum Associates.

Parker, Christopher S., and Matt A. Barreto. 2013. *Change They Can't Believe In: The Tea Party and Reactionary Politics in America*. Princeton: Princeton Univeristy Press.

Parker, Christopher S., Mark Q. Sawyer, and Christopher Towler. 2009. "A Black Man in the White House? The Role of Racism and Patriotism in the 2008 Presidential Election." *DuBois Review: Social Science Research on Race* 6 (1): 193–217.

Peffley, Mark, and Jon Hurwitz. 2010. *Justice in America: The Separate Realities of Blacks and Whites*. New York: Cambridge University Press.

Penn, Mark, and Andrew Stein. 2017. "Back to the Center, Democrats." *New York Times,* July 6, 2017.

Pérez, Efrén O. 2015. "Ricochet: How Elite Discourse Politicizes Racial and Ethnic Identities." *Political Behavior* 37 (1): 155–80.

———. 2016. *Unspoken Politics: Implicit Attitudes and Political Thinking*. New York: Cambridge University Press.

Persons, Georgia Anne. 2017. *Beyond the Boundaries: A New Structure of Political Ambition in African American Politics*. N.p.: Routledge.

Petrocik, John R. 1996. "Issue Ownership in Presidential Elections, with a 1980 Case Study." *American Journal of Political Science* 40 (3): 825–50.

Petrow, Gregory A. 2010. "The Minimal Cue Hypothesis: How Black Candidates Cue Race to Increase White Voting Participation." *Political Psychology* 31 (6): 915–50.

Pew Research Center. 2009. "Top Stories of 2009: Economy, Obama, and Health Care." December 29, 2009. http://people-press.org/report/575/.

———. 2010. "Growing Number of Americans Say Obama Is Muslim." August 19, 2010. http://people-press.org/report/645/.

———. 2016. "On Views of Race and Inequality, Blacks and Whites Are Worlds Apart." June 27, 2016. www.pewsocialtrends.org/2016/06/27/on-views-of-race-and-inequality-blacks-and-whites-are-worlds-apart/.

Philpot, Tasha S. 2004. "A Party of a Different Color? Race, Campaign Communication, and Party Politics." *Political Behavior* 26 (3): 249–70.

———. 2007. *Race, Republicans, and the Return of the Party of Lincoln.* Ann Arbor: University of Michigan Press.

———. 2017. *Conservative but Not Republican: The Paradox of Party Identification and Ideology among African Americans.* Cambridge: Cambridge University Press.

Phoenix, Davin. 2019. *The Anger Gap: How Race Shapes Emotions in Politics.* Cambridge: Cambridge University Press.

Piston, Spencer. 2010. "How Explicit Racial Prejudice Hurt Obama in the 2008 Election." *Political Behavior* 32 (4): 431–51.

Popkin, Samuel L. 1991. *The Reasoning Voter: Communication and Persuasion in Presidential Campaigns.* Chicago: University of Chicago Press.

Price, Melanye T. 2016. *The Race Whisperer: Barack Obama and the Political Uses of Race.* New York: New York University Press.

Rahn, Wendy M. 1993. "The Role of Partisan Stereotypes in Information Processing about Political Candidates." *American Journal of Political Science* 37 (2): 472–96.

Reeves, Keith. 1997. *Voting Hopes or Fears? White Voters, Black Candidates, and Racial Politics in America.* Oxford: Oxford University Press.

Roberts, Margaret E., Brandon M. Stewart, and Dustin Tingley. 2014. "Stm: R Package for Structural Topic Models." http://www.structuraltopicmodel.com.

Roberts, Sam. 2009. "2008 Surge in Black Voters Nearly Erased Racial Gap." *New York Times*, July 20, 2009.

Romboy, Dennis. 2012. "Love Would 'Take Apart' Congressional Black Caucus If Elected in Utah's 4th Congressional District." *Deseret News*, January 5, 2012.

Salter, Phia, Kelley Hirsch, and Rebecca Schlegel. 2016. "Who Needs Individual Responsibility? Audience Race and Message Content Influence Third-Party Evaluations of Political Messages." *Social Psychological and Personality Science* 7 (1): 29–36.

Schickler, Eric. 2016. *Racial Realignment: The Transformation of American Liberalism, 1932–1965.* Princeton: Princeton University Press.

Schmidt, Christopher W. 2018. "The Sit-In Movement." In *Oxford Research Encyclopedia of American History*, online ed.

Sears, David O., and P. J. Henry. 2003. "The Origins of Symbolic Racism." *Journal of Personality and Social Psychology* 85 (2): 259–75.

Sears, David O., and Victoria Savalei. 2006. "The Political Color Line in America: Many 'Peoples of Color' or Black Exceptionalism?" *Political Psychology* 27 (6): 895–924.

Sidanius, Jim, Erik Devereux, and Felicia Pratto. 1992. "A Comparison of Symbolic Racism Theory and Social Dominance Theory as Explanations for Racial Policy Attitudes." *Journal of Social Psychology* 132 (3): 377–95.

Sides, John, Michael Tesler, and Lynn Vavreck. 2018. *Identity Crisis: The 2016 Presidential Campaign and the Battle for the Meaning of America*. Princeton: Princeton University Press.

Sigelman, Carol K., Lee Sigelman, Barbara J. Walkosz, and Michael Nitz. 1995. "Black Candidates, White Voters: Understanding Racial Bias in Political Perceptions." *American Journal of Political Science* 39 (1): 243.

Sigelman, Lee. 1995. "Blacks, Whites, and Anti-Semitism." *Sociological Quarterly* 36 (4): 649–56.

Silver, Nate. 2019. "Why Harris and O'Rourke May Have More Upside Than Sanders and Biden." FiveThirtyEight, January 4, 2019.

Sinclair-Chapman, Valeria, and Melanye Price. 2008. "Black Politics, the 2008 Election, and the (Im)possibility of Race Transcendence." *PS: Political Science and Politics* 41 (4): 739–45.

Smith, Ben. 2008. "Muslims Barred from Picture at Obama Event." *Politico*, June 18, 2008.

Smith, Robert. 1996. *We Have No Leaders: African Americans in the Post–Civil Rights Era*. Albany: State University of New York Press.

Sniderman, Paul M., and Edward G. Carmines. 1997. *Reaching beyond Race*. Cambridge, MA: Harvard University Press.

Sniderman, Paul M., and Thomas Leonard Piazza. 1993. *The Scar of Race*. Cambridge, MA: Belknap Press of Harvard University Press.

Stephens-Dougan, LaFleur. 2016. "Priming Racial Resentment without Stereotypic Cues." *Journal of Politics* 78 (3): 687–704.

Stout, Christopher. 2015. *Bringing Race Back In*. Charlottesville: University of Virginia Press.

Strolovitch, Dara. 2007. *Affirmative Advocacy: Race, Class, and Gender in Interest Group Politics*. Chicago: University of Chicago Press.

Summers, Mary, and Phillip Klinkner. 1996. "The Election and Governance of John Daniels as Mayor of New Haven and the Failure of the Deracialization Hypothesis." In *Race, Politics, and Governance in the United States*, edited by Huey Perry, 127–50. Gainesville: University Press of Florida.

Swarns, Rachel L. 2008. "Quiet Political Shifts as More Blacks Are Elected." *New York Times*, October 13, 2008.

Sweet, Lynn. 2008. "Obama Tells Blacks: Shape Up." *Chicago Sun-Times,* February 28, 2008.

Swigger, Nathaniel. 2012. "What You See Is What You Get: Drawing Inferences from Campaign Imagery." *Political Communication* 29 (4): 367–86.

Tajfel, Henri. 1981. *Human Groups and Social Categories: Studies in Social Psychology.* Cambridge: Cambridge University Press.

Tarman, Christopher, and David O. Sears. 2005. "The Conceptualization and Measurement of Symbolic Racism." *Journal of Politics* 67 (3): 731–61.

Tate, Katherine. 1994. *From Protest to Politics: The New Black Voters in American Elections.* Cambridge, MA: Harvard University Press.

Tesler, Michael. 2016. *Post-Racial or Most-Racial? Race and Politics in the Obama Era.* Chicago: University of Chicago Press.

Tesler, Michael, and David Sears. 2010. *Obama's Race.* Chicago: University of Chicago Press.

Tokeshi, Matthew, and Tali Mendelberg. 2015. "Countering Implicit Appeals: Which Strategies Work?" *Political Communication* 32 (4): 648–72.

Traub, Amy, Laura Sullivan, Tatjana Meschede, and Thomas Shapiro. 2017. "The Asset Value of Whiteness: Understanding the Racial Wealth Gap." Demos.org, February 16, 2017. https://www.demos.org/research/asset-value -whiteness-understanding-racial-wealth-gap.

Tyson, Alec. 2018. "The 2018 Midterm Vote: Divisions by Race, Gender, Education." Pew Research Center, November 8, 2018. https://www.pewresearch .org/fact-tank/2018/11/08/the-2018-midterm-vote-divisions-by-race-gender -education/.

Valentino, Nicholas A. 1999. "Crime News and the Priming of Racial Attitudes during Evaluations of the President." *Public Opinion Quarterly* 63 (3): 293–320.

Valentino, Nicholas A., Vincent L. Hutchings, and Ismail K. White. 2002. "Cues That Matter: How Political Ads Prime Racial Attitudes during Campaigns." *American Political Science Review* 96 (1): 75–90.

Valentino, Nicholas A., Fabian G. Neuner, and L. Matthew Vandenbroek. 2018. "The Changing Norms of Racial Political Rhetoric and the End of Racial Priming." *Journal of Politics* 80 (3): 757–71.

Vavreck, Lynn. 2009. *The Message Matters: The Economy and Presidential Campaigns.* Princeton: Princeton University Press.

Viser, Matt, and Chelsea Janes. 2019. "Kamala Harris Enters 2020 Presidential Race." *Washington Post,* January 21, 2019.

Walton, Hanes, Jr. 2000. *Reelection: William Jefferson Clinton as a Native-Son Candidate.* New York: Columbia University Press.

Weaver, Vesla M. 2012. "The Electoral Consequences of Skin Color: The 'Hidden' Side of Race in Politics." *Political Behavior* 34 (1): 159–92.

White, Ismail K. 2007. "When Race Matters and When It Doesn't: Racial Group Differences in Response to Racial Cues." *American Political Science Review* 101 (2): 339–54.

White, Ismail K., Chryl N. Laird, and Troy D. Allen. 2014. "Selling Out? The Politics of Navigating Conflicts between Racial Group Interest and Self-Interest." *American Political Science Review* 108 (4): 783–800.

Williams, Linda F. 1990. "White/Black Perceptions of the Electability of Black Political Candidates." *National Political Science Review* 2: 45–64.

———. 2003. *The Constraint of Race: Legacies of White Skin Privilege in America*. University Park: Pennsylvania State University Press.

Williams, Vanessa. 2017. "Study: Despite Changing Demographics, the Political Playing Field Still Tilts toward White Men." *Washington Post*, October 24, 2017.

Wilson, William Julius. 1987. *The Truly Disadvantaged*. Chicago: University of Chicago Press.

Winter, Nicholas J. G. 2008. *Dangerous Frames: How Ideas about Race and Gender Shape Public Opinion*. Chicago: University of Chicago Press.

Wong, Janelle. 2018. *Immigrants, Evangelicals, and Politics in an Era of Demographic Change*. New York: Russell Sage Foundation.

Wright Rigueur, Leah. 2014. *The Loneliness of the Black Republican*. Princeton: Princeton University Press.

Yeip, Randy. 2015. "Baltimore's Demographic Divide." *Wall Street Journal*, May 1, 2015.

Zaller, John R. 1992. *The Nature and Origins of Mass Opinion*. Cambridge: Cambridge University Press.

Index

www.ingramcontent.com/pod-product-compliance
Lightning Source LLC
Chambersburg PA
CBHW060035030426

42334CB00019B/2339